BUILD YOUR OWN
ROUTER
TABLES

John McPherson

BETTERWAY BOOKS
Cincinnati, Ohio

READ THIS IMPORTANT NOTICE

Build Your Own Router Tables. Copyright © 1997 by John R. McPherson. Printed and bound in the United States of America. All rights reserved. No part of this book may be reproduced in any form or by any electronic or mechanical means including information storage and retrieval systems without permission in writing from the publisher, except by a reviewer, who may quote brief passages in a review. Published by Betterway Books, an imprint of F&W Publications, Inc., 1507 Dana Avenue, Cincinnati, Ohio 45207. (800) 289-0963. First edition.

Other fine Betterway Books are available from your local bookstore or direct from the publisher.

01 00 99 98 97   5 4 3 2 1

Library of Congress Cataloging-in-Publication Data

McPherson, John
      Build your own router tables / by John McPherson
          p.   cm.
      Includes index.
      ISBN 1-55870-459-0 (alk. paper)
      1. Routers (Tools) 2. Woodwork. I. Title.
TT203.5W37   1997
684'.083—dc20   97-20180
                                                         CIP

Edited by Adam Blake
Production edited by Katie Carroll
Cover designed by Chad Planner
Cover illustration by Jake Ellison
Interior designed by Brian Roeth

ACKNOWLEDGMENTS

I want to thank the DeWalt Industrial Tool division of Black & Decker; the Porter-Cable Corporation; Skil-Bosch Power Tool Company; Sears; and Ryobi America Corporation for furnishing their engineering drawings of the router base plates. The same thanks are extended to Onsrud Cutter supplying information on their cutter bits and the material contained in the Safety Guidelines.

Thanks to the companies that are extending the reach of the router with their products. They are the Rousseau Company; the Taylor Design Group, the developers of the INCRA line of router jigs and fences; Woodhaven for their many designs and products for the router user; and MLCS Ltd. for their comprehensive line of router bits.

Thanks to the companies who catalog and make available to us the tools, fixtures and realted products that are imporatant to our projects. Included in this list are the Beall Tool Company, Bridge City Tool Works and Woodcraft.

My thanks to MicroCADAM Inc., the developers of the computer-aided design software used to create the drawings for this book.

And finally, my thanks and love to my wife Maria who so loves router dust, particularly the deep orange dust from Padauk.

BUILD YOUR OWN ROUTER TABLES

DECIMAL EQUIVALENCY CHART

$\frac{1}{64}''$	.015	$\frac{33}{64}''$	.515
$\frac{1}{32}''$	.031	$\frac{17}{32}''$	.531
$\frac{3}{64}''$	.046	$\frac{35}{64}''$	.546
$\frac{1}{16}''$	.062	$\frac{9}{16}''$	.569
$\frac{5}{64}''$	.078	$\frac{17}{64}''$	.578
$\frac{3}{32}''$	.093	$\frac{19}{32}''$	5.93
$\frac{7}{64}''$	.109	$\frac{39}{64}''$	.609
$\frac{1}{8}''$	.125	$\frac{5}{8}''$	.625
$\frac{9}{64}''$	.140	$\frac{41}{64}''$	.640
$\frac{5}{32}''$	.156	$\frac{21}{32}''$	.656
$\frac{11}{64}''$	.171	$\frac{43}{64}''$	.671
$\frac{3}{16}''$	.187	$\frac{11}{16}''$	.687
$\frac{13}{64}''$	.203	$\frac{45}{64}''$	.703
$\frac{7}{32}''$	.218	$\frac{23}{32}''$	.718
$\frac{15}{64}''$	.234	$\frac{47}{64}''$	.734
$\frac{1}{4}''$	.25	$\frac{3}{4}''$	.75
$\frac{17}{64}''$	.265	$\frac{49}{64}''$	.765
$\frac{9}{32}''$	.281	$\frac{25}{32}''$	.781
$\frac{19}{64}''$	.296	$\frac{51}{64}''$	.769
$\frac{5}{16}''$	.312	$\frac{13}{16}''$	.812
$\frac{21}{64}''$	.328	$\frac{53}{64}''$	.828
$\frac{11}{32}''$	.343	$\frac{27}{32}''$	.843
$\frac{23}{64}''$	.359	$\frac{55}{64}''$	.859
$\frac{3}{8}''$	.375	$\frac{7}{8}$	.875
$\frac{25}{64}''$	.390	$\frac{57}{64}''$	.890
$\frac{13}{32}''$	.406	$\frac{29}{32}''$	.906
$\frac{27}{64}''$	.421	$\frac{59}{64}''$	.921
$\frac{7}{16}''$	.437	$\frac{15}{16}''$	.937
$\frac{29}{64}''$	.453	$\frac{61}{64}''$	.953
$\frac{15}{32}''$	.468	$\frac{31}{32}''$	.968
$\frac{31}{64}''$	.484	$\frac{63}{64}''$	.984
$\frac{1}{2}''$	.5	$1''$	1.00

METRIC CONVERSION CHART

TO CONVERT	TO	MULTIPLY BY
Inches	Centimeters	2.54
Centimeters	Inches	0.4
Feet	Centimeters	30.5
Centimeters	Feet	0.03
Yards	Meters	0.9
Meters	Yards	1.1
Sq. Inches	Sq. Centimeters	6.45
Sq. Centimeters	Sq. Inches	0.16
Sq. Feet	Sq. Meters	0.09
Sq. Meters	Sq. Feet	10.8
Sq. Yards	Sq. Meters	0.8
Sq. Meters	Sq. Yards	1.2
Pounds	Kilograms	0.45
Kilograms	Pounds	2.2
Ounces	Grams	28.4

TABLE OF CONTENTS

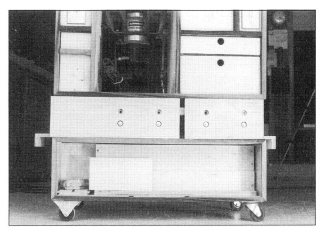

FOREWORD

HOW TO GET THE MOST OUT OF THIS BOOK

Router tables are fun to use and, for some of us, easier to use than a handheld router. I quickly bought a router table when they first came on the market. That was over twenty-five years ago. These first tables had many problems. As I used my first table, I thought about how I could make it better for my type of work. The manufacturers have improved table design since their inception, but never quite to fit what I wanted.

So I started designing and building router tables. Now, I am a longtime router-table user, and I have worked with the users of my tables, so I feel I have some insight into the problems and needs of router-table and fixture designs. You may find it helpful, when you build your own table, to know why I am recommending one solution over another; sometimes I tried the other and it didn't work.

The most important reasons for building your own table are safety, quality of cut and having a table that satisfies your particular needs. You can incorporate into your own table the functionality that you need. Commercial tables, by definition, are compromises. They are designed to both meet the needs of the largest possible range of customers and keep the product cost at the lowest possible level. Build your own table, a table that has the features you want.

The designs presented here will allow you to quickly build a table that will meet the needs of most standard routing operations. The jigs and fixtures in this book are designed to fit with these tables as a system, a system that helps you make the cuts you need. While there are numerous jigs and fixtures described in the book, there is no compelling reason to try to build all of them. Build what you need, and when you need more you will have the ideas and plans available to build them.

Having a good router in your shop is like having a Porsche in your garage. Having a router table in your shop is like having a German autobahn to drive your Porsche on. This is a good analogy, but where it fails is, though the Porsche is designed to be driven on autobahns, no router is designed for the upside-down world of router tables. The engineers who design routers have a flat-earth philosophy. They know that things will fall off if you go to the other side of the earth's surface, and this is a similar case when the router is turned upside down. The table design and the use of the equipment must compensate for this flat-earth philosophy. In developing these designs, I have taken various steps to minimize the inherent mismatch between the router design and the table application.

ROUTER-TABLE ANATOMY

A router table is comprised of three primary parts: the router, the table surface and router plate, and the fixturing. The table's height, the storage provisions and size are all user-specific parameters. Notwithstanding their apparent secondary role, these parameters will determine your satisfaction with the resultant design.

The book first looks at routers and router bits. This overview will help you choose the right router and table combination for your needs. In the next chapter, I make recommendations for table surfaces and router mounting. Chapter three covers the fences, and chapter four the jigs and fixtures. These items then appear throughout the book in the cutting and building sequences. The last three chapters cover the building of three different router tables. Each table design has its own solution to storage.

My philosophy and the philosophy followed in the designs of these tables is if accessories are used with the tool, they should be stored with the tool. Routers, probably more than any other tool in your shop, demand an inordinate amount of storage. The table saw with its miter, fence and some blades will do most of the cutting a woodworker needs to do. The same is true for a drill press. A set of drill bits and a fence will take care of over 95 percent of the woodworker's drilling needs. The router, on the other hand, needs its bits (there are hundreds available), all types of jigs and fixtures (none of them are small) and all the little pieces that come with router accessories. If the router is going to be used as a power hand tool as well, add another set of jigs and fixtures that will need storing.

The three router-table designs covered are the job-site table, the shop table and the contractor's table. Their primary differences are size and storage organization. Each has a different solution for handling the router's power "on-off" control. All the tables have switched power control for using the router externally or for plug-in accessories, like a shop vac, that automatically turn on when the router is turned on.

The job-site table is a bench-top router table for the small shop and for fabricators and installers at the job site. It will support circular saws, miter saws and saber saws. You can mount this table module on a low-level bench like the Black & Decker Workmate. You can also use it with legs or with a wheeled storage box. This wheeled box-and-drawer combination allows for easy movement and lots of additional tools and fixtures. The job-site router table is an ideal design for the garage or small shop.

The shop router table is a full-height unit. The height is the primary difference between this table and the job-site table. It also is a good small-shop table. In a commercial shop it makes a good table where cuts and sequences for prototypes can be developed. I have used the shop-table design more than any other over the past five years.

The contractor's table got its name from the woodworking catalogs. The largest table in a catalog is always the contractor's table. This is the largest table described here, ergo, it's *our* contractor's table. This table's top surface is $36'' \times 24''$. It has the most storage space and is designed to be used with large variable speed (3-plus hp) routers and/or with large fence systems like the INCRA Ultra. The contractor's table features four-point power switching. This four-point control allows the router motor to be turned on or off at any of the table's four corners. This is an important added feature since, like all the tables, the contractor's table is designed to be used from any of its four sides.

Router-table fences come in all sizes and varieties. An early question will be *Make or Buy*? The safe answer is to do both. Plan to use commercial fences, but go ahead and make some of your own. The sliding miter fence described in chapter three is not available commercially, so it must be made. You will also find that hybrid fences—adaptations of commercial fences—work well with your router table.

The jigs and fixture designs described in this book can be used with any of the tables. The job-site and shop tables have the same size top, so the jigs designed for one of these tables can be used with the other table. For the contractor's table, many of the jigs are increased in size to accommodate the larger table, but generically they are still the same tool. The jigs are designed to be not only functional, but also attractive. I find good-looking tools make better-looking furniture.

Read the entire book before you start cutting. Don't be turned off by the decimal notation. Dividing an inch into 100 parts is really easier than dividing it into 128 parts.

Spend some time studying and understanding the various parts and their relationships to one another. In many cases, the given dimensions are those I used myself. Often these dimensions are arbitrary and can be changed. When making parts, particularly the various shop jigs, I use the wood I have available. These random length and width cutoffs are now immortalized in this book's drawings. After building the cases, you will have leftover pieces that you too can immortalize.

CHAPTER ONE

ROUTERS AND BITS

Routers come in all shapes and sizes. Some are designed for specific applications. The majority of routers available in the marketplace are for general use. The discussion that follows is directed mainly toward this general-purpose type of router. Special-purpose routers are discussed in instances when their design or application makes them suitable for use in conjunction with the router table.

ROUTERS

The first order of business is to take a look at routers. There is not a router manufactured that is designed for use in a router table. The consequence of this is you must watch for a number of things when you use your router in the upside-down world of router tables. The table design should complement or, if necessary, compensate for the router's design. Fortunately this is not a significant problem for either the router or the table. After discussing routers, router bits and some tools used with your router, this chapter ends with a summary of considerations that you should review prior to using your router in a table. These considerations will make more sense after we look at routers in general.

Router Horsepower

Two primary characteristics of general-purpose routers distinguish them from the other members of their family: power and cut entry. Routers with a horsepower rating of 1 hp to 1½ hp are the norm. Routers with horsepower ratings at and above 1½ are generally classed as *production* or *industrial* routers. They are more powerful and are designed for high-

ROUTER ASSORTMENT
All these routers have one thing in common: None were designed to be used in the upside-down world of router tables.

duty cycle (power on) applications. A production router will have a much longer life than the lower-powered routers when used in similar conditions. The higher-powered routers are the only ones that offer variable speed control, a feature required by certain large cutter bits specifically made for a router table.

Router Anatomy

Cut entry is the method used for bringing the cutter in contact with the workpiece. Entry from the side of the workpiece is the normal method. Direct entry into any position on the workpiece surface by plunging the rotating bit into the workpiece is the other method—hence the name *plunge* router. Both normal and plunge routers work well in router tables. When used in router tables, plunge routers are used as normal routers, i.e., they are used in a fixed depth (height) mode and do not plunge into the workpiece. Since plunge routers can be used either as fixed or in the plunge mode, they are the most general purpose.

ELEVATION METHODS: PORTER-CABLE
The Porter-Cable fixed-based routers use a common method for height adjustment. A spiral ring cut in the base will ramp the motor unit either 1″ per revolution or 2″ per revolution depending on the router model.

ELEVATION METHODS: BOSCH
The Bosch fixed-base routers use a spiral ramp that is the top of the base casting. The motor unit is raised or lowered by riding on this ramp.

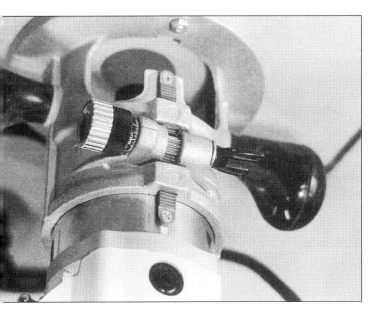

ELEVATION METHODS: DEWALT
This DeWalt router is an example of the rack-and-pinion type elevation control. This method of height control is always visible to the table user.

Some models though, without modification, do not have the depth/height control necessary for use in a table.

Depth Adjustment

Of our so-called normal routers, two methods can be used for depth adjustment. One is the rack-and-pinion, and other is the spiral. The spiral can act as a thread, using grooves in the base for the lead pitch, or it can be a spiral ramp that wraps around the router base.

Bit Elevation

Looking at the three methods of adjusting the bit elevation, the rack-and-pinion method would appear to be preferable for use in a router table. This is not the case. When I adjust the bit height, I look and measure from the table's top using one hand to control the height adjustment and the other to hold the workpiece or a scale. Working this way, I can't see the elevation scales on the router. If the height adjustment is critical, I often place the router fixed to its plate on the table top, but still tend to work off the plate surface, again not looking at the elevation scales. With the router and its plate sitting on top of the table, it is easier to use and read the rack-and-pinion or spiral-ramp designs. Conversely, when either of these router types are mounted in the table, height adjustment can be a problem. Both rely on gravity to keep the router motor from dropping out of its base. In the Bosch design, the router motor is stopped with a spring-loaded retaining pin before leaving its base completely. Since they are gravity designs, extra care must be taken when adjusting a particular bit height. Note the position of the elevation indicator before adjusting to a new setting.

ROUTER SET FOR HEIGHT ADJUSTMENT
Router height/depth controls were designed for using the router in an upright position. You can remove the router from the table and set it up as shown here to make adjusting the router-bit height easier.

With routers like the Porter-Cable 690 series that use a slip ring for height adjustment, you have to stand on your head to read the scale, whether the router is mounted or is sitting on the tabletop. The elevation ring on models 7518 and 7519 can be read from the side if you bend down a little. It turns out, though, this isn't a problem for the Porter-Cable elevation control. A half-revolution turn of the motor on the 690 series produces 1″ of elevation change, and one complete revolution of the motor on the 7518 and 7519 is equal to 1″ of elevation change. You learn quickly how much of a turn will produce the desired change in bit height.

For all router types, you can place the router plate in the top opening with the router in an upright position, allowing you to use the scales and controls as they were designed to be used. To position the router in the top this way, the power cord must be disconnected—an added safety feature.

When you make a measured height cut with a table saw, your interest is with an absolute cut dimension. There are no blade height scales so after using a gauge or eyeballing the height, the final height is set by incremental adjustment. Try it, and if it's not right, change it. The same trial-and-error method is used with a router. You are normally looking for the incremental change from the last cut.

Selecting a Router

The particular method of depth/height adjustment the router manufacturer uses doesn't play an important role in selection of a router for router-table use. Selection is based on the type of cutting that will be performed with the router table. If the table is going to be used frequently for heavy production-type cutting or a high duty cycle, or if you will be using large cutters requiring the speed-control feature, then a production-type router is called for. If speed control and continuous heavy cutting are not requirements, get a good commercial router for your table. Routers used in a router table are subjected to forces of far greater magnitude than those experienced by routers used as handheld tools.

A familiar comparison might be the difference between drilling with a handheld drill motor and drilling with a drill press. You know that for hard, dense materials or end grain the drill bit will often just bounce off the surface and make drilling a hole hard to do. Set the same workpiece in the drill press, and the hole is easily drilled. The difference is the controlled, increased force of the drill into the hard material.

The router table is like the drill press. The force of the workpiece against the cutter bit is controlled and focused. This means that the router is subjected to far greater forces—and, in some cases, far greater abuses—than when used as a handheld device. The router used in the table must be of quality design and construction to withstand this abuse. It must also have the power to cope with the additional strain caused by the cutting. The minimum horsepower rating is 1½ hp for the general router-table application.

Many plunge routers offer extremely fine elevation adjustment in the router-table application, however, gross adjustment can be tedious. The pitch of the height-adjustment screw is normally 20 threads per inch. If you want to change the bit height from the last setup by 1″, you must turn the knob 20 complete revolutions. Many early routers used a 32-threads-per-inch pitch for depth adjustment. Although that offered fine depth adjustment, setup time was considered inordinate; and the more modern designs went to the rack-and-pinion or a coarser pitch (½ or 1 thread per inch) for elevation control.

Notwithstanding the elevation control possible with plunge routers, my advice is to have a dedicated fixed-base router for the table. Select a router with a

EARLY ROUTER DESIGN
Early routers have a number of common characteristics with today's routers. They had a large number of cutter shapes available, and they were equipped with fences and edge guides for controlling the cuts.

COLLETS
Collets are an important part of the router. They should be well maintained and replaced when worn. In the upper left is an example of a collet nut and ¼″ sleeve. This style collet is an integral part of the motor shaft. Take particular care with this type of collet since they can be expensive to replace.

base that can be separated from the motor and buy a second base. You can use one base with the table and the other for handheld applications. One manufacturer, Porter-Cable, has three bases for its basic motor: a standard, a D-handle and a plunge base. The three bases allow for a high degree of flexibility in router usage. Being able to separate the motor from the base allows easier bit changing and another very important feature: You can leave the fence in its set position when changing bits.

Changing bits is greatly simplified when you don't have a separate base and plate to contend with. A combined base and plate also offers greater cutting accuracy. (The reason for this is discussed in chapter four.) Also, you can leave the fence in place when changing bits, which is both a time-saver and a benefit when the next cut must reference off the last cut. With the fence in place, you will know the last cut setting.

Having a plunge router in the shop is almost mandatory. Making or buying a plate for your plunge router so it can be used in the table allows you to take advantage of all the benefits of the plunge router. Chapter three discusses the various plate styles and options. Changing from one plate to another is easy. Three or four screws hold the plates to the router base. From my experience, the plunge router is a little more flexible for overhead routing of the type explained in chapter four. (See The Planing and Dado Jig.)

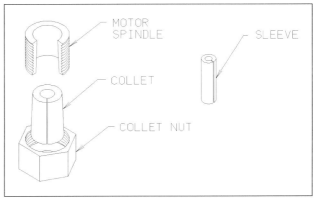

COLLETS

ROUTER COLLETS

Many routers are offered with only ¼″ collets. Some come with both ½″ and ¼″ collects or offer the ¼″ collet as a purchased option. Others come with a ½″ collet and a ¼″ sleeve. The sleeve has a ½″ outside diameter and a ¼″ inside diameter.

I have sometimes experienced trouble separating the ¼″ bit from the sleeve-type collet. The problem comes from attempting to grip the sleeve to pull the bit out without damaging the sleeve surface. Axle pegs, used in some of the jigs and fixtures, have a ⁷/₃₂″ diameter and are handy for pushing the bit out.

The collet is an important part of the router design. (Read the information contained on pages 151-152 to learn more about collet maintenance.) Certainly, when the router is used in the table application, the collet is subjected to much greater force than when the router is used normally, and so proper collet maintenance is necessary.

Since many router bits are only available with ½″ shanks, it makes sense to get a router which accepts either size bit. The 1½ hp router will come with collets sized for both ¼″ and ½″ bits. The question of total power and variable speed control is answered by the bits that will be used.

ROUTER BITS

Router bits can be classified into two primary sets. One set consists of router bits that can only be used with a table-mounted router. The other set is comprised of those bits that can be used with either a table-mounted or hand-held router. One distributor of router bits prints a pictograph, or icon (shown here), next to the bit description to tell the potential buyer that this bit can only be used with table-mounted routers. As with pictures in general, this icon tells the story quickly. Hopefully, the router manufacturers know that it doesn't mean "stamp out routers." I have also noticed that router manufacturers don't use this particular way of telling their customers that the bit can only be used in router-table applications. (Who wants the bar sinister drawn across their product?) All manufacturers do include this information with a bit's specifications.

A subcategory of bits that can only be used in router tables includes bits with restrictions on the maximum allowable rpm for the particular bit. Many of the larger bits can only be used with routers having a variable speed control. I looked at a router-bit catalog that listed 117 bit types. Of these 117 bit types, 14 carried the note, "Not for use in handheld routers." Six of the 14 bits required a variable-speed router. All these bits are available only with ½″ shafts. Use this information when making your decision on which router to buy. If you want to use a specific bit, you must have the router equipped to use it. A word of caution: Bits themselves are not marked or labeled with this information. And it may or may not be included on the bit package, a package that is easily lost or thrown away. It seems that including the maximum rpm would be an easy thing to include along with the part number on the actual bit. For that matter, manufacturers could also include the "Not for use in handheld routers" pictograph on the bit.

As router tables become more prevalent in small shops, more and more of the newly designed bits will

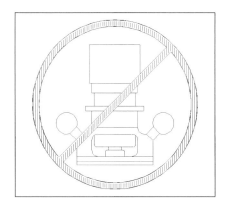

PICTOGRAPH

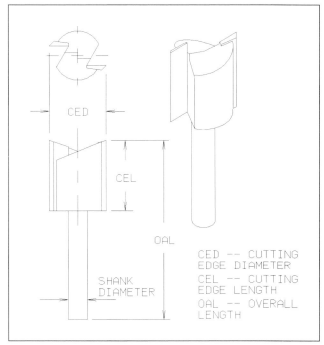

CED -- CUTTING EDGE DIAMETER
CEL -- CUTTING EDGE LENGTH
OAL -- OVERALL LENGTH

ROUTER BIT PARAMETERS

be for table usage only. Some bit manufacturers offer bits that a few years ago would have been patterns that could only be cut with a shaper. The majority of these new bits can only be used with a table-mounted router. Even some that don't carry the proviso, "Not for use in handheld routers," should only be used with a table or with very large workpieces. When in doubt, use the bit in the table configuration.

Another force driving the router-bit industry is the exploding use of routers for the shaping of solid-surface materials. Most solid-surface cutting is accomplished by bringing the router to the workpiece. The normal solid-surface workpiece—a countertop or some equally large and heavy piece—is too large for a shaper to handle in a small shop. Fortunately, all these bits work well with hardwoods; and, since the hardwood is lighter and generally smaller than a sheet

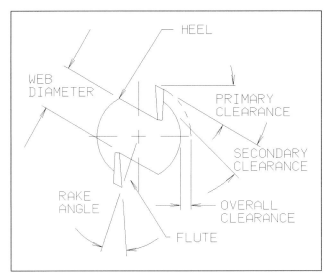

ROUTER BIT GEOMETRY

of Avonite, the bits work well in the router-table application.

The size of the workpiece is normally the deciding factor for when to bring the work to the router and when to bring the router to work. If it's easier to control the router than the workpiece, bring the router to work. Use the router as it was designed to be used, as a handheld power tool. Conversely, when the router and its power cord overwhelm the workpiece, mount the router in the table and bring the work to it. The router table makes a good tabletop to hold the workpiece, and often the router plate offers a better, more stable base than the base plate that comes with the router.

Router-Bit Design

As a router-bit user, you are interested in the bit size and the type of cut the bit makes.

The more esoteric terms describing the bit's design and cutter geometry are not typically found in the router-bit catalogs. (The exception to this is the number of flutes.) Some other general terms are defined here so that if you do run into them, you'll know what they mean.

Rake—The angle between the top cutting surface of a tool and a plane perpendicular to the surface of the workpiece. Like its namesake, the rake angle defines whether you are chopping at the leaves (high rake) or shearing them from the lawn's surface (low rake). The rake angle is also sometimes referred to as *hook angle* or *shear angle*.

Cutting flutes—The space in front of the cutter is the flute. Like a chimney flue, the router bit flute is a channel that allows the cut wood to escape. Flutes are like gullets on a saw blade. For each gullet there is a tooth, and for each flute there is a cutting edge. Since more flutes mean more cutters, increasing the number of flutes increases the quality of the cut. Single-flute designs are used for fast cutting. The resultant edge does not have the quality/smoothness of a multiple-flute router bit. Some small bits have only a single flute since there is not the material for multiple flutes.

Spiral bits come with single or double cutting edges. They are available with up, down and up/down cutting spirals. The "up-down" terminology refers to the direction of the wood removal when the router is being used as a handheld tool. Use the down spiral for keeping a clean top edge and the up spiral when the far edge is of concern. The up/down spiral cutter is best for double laminated boards (boards laminated on both sides) since it will give a clean top and bottom edge.

Cutter Material—The two primary choices for the cutter material are high-speed steel (HSS) and carbide. High-speed steel is best for cutting plastic, aluminum and wood. High-speed steel has a sharper edge than do the carbide cutters, but it will not keep its edge as long as a carbide cutter. For overall longer tool life, the carbide tools are the best to use. Both materials can be sharpened, but often the cost of sharpening the HSS is greater than the cost of a new bit. If you do your own sharpening, this won't be as much of a problem. You have to decide what your time is worth. Remembering that clean cutters will cut better than gummed-up ones. Throw old and damaged bits away.

Cutting Speed—I mentioned that certain bits have a maximum rpm rating. This rating is usually less than the router's rpm rating. The reason for limiting the allowable rpm is that these bits have large diameters.

Look at the points that represent the cutting edge of a ½″ dado bit and a 3½″ raised-panel bit. The point on the ½″ bit travels its circular course at a speed of 576 inches per second. This calculation is based on a router turning at 22,000 rpm. The corresponding point on the raised-panel bit travels 4,032 inches per second, 7 times the speed of the ½″ bit. No wonder the router-bit manufacturer wants the maximum rpm limited for these large-diameter bits. For example, a 3½″ raised-panel bit has 18,000 rpm as its recommended maximum speed. When I use this bit, I wait

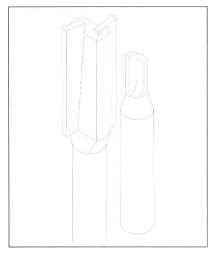

SINGLE AND MULTIPLE FLUTES

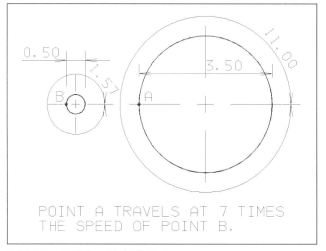

POINT A TRAVELS AT 7 TIMES
THE SPEED OF POINT B.

POINTS ON 1/2″ and 3-1/2″ BITS

for the last couple of passes to bring the speed up to the 18,000 rpm. The first passes remove wood, and the final passes with the cutter at max speed clean the edge. The larger the bit diameter, the faster the cutting speed at the workpiece surface, and, therefore, the cleaner the resulting cut.

Another ratio to consider is the ratio of the shank diameters. For the ½″ shank versus the ¼″ shank, there is twice the surface contact with the collet of the ½″ shank and therefore twice the holding force. The ratio of the cross-sectional area of the shafts is four. This is four times the area for the ½″ shank, therefore four times the strength of the ¼″ shank. When you have a choice, buy the bits with ½″ shanks. You will find some bit styles only come with ¼″ shanks.

Body Design—As the size of a bit increases, the geometry of the basic bit changes. To improve the balance and limit the bite of the cutter, the standard body of two wing cutters has, or is in the process of evolving toward, the solid-body design. The solid body fills the area (volume) between the cutters, giving the new design greater mass (inertia) and better balance. The chip-limiting feature limits the possibility of kickback by limiting the bite. A good rule of thumb is that if the bit *must* be used in a router table, i.e., its size and shape dictate its use only in a table, then it's best to be using a solid-body design. This is not to say that technology has made your old bits obsolete, but if you are buying a new bit, buy the best and safest available. It's like driving a car with or without an airbag. Driving a car with an airbag is safer, but if your car doesn't have one, you're probably not going to take the bus.

Specialty Bits

Specialty bits are bits designed for special cuts or applications. I group them by how I use them or if they are part of a set of bits designed for particular cutting operations. Rail-and-stile bits or tongue-and-groove bits are examples of sets. Some, like the pattern bits, aren't so much specialty as they are special: They do a particular job very well. Others are true specialty bits because they have only one application. The glue-joint bits or the drawer-joint bits are examples of this class.

Most specialty bits do not come with instructions on how to accomplish their particular specialty. I have cut a lot of wood searching for the right setup to use with some of the bits that don't include this information. The bits sold by MLCS and Sears are exceptions. Both companies include information on how their specialty bits were designed to be used, including setup information. I have cut a lot of wood searching for the right setup to use with some of the bits that don't include this information. The problem could be simplified if you knew what the bit designer had in mind and what was planned to be accomplished when the bit was designed.

PATTERN BITS

Pattern bits have a bearing surface used to guide the cutter. The bearing can follow a pattern, or a surface of the workpiece can be used as the pattern. More and more bits are coming on the market with bearings. Some, designed for use with solid-surface material, have nylon bearings that won't mar or burn the workpiece.

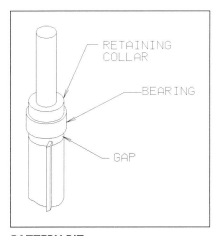

PATTERN BIT

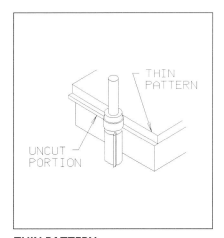

THIN PATTERN

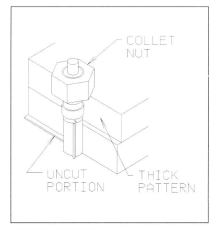

THICK PATTERN

The bearing of the true pattern bit is at the base of the bit. This is the strongest and most stable part of the bit.

Look at the drawing of a typical pattern bit. The space between the bearing and the cutter must be accounted for when designing the pattern. Using a pattern that is too thin can leave a portion of the workpiece uncut. A pattern that is too thick may limit your ability to cut the complete edge of the workpiece in one pass.

Since a thick pattern leaves an uncut portion at the bottom, you can use the thickness of the pattern to control the depth of the cut. Conversely, the uncut portion can be trimmed away by using the cut portion as the pattern for a second pass with the router.

Another problem that you may experience with a pattern bit is a short shaft. This condition produces the same problems experienced with a pattern that is too thick. Two similar pattern bits are shown above. The difference is their shaft length. The one of the right is manufactured by MLCS. The shaft is 1½″ long, a good length for this class bit. The bit on the left was produced by a manufacturer no longer in business. With its 1″ shaft, its uses as a pattern bit are limited. The collet nut ends up so close to the pattern bearing that, when used in a table, there is no space for the router base or the router plate between the collet nut and the bearing collar. With a longer shaft there is room for the plates.

Examples of special edge-shaping bits are the multiform pattern bit and the various crown-moulding bits.

Multiform. The multiform bit allows the cutting of numerous profiles. It's a handy bit to have in your

EXAMPLES OF GOOD AND BAD PATTERN-BIT DESIGN
Pattern bits should have shafts long enough to allow the bit to be used with the pattern and still have good depth control. Of the two similar styles shown here, the one on the left does not have a shaft long enough for many of the cuts you will want to make.

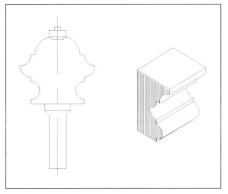

MULTIFORM PATTERNS

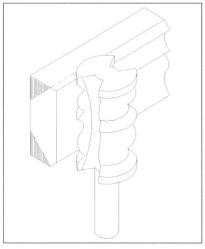

CROWN MOULDING BIT

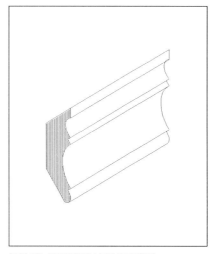

SEARS CROWN MOULDING

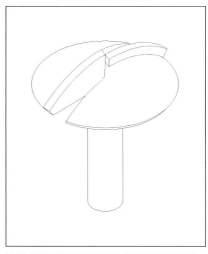

WOODHAVEN COVE CUTTING BIT

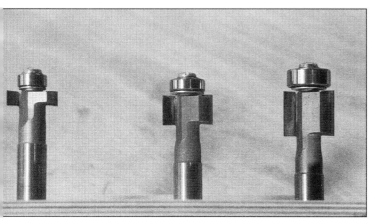

INLAY BITS
These inlay bits which can be used with patterns or use the workpiece as a pattern, all have long shafts that greatly increase their suitability for doing inlays and rabbets.

kit. One problem I have is remembering how I cut a particular piece. The first one is easy; you just keep cutting and experimenting until you have the profile you want. Getting back to that particular sequence of cuts can be a problem. The best solution is to cut all the moulding you need at one time.

Inlay. These inlay bits (above), manufactured by Bosch, were developed for cutting inlay slots in solid-surface material. They work well with hardwoods. Three bearings and three cutters offer nine possible cutting combinations.

Crown Moulding. You can use single-pass crown-moulding bits or a set of bits like those sold by Sears, or you can purchase a cove-cutting bit and design your own moulding.

The single-pass crown-moulding bits are vertical

bits, that is, the workpiece is held vertically against the fence for cutting. These bits are tall, as opposed to having large cutting diameters, which makes them safer to use. The single-pass terminology means the complete profile is cut in a single pass. For most crowns, it is still necessary to work your way into the cut using the fence to control the amount cut away in any one pass. After the moulding has been cut, the 45° ends are cut. I normally use a table saw to cut the ends. A typical profile is shown above, left. This particular style bit is one of three patterns offered by MLCS.

The heart of the Sears kit is the cove cutter. The other bits in the set may or may not be duplicates of bits you already have. Besides the cove bit, the set includes a core-box bit, a V bit and a bead-style bit. Directions are included for cutting eight different profiles. It makes a very good starter set if you haven't made crown moulding before. I also use these bits for cutting mirror and picture frames.

The Sears bits have ¼" shanks. For larger and more demanding cutting, Woodhaven offers a good cove-bit design. It has a ½" shank and is available with both a 1¼" and a 1¾" cove radius. These bits can replace the table saw for cutting large coves.

A number of bits are used for joining wood. Some are used for right-angle joints, while others are used for joining boards horizontally, i.e., making a wide board from a number of narrow boards. The most common right-angle joint bits are used to join drawer sides to fronts and backs. These bits are variations of a more versatile bit, the lock-miter bit.

LOCK MITER

Though versatile, the lock miter is still an example of a true specialty bit. Its only function is to form right-angle joints, which are faster to cut and stronger than plate or biscuit joints. With prototype work, joints that stay together without glue are beneficial. Examples of this bit are shown at right.

One bit has a solid-body design and is used for cutting ¾″ to 1″ material. The other is a more traditional or standard body design and is used for cutting ½″ to ¾″ material. With the traditional body design, setting the bit height is much easier since you can see where the cut will be made on the workpiece. With the solid-body design of the type shown in the photograph above, right (manufactured by Onsrud and sold by Onsrud and Porter-Cable), the height is established either by trial and error or by understanding what should line up with what. The lock miter bit drawing shows the profile of the solid-body design.

Identify the point on the cutter that is reversely symmetrical to the cuts in the two workpieces. The height of this point, with respect to the table surface, must be exactly half of the workpiece thickness. It's identified in the drawing below, right, as the "joint center point." To establish the proper height, first do an eyeball setting and make a cut. Using a micrometer, measure the distance as cut on the workpiece from the center point to the edge and then adjust accordingly. The fence to cutter tip is 0″ at the top of the cut and the workpiece thickness at the bottom of the cut. See the sidebar on the next page, "Cutting Tip for Lock Miters," for a fast way to check your settings.

The beauty of the lock-miter joint is that only one setup is required to cut the components of the box, whether a large carcass or a small drawer. Another benefit is you know how to cut the pieces. Since they will form 45° miters at the corners, they are cut to the outside dimensions of the desired box.

The drawer- and glue-joint bits are variations of the lock-miter joint bit.

Drawer-joint bits come in both the traditional and solid-body designs. Shown on the left in drawing 115 is the Sears drawer- or box-joint bit. The Freud drawer-bit on the right has the solid-body design. The bit in the center is a special cutter designed for drawers with ¾″ rabbeted faces and ½″ or ⅝″ sides. For all of the drawer-joint bits, hold the bit height constant and move the fence to cut the sides. The drawer style determines which type of bit to use.

LOCK MITER BITS
The lock miter joint can be used for carcasses or drawers. This strong joint allows pieces to be fitted without gluing. Another advantage is the pieces forming the sides can be cut from one table setup. Since the corner formed is a true 45° miter, the length of the pieces forming the sides is the side dimension.

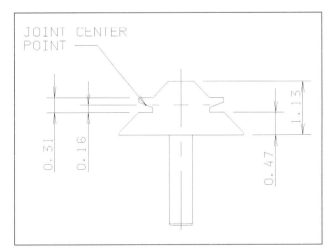

LOCK MITER BIT

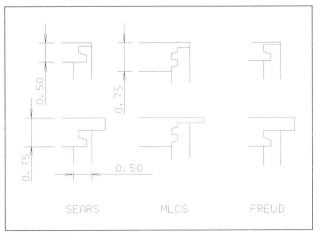

DRAWER JOINTS

CUTTING TIP FOR LOCK MITERS

Find a 6″ to 8″ length of scrap the same thickness as the workpieces and tack a backing board to it. With the backing board on top, run the scrap workpiece through the cutter about halfway. Now, position the scrap workpiece against the fence with the uncut portion of the scrap facing the bit and again cut halfway down its length. Remove the backing board and cut the piece in half. Trim to remove any double cut or uncut portion at what

was the scrap workpiece center. Orient the two pieces and check the fit. The end miters should be cut to the edge of the stock and should align when the pieces are joined. The cutting sequences are shown below.

If the end miters do not align, the bit is either too high or too low. The type of fit you end up with will tell you whether to lower or raise the bit. Remember, when you adjust the bit, you also move the 45° miter edge with respect to the fence.

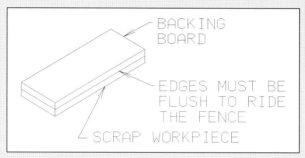

BACKING BOARD

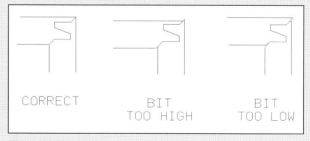

LOCK MITER TEST CUTTING

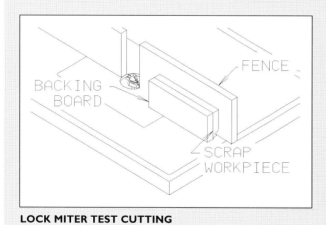

LOCK MITER TEST CUTTING

EXAMPLES—LOCK MITER JOINTS

DRAWER JOINTS

I use ½″ ply for the four sides of a drawer box. The Freud bit is the best for this type of construction. Like the lock-miter bit, the Freud bit uses a single height and fence setting to cut both the vertical and horizontal pieces.

For a ¾″ drawer front that is an integral part of the drawer box, the other drawer-joint bits work well. If the back is attached with the same joint, it must also be at least ¾″ stock.

Glue Joint. A glue joint is sort of a cross between a lock-miter joint and a tongue-and-groove joint. Its purpose is to both increase the surface area that is

glued and to offer some mechanical support to the joint. The glue-joint bit is frequently used to build up the panels for rail-and-stile cabinet doors. The resultant panel will not warp like a single wide board will tend to do.

Like the lock-miter and drawer-joint bits, the glue-joint bit must be centered on the workpieces. For the joint to properly join, the workpieces must be flat and of the same thickness. This often means having stock milled to the required thickness or having a planer. Make the cuts with one workpiece faceup and with the mating half facedown. Before cutting, lay the pieces out and check for grain patterns and other

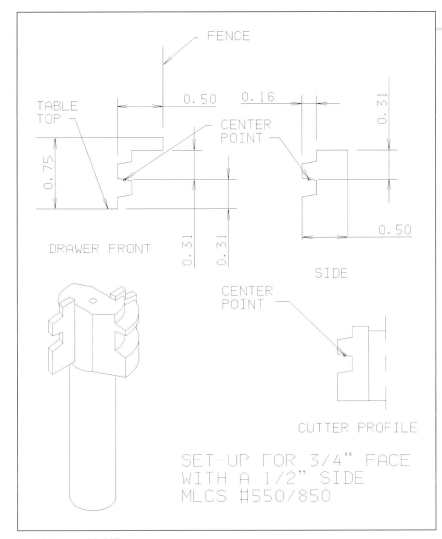

FENCE

0.50   0.16   0.31

TABLE TOP

CENTER POINT

0.75

DRAWER FRONT

0.31   0.31

0.50

SIDE

CENTER POINT

CUTTER PROFILE

SET-UP FOR 3/4" FACE
WITH A 1/2" SIDE
MLCS #550/850

MCLS DRAWER BIT

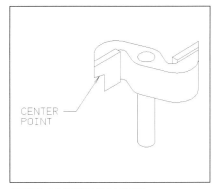

CENTER POINT

SEARS DRAWER/BOX BIT

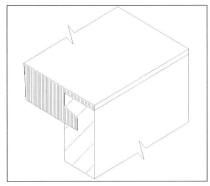

FREUD DRAWER BIT—SIDE VIEW

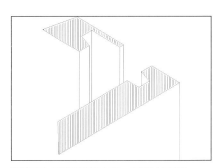

FREUD DRAWER BIT—TOP VIEW

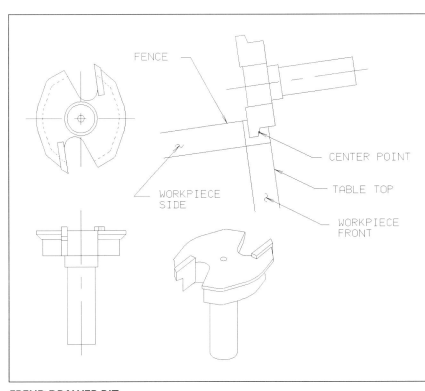

FENCE

CENTER POINT

TABLE TOP

WORKPIECE
SIDE

WORKPIECE
FRONT

FREUD DRAWER BIT

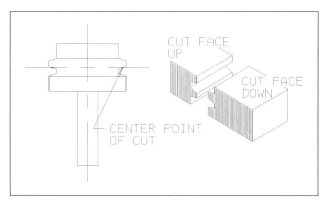

GLUE JOINT

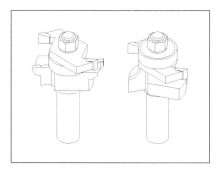

RAIL AND STILE CUTTERS

features that can either enhance or detract from the finished board's appearance. With patterned wood like birch, if you take a little care and are willing to use extra wood to match the pattern, you can come up with beautiful door faces. Conversely, it is also easy to come up with a door face where one strip is highly patterned and the adjoining strips are bland.

Raised-Panel Doors. You can build a raised-panel door with three special bits. These bits are the stile cutter, the rail cutter and the raised-panel bit. They are often sold in sets which also include a glue-joint bit for making the door panels and a door-lip bit for cutting the door's outside edges and for drawer faces. Single-bit arbors have removable and reversible cutters. In one setup, the inside edges of the rails and stiles are cut, and in the second configuration, the complementary cuts are made in the rails.

Raised-panel bits are available in the vertical style like the crown-moulding bit previously described or with flat, large-diameter cutters. I prefer the flat cutter for two reasons: I do a large number of doors with arched or cathedral tops, and I prefer to work with the panel flat on the router table so that I have more control of the cut than I do when the panel is held vertically. If you don't have a variable-speed router,

you must use the vertical cutters. See the vertical miter fence described in chapter three to make this type of cut.

ROUTER ACCESSORIES AND AFTERMARKET PRODUCTS

Speed Control. Electronic speed controls are sold which allow you to reduce the motor's rpms. I have not used any of these controls but have noted that they are designed for both handheld and table-mounted routers. Some router manufacturers do not recommend the use of a speed control with their product. Read your owner's manual carefully.

Elevation Control. This knob can be used with the Porter-Cable 6931 plunge base for elevation control when the plunge-type base is used in a router table. Since this particular router base is not designed for table applications, the best solution is to buy the Porter-Cable 1001 base. Use the motor with the plunge base for handheld use and the fixed base for the table. All other plunge routers that I am familiar with have the required elevation control for use in a router table.

Template Guide Bushings. Template guide bushings are available for all routers, but the de facto standard is the Porter-Cable set. In the early days, when other manufacturers were offering template guide bushings formed from dimpled tin, Porter-Cable offered the machined inserts that are still available today. Adapter plates are available for using Porter-Cable bushings with just about any router.

Today, a few of the template guide bushings identify the template they are designed to work with, but most merely state that they are for general routing. I have cut all of my bushings to a ¼" shoulder. Doing this allows me to use the bushings with any pattern I might have. Additionally, if the bushing has an outside diameter of ½", ⅝" or ¾", I make expander rings since I have drills with these diameters. I make the outside diameter of the expander ring whatever size I need to do a particular job. These modifications are shown opposite, top right. The expander rings are made like insert rings for the router plates. This technique is explained in the next chapter.

MEASUREMENT TOOLS

Measurement tools that are handy when working with the router table include some form of a height/depth/edge gauge, a dial caliper and a scale. A micro-

ELEVATION CONTROL KNOB
With the addition of this elevation control knob, the Porter-Cable plunge router can be used in a router table. The better solution is to use the plunge router motor unit with a fixed base when you use it with the table.

PORTER-CABLE TEMPLATE GUIDE BUSHINGS
The Porter-Cable template guide bushings are the de facto industry standard. Increase their usefulness by cutting the bushing shoulders so they are all the same length. Expander rings, like those shown in the photograph, are easy to make and further increase the cutting flexibility of the bushings.

positioner for the fence and the various fixtures, along with a calculator, are beneficial when you get into the more demanding types of cuts. The use of the micropositioners is explained in chapter four, "Building Router-Table Jigs and Fixtures."

The block shown on the next page fits on the scale as the bench rule hook described on page 72. In this application, it is used for height/depth readings and settings. The size of the hook allows the scale to be set on the table surface with the hook spanning the router-bit opening for precise height settings.

ROUTER TOOLS

The only tools required when using the router are the collet wrenches. They come in all sizes. Something to think about is their color. They are normally either black or zinc-coated. Having a color that will contrast with the router table's top is worthwhile. Black wrenches lying on a black table surface or a black router plate are almost invisible—that is, until you turn the router on and start pushing the workpiece into the cutter.

MAINTENANCE TOOLS AND SUPPLIES

The following maintenance tools and supplies should be included on your required accessories list.

Collet Brushes. Read the material on pages 151-

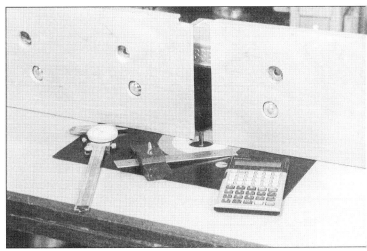

MEASUREMENT TOOLS
Good measurement tools are a must to make fast setups and accurate cuts. As a minimum, you need a dial caliper and a good scale. The scientific calculator isn't mandatory but can be handy.

152. After reading it, you will probably want to buy a set of brushes.

Brush. A brush for cleaning the router is a must. You can use an inexpensive varnish brush with the bristles cut back so they are strong and stiff. As discussed in the next section, the accumulation of router dust in the router can cause problems with the clamping and the elevation controls.

Cleaners and Lubricants. You can add life to your

SHOP-MADE HEIGHT/DEPTH SCALE
Measuring the bit height on a router table can be a problem. The openings in the plate and the fence make it difficult to place the scale. With the addition of the hook shown here, the measurements become much easier.

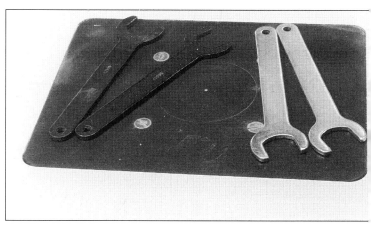

BLACK AND WHITE COLLET WRENCHES
Black collet wrenches can disappear on black insert plates. Add some white stripes.

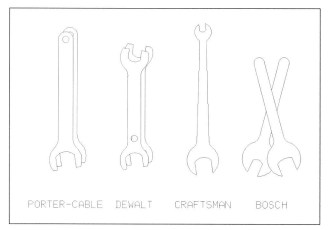

PORTER-CABLE   DEWALT   CRAFTSMAN   BOSCH

COLLET WRENCHES

router bits by keeping them clean and the bearings lubricated.

Dressing Stones. Both carbide and high-speed steel bits can be honed with diamond-covered dressing sticks. These sticks are relatively inexpensive and, if nothing more, keep the cutting edges clean. Use them like a strop.

Highland Hardware offers a router maintenance kit (part number 10.52.01) that includes all of the above tools except for the modified varnish brush. The collet brush is for ½" collets. If you need a ¼" collet brush, the only one I know of is from Onsrud Cutter.

DUST BUILDUP

Accumulated router dust can cause two serious problems with your router. The first problem is the possible hindrance of clamping the router to its base. The photograph opposite, top left, shows how dust accumulation will, over time, build up and eventually prevent complete clamping.

When the router isn't properly clamped to its base, the router can spin out of the base—a very disconcerting event. The router can also spin out due to negligence. For this reason, the floor of the router cavity in the table should be as close as possible to the bot-

tom of the router. If the router does spin out, it will hopefully stay in the cavity, minimizing the possible damage to you and the router. I have had this happen and, thankfully, the router stood on its base on the cavity floor without tipping. I was also thankful for the nearness of the on-off switch in the table.

The other problem that must be contended with is how dust buildup affects the elevation control. With the rack-and-pinion design, the dust can collect in the rack, jamming the pinion gear. To clear the jam, remove the router and clean the rack and pinion. Sometimes you must use a toothpick or some other sharp point to pick the compacted dust out of the rack gears. See opposite, top right, to see what I mean.

With the spiral's design, dust can build up in the races, locking the motor to the base. You can have a real problem freeing them from one another if you wait too long between cleaning. This form of dust buildup is shown opposite, lower right.

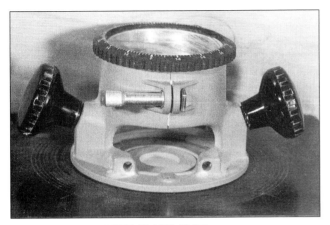

DUST BUILDUP IN THE CLAMP SLOT
This dust buildup that can be seen at the bottom of the clamp slot, if allowed to accumulate, will prevent the secure clamping of the router motor to the base. A motor not securely clamped will spin out of the base when turned on.

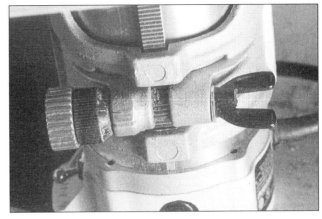

RACK-AND-PINION DUST BUILDUP
Router dust buildup, like that shown here, will jam the rack-and-pinion gears. If you do not clean it before adjusting the height, you will need to disassemble the clamp/pinion assembly to free the jam.

The cutting method and the use of inserts in the router-plate opening both affect the possible dust buildup. Sometimes just one or two passes of a work-piece will throw dust down where it must be cleaned, while other times, you can go all day without the need to clean out the races. Look for the dust accumulation and clean it out before it starts causing problems.

ROUTER CONTROL LOCATIONS AND MARKINGS

On-off switch—The on-off switch plays a secondary role when the router is used in a table. It is not important to have the switch readily accessible. Get in the habit of switching the router off whenever you bring the motor up on the table. Two switches—one on the router and one on the table—must be thrown in order to power the router. You may forget to turn the router's switch back on when remounting the router, so be safe and make it a habit to always turn the router table's switches back off whenever you find that the router doesn't start. Another thing to remember is that the router in the table will normally be in the "on" state. Get in the habit of switching it off whenever the motor is removed. If you take it out and put it in another base for hand routing, you don't want to be surprised when you plug the router's power cord in.

Without a doubt, the safest method for disabling power is to unplug the extension cord that powers the table. There is no inadvertent way the router can be turned on. The router's power cord is still plugged in, but it's plugged into a dead circuit.

Elevation. The elevation controls are important to

SPIRAL DUST BUILDUP
Dust buildup in the grooves of the spirals has the same effect as the dust buildup in the rack-in-pinion design. The motor will jam in the base and can be extremely difficult to free. Keep a brush handy and clean the grooves frequently.

have accessible and visible when the router is mounted in the table. The mounting suggested in chapter three allows this visual and physical access.

For the Porter-Cable ring-type elevation control, the etched scale line may not be visible. When it's not visible, draw a pencil line on the motor body to reference the ring. The graphite from the pencil is a good lubricant, so don't worry about marking up the motor body.

The engraved scale on a router like the DeWalt 610 is hard to see since it is black-on-black. You can improve the elevation control by brushing white paint into the engraved scale and then rubbing the outer surface clean. The index mark from the cast is also rather coarse, so I engraved a new, thinner index line on the base housing and filled it with paint. The result is shown at lower right.

You can change the height setting more easily when you can read the engraving on the elevation scale. This form of elevation control is handy, not only for incremental height changes, but also for moving from one height position to a second height position. Its use is similar to using turrets on a plunge router.

For the Bosch, if you work in inches, you have to remember that one division is equal to $1/32''$. From the looks of the casting shown opposite, top right, it would appear that Bosch wants to eliminate fractional notation. Not a bad idea really.

Plunge routers are adjusted using the elevation knob. Note that the plunge stops and screw-in turret stops all have a tendency to loosen and fall out when the router is mounted upside down in the table. There is a good chance they will drop into the router dust and end up in your shop vac. Either tighten them or take them off when the router is used in the table.

Speed Control

Location—With the spiral elevation control, the location of the speed control will vary depending on the height of the bit. Learn where the control is located and which way to move it to change the speed.

Marking—Why is it that a router manufacturer will offer variable-speed control and then disguise the settings with some arcane mnemonic like 10,000 rpm equals *A*? Wouldn't it be just as easy to silk-screen a *10* as an *A*? Another manufacturer uses broad stripes as leaders to the numbers silk-screened to the control slide. The problem is that the numbers cannot be seen when the router is table-mounted. For the table application, it would be nice if the thickness of the stripes reflected the greater or lesser speed. The human factors of some designs leave much to be desired. The table's human factors for elevation control aren't much better. The way the tables are designed, you must either stand on your head or use a mirror to read the speed-control settings.

Clamping. The router base/motor clamp or router's depth clamp, in the case of plunge routers, must be easily accessible. Certainly from a safety standpoint, this is the most critical control when the router is mounted on a table.

PENCIL MARK TO REFERENCE HEIGHT CHANGE
Porter-Cable has an elegant method for adjusting the depth of a cut, but when depth of cut becomes height of cut with the router mounted in the table, you probably can't see the index line. Make your own index line with a pencil mark.

DEWALT ELEVATION MODIFICATION
This DeWalt height/depth control knob has been modified by filling the index knob engraving with white paint. The scale can now be read when the router is mounted in the table. Note also the thin line above the casting index. This line was added to increase the precision of the adjustment. It would be better to scribe it below the cast index.

Earlier Porter-Cable 690 series routers had a smaller wing nut for clamping the motor to the base than today's routers do. The old style is easy to enlarge with a couple of cut blocks that are hogged out to fit the wing nut and then glued over the small wings. I have made this modification, as shown at the bottom of the page, for both the standard base and the D-handle base.

There is no perfect router or perfect solution for the table application. I have used many routers and have tried many possible solutions. All the routers and some of the solutions have worked well. All of them left something to be desired. But after all, it is an upside-down world.

BOSCH ELEVATION CONTROL
Like the spiral index, the Bosch index may not be visible when mounted in the table. Again use your pencil. From the looks of the casting it would appear that old man Bosch wants to stamp out fractional notation.

PLUNGE-ROUTER TURRETS
Most plunge routers suffer a common problem when used in a table. The turrets and depth bars tend to loosen and fall out, dropping onto the base of the table's router cavity. As you can see, they can be easily lost to your shop vac. Either keep them tight or take them off when the router is used with the table.

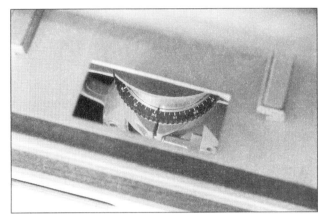

USING A MIRROR
One way to turn the upside-down world upright is to use a mirror. This technique is also handy for checking the router speed setting when using a variable-speed router.

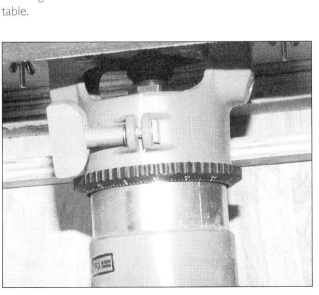

ENLARGED WING NUTS
The leverage and ease of use of the router can be enhanced by increasing the size and grip of the clamping wing nut. The modification shown here is on an earlier Porter-Cable design. Their current models have increased the size of the wing nut. Upside-down routers must be securely clamped, and small wing nuts wreak havoc on the carpal tendon.

CHAPTER TWO

BUILDING ROUTER-TABLE TOPS

Before building the top for your router table, decide its size, the surface material and what type of plate will be used to hold the router. Remember that you will be living with your choice for a long time. The most important decision is the selection of the standard plate. All the surface materials discussed offer good lasting results. Two table sizes are presented, and each has advantages and disadvantages with respect to the other. As with router selection, you must consider the type of cutting you plan to do.

Review the features of the three router tables covered in this book and see what best meets your needs. If you plan to combine features from the individual table designs, determine if these combinations will affect the table size. My feeling is that most of them won't.

If you will be using a large variable-speed router or a fence system like the INCRA Jig Ultra, you are best served with the larger table size. Conversely, if portability or shop space are important parameters, you will probably want one of the smaller tables.

Use what you are familiar with or what is available to you for the table surface. Both the plastic laminate and the solid-surface materials can require you to purchase large sheets, resulting in unusable remnants. That's the nice thing about good wood: There is no such thing as remnants. Sometimes the cutoffs wait for their calling, but they always get called. Making the top with birch ply is the simplest and easiest way to go.

The plates to hold the router can either be purchased or made. You will probably want to use both. To do this, pick a commercial plate for your standard. Make your shop-made plates then to this standard size.

ROUTER PLATES

The router plate is an important part of the table design. Certain commercial plates can be purchased with removable insert rings. If you are buying, this is the type to buy. These purchased plates also come with starting pins that are well designed and, if they don't get lost, will be invaluable for certain cutting operations. If you make your plates, it probably won't be possible later to use a purchased plate without some shimming or cutting. Two standard-size commercial plates are used in this book. The one manufactured by the Rousseau company is $9'' \times 12'' \times \frac{1}{4}''$. The other, manufactured by Woodhaven, is $9\frac{1}{4}'' \times 11\frac{3}{4}'' \times \frac{3}{8}''$. Both plate sizes are offered with removable insert rings. The smallest opening in each plate is sized for the Porter-Cable template guide bushings. Each of the plates is large enough to handle just about any router you select. If you will only use one of the smaller routers, you can use a smaller plate size for your standard. If you want to be able to add a jigsaw or some other tool to the table, use one of the larger sizes.

Next, decide where the plate (and thus the router bit) will be located on the top's surface. For the two table sizes covered, three locations are specified. The reason for the three locations is to give you the best-sized table half or quadrant to work with. Looking at the contracter's table top, you can see that, depending on the fence type and the plate location with respect to the table, you can form varying work surfaces. When working with large workpieces, you want to maximize the surface area supporting the workpiece. Working with smaller or vertical pieces will be easier if you work in a smaller quadrant, placing you closer to your work. The type of fence you use will also influence the location of the plate. Review the material in chapter three before making your decision about plate location.

As you can see on the next page, there are four

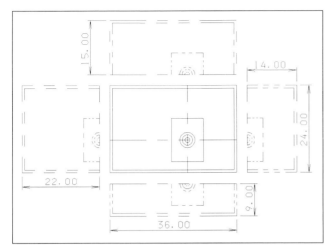

CONTRACTOR TABLE CUTTING QUADRANTS

distinct work areas that can be used for specific cutting. The size of the workpiece and the type of cutting being performed determines which area is best suited for the particular cut.

Plate Materials

The choices to make for shop-made plates are material and material thickness. Plate blanks can be purchased in polycarbonate (generic Lexan), acrylic and high-density phenolic. The polycarbonate is shatter resistant but not as stiff as the acrylic. For the large plate sizes used here, the polycarbonate is not my favorite since it tends to sag with heavy routers. Both materials can be purchased in ⅜″ × 12″ × 12″ blanks. The rub is that the 12″ × 12″ dimensions are nominal. The blanks may come as 11¹⁵⁄₁₆″ squares. If the standard plate opening is 12″, i.e., you are using a Rousseau plate, this means some shimming.

The acrylic material makes the best plate for a plunge router. It allows you to view the cutting area before you take the plunge. In fact, the clear plastic is a better choice for the router base whenever it is used as a handheld tool.

Another good plate material is ½″ Finnish or Baltic plywood. The ½″ stock is strong, and it cuts and machines well. The fact that it is not really ½″ thick is of no concern since the plate will be rabbeted to fit the opening. The same is true for the ⅜″ acrylic or polycarbonate when matching a standard ¼″ plate. For the ⅜″ standard plate, it may be necessary to shim the acrylic or polycarbonate. This shimming and trimming is described in the instructions for each top.

MAKING THE ROUTER-TABLE TOP

The finished top is a perfect rectangle with hardwood borders. The top surface can be solid surface, plastic laminate or finished Finnish birch. For the plastic-laminate and birch tops, cut the base materials from ¾″ birch stock. For the solid-surface top, use ½″ Finnish birch as a base for the ½″ solid-surface material. The resultant top thicknesses are therefore ¾″ for the birch top, ¾″ plus the laminate thickness for the plastic-laminate top and 1″ for the solid-surface top. In each case, the top will be mounted on the table's ¾″ subtop, resulting in 1½″ to 1¾″ total thickness of the complete top assembly.

Making a Birch-Ply Top

To make a birch-ply top, lay out and cut the top from the Finnish birch sheet. (Cutting diagrams for the tops are shown in chapters five, six and seven.) The steps outlined below are for making a birch top with a 9″ × 12″ plate opening. The variations for the other plate size and for solid-surface and plastic-laminate materials are covered following this basic sequence.

1. Lay in the plate opening. Note that the opening is cut ¾″ less than the selected plate size. The final plate opening will be cut using a ⅜″ rabbeting bit.
2. Scribe the center lines onto the top.
3. Using a jigsaw, cut out most of the hole material. Make sure you stay slightly inside the plate-opening lines.
4. Position and secure 3″-wide by ½″-long strips of birch ply along the lines representing the plate opening. These strips will guide the bearing on the pattern-cutting bit mounted in the router. Place enough ¾″ and ½″ stock over the hole to insure that the router remains flat with respect to the top surface. You can also use double-backed tape to attach a spacer to the router base.
5. Elevate or bridge the top so the cutter won't cut the bench top and, using a pattern bit, cut the final opening.
6. Use this opening as the pattern to guide the bearing. Cut the ⅜″ rabbet. The depth of the cut is the thickness of the selected plate. Take small cuts to reach the required depth. Use a dial caliper to check the depth.

DRILLED CORNER HOLES
Drill the corners first to allow an exact match with the plate corner radius. The hole centers must be accurately located for this method to work properly.

7. The final step is to fit the corners. The Rousseau plate has ⅜″ radius corners which will not fit the ⅝″ radius corners cut in the top using the pattern bit (¼″ radius bearing plus ⅜″ rabbet). You can do one of two things: You can sharpen up the corners with a chisel, or you can drill holes in the corners. By drilling holes in the corners, you will make an opening that minimizes the dust buildup. The corners collect dust. It is necessary to clear accumulated dust away whenever you lift the plate. The holes will help keep the corners free of this dust accumulation. Drill these holes before cutting out the plate opening.

Making a Laminate Top

When the top is covered with a plastic laminate, some woodworkers opt to cover both sides of the wood to keep the wood under uniform stress. I never bother with covering the underside and have never experienced any problems. On the other hand, if you use the laminate covering, chances are you will have an excess of material, so covering both sides is not a problem. Belts and suspenders are always the safe solution.

To make the top, cut the birch piece slightly over-sized. Next, cut the laminate slightly larger than the oversized birch blank. Bond the laminate to the top with contact cement. Follow the manufacturer's directions for applying the contact cement. Two coats are always better than one, and, in this case, go with the conventional wisdom. Make sure the laminate is flat and there are no air pockets or bubbles. A J-roller is the best tool to use for this bonding. A wallpaper roller, though smaller, will get the job done, as will a block of wood and a dead-blow hammer. Start the rolling or hammering from the center and work your way out toward the edges. Make sure the edges are tight.

Since the laminate is sticking out past the edge of the birch piece, use an offset spacer to cut the laminated top to its final size. Position this spacer strip between the edge of the birch and the saw's fence.

I have a Delta Unifence with this feature built into its fence design. If your fence doesn't have this feature, use double-backed tape to attach a straight spacer strip to the fence. This strip should be the length of the fence and have a height less than the thickness of the birch sheet. Cut two of the top's sides, one on each axis, using the offset. Now, using these trimmed sides and a normal fence setup, cut the parallel sides to the final dimensions.

An alternate trimming sequence is to cut the birch to its final size and then bond the oversized laminate to it. Use a flush-trim router to cut the excess laminate away. The resulting edge may not have the quality of the saw-cut edge. If your table saw is wide enough to do the trimming, use the saw.

Another variation is to cut the laminate piece oversized, and then cut the birch slightly larger than the laminate piece. This method does not require the use

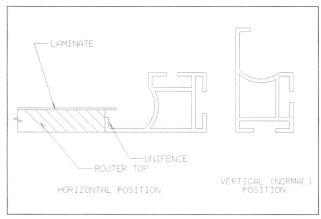

OFFSET EXAMPLE

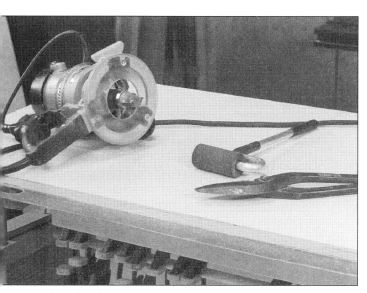

APPLYING AND TRIMMING THE LAMINATE TOP
Useful tools for making plastic laminate tops are a good pair of tin snips to cut the laminate, a J-roller for the pressure bonding of the laminate to its substrate and a large-diameter pattern bit to trim the edges.

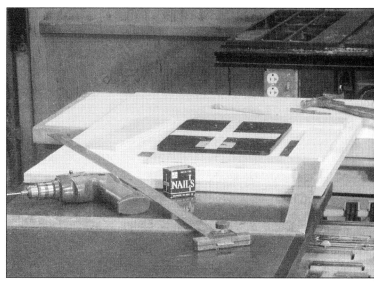

FORMING A CUTTING PATTERN
Border the plate with strips, as shown here, to create the cutting pattern for the router plate. Start with the placement of the plate and then border it with the precut strips.

CUTTING THE ROUTER-PLATE OPENING
The actual opening is cut ¾″ undersized. Use a ¼″ bit with a 1″ template guide bushing.

CUTTING THE FINAL PLATE INSET
Cut the final plate inset with a ⅜″ piloted rabbet bit. The depth of the cut is the router plate thickness.

of the fence offset, but does require care in positioning the laminate to the birch.

The plate opening can be cut as described in the directions for making a birch top, or by using a variation of the insert method. For either method, start by scribing the center lines onto the laminate top and then lay in the plate opening. Use a marker pen to highlight the scored line. Any kitchen cleaner can be used to remove the excess marker ink.

1. Position and fix the router plate to the underside of the top.
2. Border the plate with scrap ½″ strips of birch ply, tacking the strips to the top.
3. Using a 1″ outside-diameter guide to bushing with a ¼″ spiral bit, cut out the router plate opening. This opening will be ¾″ undersized. Jump ahead to the next section and review the material on inlays.
4. With the top side up, cut the ⅜″ rabbet as described in making a birch top.

CENTER LINE LAYOUT

Center line layout is a technique to establish both a workpiece's center and the positional relationship between parts. Two or more parts can be positioned with respect to one another by matching their center lines.

Step 1. To find the center, measure the width and divide it by two.

The result of this calculation, of course, is the halfway point.

Step 2. Measure from one side of the board and mark the center point.

Step 3. Repeat the measurement from the other side of the board and mark it.

You will end up with two marks something like this II separated by probably less than 1/16". (In theory, the marks would not have any space between them. As any woodworker knows, however, there *will* be a space.) The point midway between the two marks is the board's center in the width dimension. Note that it doesn't make any difference if the marks were short of the center or slightly past the board's center. The marks still bracket the true center.

Step 4. Repeat the double measurement for the board's other dimension.

Step 5. Use a try square to lay in and extend the center lines on the workpiece.

If the workpiece is too large for the try square, repeat the double measurement at each end of the board and use along straightedge to lay in the lines.

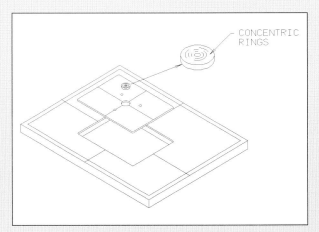

EXAMPLE OF MATCHING CENTER LINES

Match these center lines with center lines on other workpieces. For example, match the center lines of the plate and the top to establish the plate's position on the top. The eye is very discerning in its ability to see minute differences in the alignment of the lines. If the lines "look" as if they are in alignment, they are aligned. If the cardinal axis doesn't line up as in the example here, check your center line measurements and correct the offending line. As will be described for the construction of the router-table carcasses, measuring from the edges can cause a buildup of errors in the layout. By doing the layout and measurement from the part's center, these errors and the accumulation of tolerance buildups are eliminated.

The final touch is to mark the insert rings. Instead of drawing the axes on ring, lay in two or three concentric rings with, for example, ½", ¾" and 1" diameters. Use these rings as an aid in fence and fixture positioning with respect to the bit's center.

Making a Solid-Surface Top

I am most familiar with Avonite, one of the manufacturers of solid-surface materials, but the following discussion also applies to solid-surface materials produced by other manufacturers.

One reason for using solid-surface material is that it looks so nice. I call these *designer tables*—they cost more but don't offer much of a utilitarian advantage.

The best way to get the material is to buy it either as scrap or as a finished cut piece from a shop that works with solid-surface materials. This shop will probably be in the business of doing kitchens and bathrooms. Their scrap cutouts from stoves and sinks are normally large enough for the material you need. This won't give you much of a color selection but it

does keep the cost down.

Cut the plate opening the same way you cut inlays or inserts. There are bushing sets available to cut inlays such as mock dovetails or other decorative shapes.

Cutting inlays is best accomplished using a female pattern. The standard plate (either purchased or shop-made) is the male pattern used to create the female. To cut an inlay, you'll need either a bushing guide and a bushing-guide expander, or two bushing guides of the required diameters. You'll make the insert cavity in the workpiece with the guide riding on the female pattern. You then cut the male insert using the same pattern but with the expander placed on the guide. The expander diameter is the guide diameter

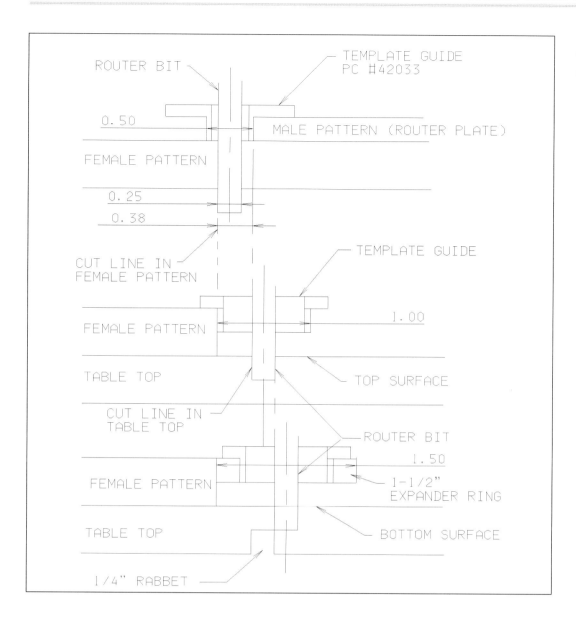

plus the bit diameter. For our application, we already have the male insert; it is the router plate.

The pattern guides used in this example are from the Porter-Cable template guide kit. All routers will support the Porter-Cable guides, either as manufactured or with the purchase of an adapter. Of course, you can use any guide set.

1. Cut the solid-surface material to size. Use a 20° hook solid-surface blade like the Forrest Solids Planer for this cutting.
2. Scribe the center lines on the top's surface. See sidebar on page 32.
3. Cut the female pattern using a ½″ guide and a ¼″ bit. The standard plate can be screwed to the female pattern for this cutting if the template shoulder has been cut down to ¼″.

Review the steps in the drawing above which shows first how to cut the female pattern and then how to cut the top. Notice the relationships between the male and female patterns and the bushings.

4. Lay out center lines on the pattern.
5. Align center lines on the solid-surface top with the center lines on the female pattern and fix the pattern to the top.
6. Using a plunge router with a 1″ guide and a ¼″ bit, cut the opening border to the depth of the plate thickness (¼″ or ⅜″). After getting the depth of the cut just right, cut the border slot in one pass of the router. Don't precut the hole with a jigsaw. Cutting the solid-surface material with a saw can cause stress and fracture at the corners. The cutout piece can be

trimmed and used as a filler plate, so take care with this cutting. Don't wander into the plate area with the router cut.

7. Reposition the female pattern to the other side of the top. Secure the top and the center (cutout) portion to a backing board or the bench top so that when the center is cut free, it will not cock or turn and jam the cutter bit. Using a 1″ guide with a 1½″ expander ring, cut away the remaining ⅛″ or ¼″ of material and free the plate cutout piece. The resultant opening now has a nominal ¼″ ledge to support the router plate.

CUTTING THE SOLID-SURFACE BASE

The solid-surface material will be bonded to a ½″ birch-ply substrate base using 100 percent silicon adhesive. Do this bonding after the substrate has been bordered. See "Top Borders" and "Attaching the Top to the Table" in the following sections before bonding the top to the substrate. Use the opening in the solid-surface top as the pattern guide to cut out the plate opening in the substrate. Place a piece of scrap in the center area to keep the router base flat and perpendicular to the cut or, as mentioned before, tape a filler block to the router base.

Making Tops With a 9¼″ × 11¾″ Plate Opening

The Woodhaven plate has a ¾″ corner radius. Use the insert method for any of the top materials to make the opening for this plate. If you form the plate opening by using the modified insert method outlined in the directions for making a laminate top, the resultant

CORNERS
Use the ⅜″ rabbet bit with a ½″ bearing to cut a ⅝″ corner radius. The Woodhaven plate shown here has a ⅜″ corner radius. The resulting mismatch will not be a problem.

corner radius will be ⅝″. There will be a slight opening at the corners that ensures the plate will not bind with the top.

Top Borders

After you have cut the plate opening, you're ready to border the top with hardwood. Try to get good, straight-grained lumber to use for these border strips. You can use a number of methods to attach the strips to the top. Dowels or biscuits work best. Glue alone is adequate and certainly is easier to do. For the solid-surface top, a tongue-and-groove joint is recommended. The ½″ birch base is the tongue.

If you use a solid-surface top, then pick a complementary color for the border just as you would for

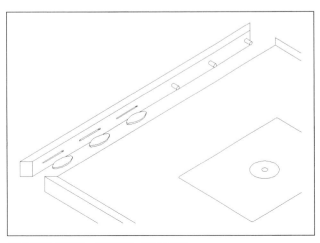

BORDER JINTS—DOWEL, BISCUIT

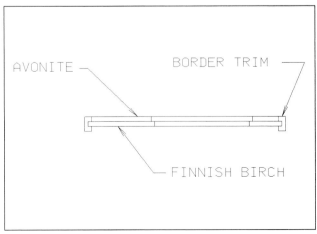

AVONITE — BORDER TRIM

FINNISH BIRCH

TONGUE AND GROOVE

kitchen countertops or a coffee table. You can do a lot to enhance the final appearance of the table for very little additional effort or expense.

Normally 1″ hardwood is milled to a $^{25}/_{32}″$ or larger thickness. After you attach the borders to the top, sand them flush with the top surface and then cut to the nominal ¾″ dimension.

Use your table saw to trim the top to its final outside dimensions. Over the life of your router table, a true rectangular top will save you time—lots of time—setting up cuts. The table's edges should be parallel to the center lines that were previously scribed in the top. After the borders have been glued to the top, their edges should be parallel to the center line. If not, you can use MFD plywood to make a cutting guide to reference the table saw trim cut to the center line.

For the smaller tops, a framing square tacked to the top will ensure not only a parallel edge but also one that is perpendicular to the adjoining edge. Drilling ¹⁄₁₆″ holes in the framing square's legs will allow you to use 18-gauge nails to position and retain the square. Turn the top over for this cutting and trimming, and the nail holes will never show. The long leg of the framing square rides the fence, as shown in the photograph on the next page.

The absolute size of the table is not important. What is important is that the top is square. Each of the sides must be at 90° angles to the adjacent sides. To achieve this squareness, it may be necessary to cut away more border material. You'll never know the difference between a top having all ¾″ borders and

FLUSHING THE TOP BORDER STRIPS
A plane can be safely used to flush the hardwood borders to the laminate. Do a final sanding with a 60 micron or finer grit paper.

one having one or two ¹¹⁄₁₆″ borders.

For the birch and laminate tops, glue the borders to the edges. Using a damp rag, make sure all the glue is removed and the joint line is cleaned before the glue has dried.

With the solid-surface material, the top is fitted to the border frame. Use the solid-surface top for the pattern when you glue the border strips to the top substrate. You want a tight fit. Bond the top to the substrate with the 100 percent silicon glue. The border strips can be bonded to the solid surface using Eclectic Products FAMOBOND Melamine Adhesive.

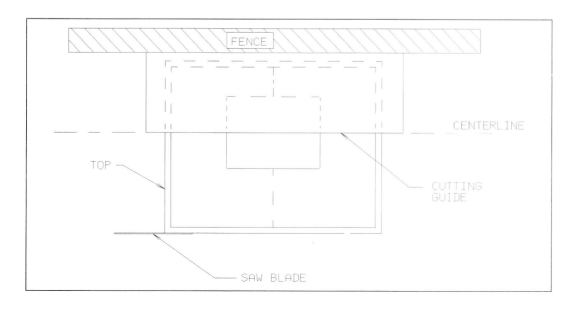

CUTTING GUIDE— CENTERLINE TO EDGE

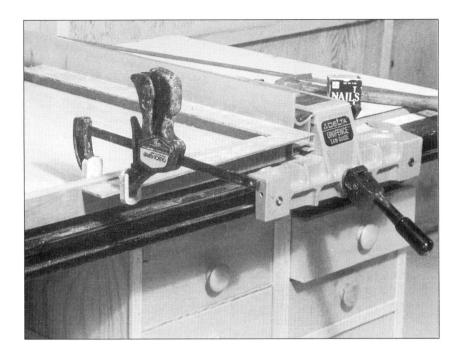

After you attach the borders, make sure there is no lip or edge that can catch a workpiece or jig at the transition line between the top and its border. If the borders are higher than the top surface, cut or sand them flush. The birch top has quite a lot of veneer thickness, and you can quickly accomplish this sanding. With the laminate top, take care to create a flush interface without marring the laminate top. I sometimes lay masking tape over the top where it joins the border and sand down until the tape starts to disappear. I then use a scraper to complete the task. The scraper will not mar the laminate surface when used properly.

I use an old planer blade as a scraper to clean the tops of many of my laminate-covered workstations and benches. I have been scraping dried glue off some of them for over five years, and they still look fine. My wife, however, will not let me use the scraper on the kitchen countertops.

If the borders extend below the top surface, carefully sand a transition bevel, eliminating any corners or edges. A slight round or chamfer will not affect the use of the table.

Use a 60-micron or finer grit paper to sand the solid-surface or plastic-laminate top. Sand the complete top surface to obtain good texture for the top.

Attaching the Top to the Table

Don't permanently attach the top to the table. Instead, use dowels for locating pins and then use a couple of screws to hold the top to the subtop. You will drive the screws from the underside anywhere in the router cavity. The dowels are blind. Start by drilling three dowel holes in the subtop over the dividers as shown below.

1. Use tape or hot glue to attach spacer blocks either to the inside of the top border or to the sides of the table so that the top will be properly positioned when placed on the subtop. Use dowel centers in the dowel holes in the subtop and place the top on the table, thereby marking the hole location in the top. Drill the stopped

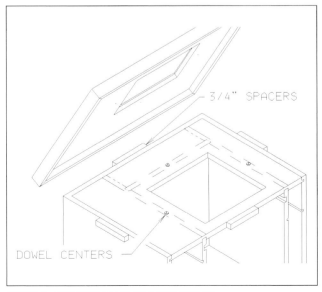

DOWEL CENTERS AND SPACER ROLLS

holes in the top about ½″ deep. Make sure you don't drill through or into the top material. Check the fit and, if desired, glue the dowels to either the top or the subtop.

You can drill the dowel holes in a solid-surface top before you bond the solid-surface to the ½″ substrate. You will be able to drill through the substrate and into the subtop without resorting to dowel centers to establish the mating-hole locations.

2. Use the top to cut the opening in the table's subtop. First remove most of the waste with a jigsaw.
3. Now, with the top in position, trim to the top opening using a pattern bit.
4. Next attach the selected router base to the plate. Mounting dimensions for the routers discussed are shown in the next section.
5. Accurately lay in the mounting-hole locations. Establish the plate's center first and then mark the hole locations. Place masking tape on the plate so you can see and, if necessary, change the hole center points.
6. Drill and countersink the holes. When the base is attached, the screwhead should be slightly under the top's surface.

If you use the Woodhaven plate, you may have to cut away some of the subtop to allow the router, attached to its plate, to be positioned. The cuts required for the Porter-Cable 5718/19 base are shown on the next page.

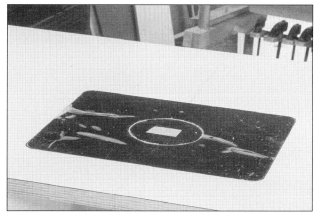

FITTING THE STANDARD PLATE
Do a final check for the fit of the plate to the opening. The plate should not move with respect to the router-table top.

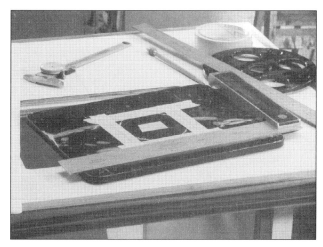

ESTABLISHING THE MOUNTING HOLE CENTER
If possible, use exact dimensions to locate the router mounting holes. Tracing the router base plate isn't accurate since the center location is unknown. Notwithstanding, use the base to check your layout.

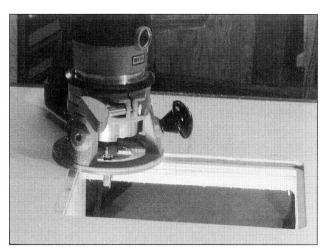

TRIMMING THE SUBBASE OPENING
The opening in the subtop is cut with a jigsaw and flush trimmed with a pattern bit.

RECESSED SCREW HEADS
The countersink for the mounting screws must be deep enough to ensure the screw heads do not protrude above the top's surface.

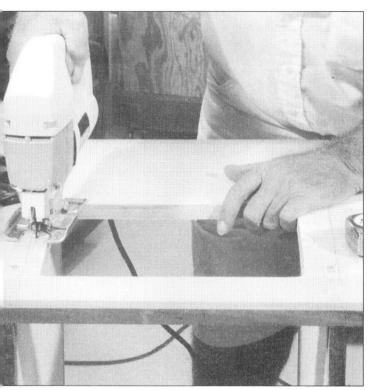

REQUIRED CUTTING
For some routers, like the Porter-Cable 7518, you need to cut away some of the subtop to use an 11¾″ plate. As shown here, a couple of 1″ scallops on each side solves the problem caused by the distance of the router handles from the plate.

TRIMMING AND SHIMMING PLATES

If the material is too thin, i.e., not as thick as the standard, try using edge bonding "ironed" onto the thin stock. This method of shimming normally works well and will last a long time.

To increase the overall size of an acrylic blank, bond wood strips to the acrylic with contact cement. A small tube of contact cement is easier to use for this type of fix than a large, messy can of cement.

Border an undersized blank of acrylic or birch with wood stock and then cut to size. You will save material that would otherwise be too small to use. For the trimmed birch, use aliphatic resin glue, e.g., Franklin Titebond. When bonding wood to solid-surface material, I recommend using Eclectic Products FAMOBOND Melamine Adhesive. Making a solid-surface filler plate for the table having a solid-surface top will require bordering the piece previously cut from the top to bring it back to its required size.

SHOP-MADE PLATES

I find many reasons to make additional plates for my router tables. One reason is that I want a larger bit opening. I use a primary router with the table and other routers in the handheld mode. Sometimes I want to use these other routers in the table. I may not want to go the expense of purchasing a new plate and then waiting for it to arrive. Often I want a plate for some nonstandard or special-purpose application which dictates a shop-made plate. A number of these special-purpose plates and applications are covered later in this chapter.

The material you use to make the plate depends on the application. I use ⅜″ clear acrylic when I need to see what is going on and birch ply the rest of the time. Cut a rabbet in the plate to bring the thickness down to the standard plate thickness. If your plate material is too small or too thin, review the sidebar below, left, on the various options for bringing the material up to the required size.

1. Cut the blank to the required outside dimensions (9″ × 12″ or 9¼″ × 11¾″).
2. Scribe center lines on the blank.
3. Round the corners and check the fit. Use the standard plate or a corner pattern and pattern bit for rounding the corners. The standard plate can be fixed to the plate blank using the router mounting holes and wood screws. Corner patterns are described in chapter four, "Building Router-Table Jigs and Fixtures."
4. Using the center lines as the primary axes, lay in the mounting hole locations. Determine the size you want and lay in the circle opening for the router bit. You can make insert rings for the shop-made plates. Review the sidebar on the next page before cutting the router-bit opening.
5. Drill and countersink the router mounting holes. These holes can also be drilled and counterbored to use pan head screws. This method will allow you to compensate for layout and drilling tolerance errors.
6. Drill out the center opening. See the sidebar on insert rings on the next page. Check the fit and make sure the plate is level. Be sure the center lines are clearly visible. If not, highlight them with a thin pencil line. The center lines should line up with the center lines previously

INSERT RINGS

Having insert rings for shop-made plates is always worth the time invested. Rousseau and Woodhaven plates have multiple insert rings which are the best. For shop-made plates a one-ring insert is the best solution. Multiple rings can be made for varying sized bit openings but having a nested set cut from wood is pushing. You can also make insert rings for your commercial plates. The minimum bit opening for the Rousseau and Woodhaven plates is a 1¼″ diameter hole sized to accept Porter-Cable template guide bushings. For either of these plates or any of your shop-made plates, try to have three little ring plates: one for use with ¼″ bits (⁹/₃₂″ opening), one for ½″ bits (⁹/₁₆″ opening) and one for ¾″ bits (¹³/₁₆″ opening).

First, decide on the size of the primary opening in your shop-made plates. This no-insert size is normally the opening required for the largest diameter bit you will use with this router and plate combination. The tool used to cut this opening will be a function of the size required and the cutting tools available. A drill press and a Forstner drill bit works well. For me, it means the largest opening cannot be more than 2″. This is the largest Forstner bit I have. For large hole openings, use the router or a drill press with a circle cutter.

First, let's look at the method used for drill-press cutting. The desired cross section of the final opening in the plate and the insert will look like the drawing on the right. Using a Forstner bit, drill to a depth equal to the thickness of the insert stock. This is nominally ¼″, but since most ¼″ birch ply is thinner than that, use the actual stock thickness. If the resultant depth cut leaves the insert slightly proud of the plate, sand the insert flush. If the sanding removes some of the top layer of veneer, don't worry, just turn the insert over. It will never show.

CIRCLE CUTTER

Use a circle cutter of the type shown here to cut the insert circle. This particular style of cutter can cut circles from 1″ up to 6″ in diameter. It can be adjusted to about any accuracy required. Sometimes you need to cut a few trial blanks before you get it just right. The desired fit is a tight one where it is necessary to tap (not pound) the insert ring into the plate opening. If the fit is loose, the insert can be dangerous. You will find that, like a flying saucer, the insert will first hover over the router bit and then when it catches the bit, again like a flying saucer, take off for spaces where no man has gone before. If this happens you may find that you have cleared your alimentary canal and worst, the router plate will be damaged. Don't use loose-fitting inserts. A consideration is to use these shop-made inserts only when the fence is acting as a clamp and keeps them in place. For the small 1¼″ diameter inserts make sure you have a good fit. They can be used very effectively with the sliding fence.

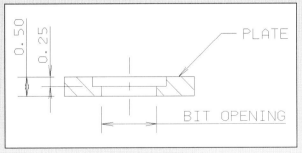

CROSS-SECTIONAL VIEW OF INSERT OPENING

scribed on the top. Apply tung oil to the plate. After the oil has dried, sometimes you need to reinforce the lines again. Finally, coat the plates with a lacquer or a polyurethane finish.

If you use pan head screws to retain the router, the router will float and you won't know exactly where the router center is. A good way to align the router to the base is to put a V-groove bit in the router. Raise the bit until it is flush with the plate surface. Clamp a straightedge to the plate along a center line and try to line up the tip of the V-bit with the straightedge. Secure the router mounting screws.

If you later remove the router base, repeat this alignment procedure when you reattach the base, or the router in the case of plunge routers.

STEPPED INSERTS

Stepped inserts can be cut from either ½″ material or two concentric rings of ¼″ stock that is glued after cutting. A stepped insert has a cross section like this:

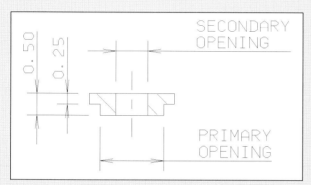

STEPPED INSERT
This type of insert has more surface contact with the plate and therefore greater retention force holds the insert. For a ½″ blank, cut the circle to fit the hole. Next, rabbet the insert to fit the inside diameter. Finally, cut or drill the inside bit opening hole.

For a ¼″ blank, cut the individual circles and, using the plate hole as a pattern, glue them together. Now, drill out the relief hole for the bit opening.

CUTTING THE INSERT CIRCLE USING THE CIRCLE CUTTER
After you establish the correct setting for the circle cutter, cut a number of inserts for later use.

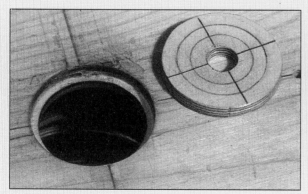

INSERT WITH CENTER LINES AND CONCENTRIC RINGS
The addition of center lines and concentric rings to the insert will aid in the setup of fences and jigs.

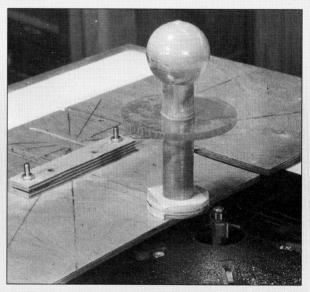

CUTTING THE INSERT USING THE FENCELESS FENCE
The sliding or fenceless fence is best since the setup is retained when the trial insert is removed to check the fit.

USING PAN HEAD SCREWS

If you use flathead screws (countersunk holes) to attach the router to the plate, the screw hole locations must be exact. To allow yourself a little margin of error, use a slightly oversized hole and counterbore and then attach the router to the plate with pan head screws. The amount of float (see diagram) is a function of the size hole drilled.

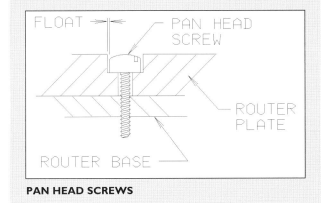

PAN HEAD SCREWS

RECOMMENDED PLATES AND ROUTER POSITIONING

The drawings shown here represent a cross section of router types suitable for use in a router table. It certainly is not an exhaustive list nor does it mean that the suggested mounting is the only mounting possible.

To mount a router, first decide what the router's orientation will be when it's mounted in the table. The elevation and clamping controls are the primary considerations. If you don't have the dimensions of the mounting holes, use the router's base plate for the template. Try to establish the center accurately. The Rousseau plate has concentric rings molded into the plate's bottom side to aid in this alignment. Another method is to tape over the opening in the router's base plate and, using a V-groove bit in the router, mark the plate's center. Remove the base plate from the router and line up the plate's center with the base plate's center. Rotate the base plate until the desired orientation is achieved. Now mark the mounting hole centers.

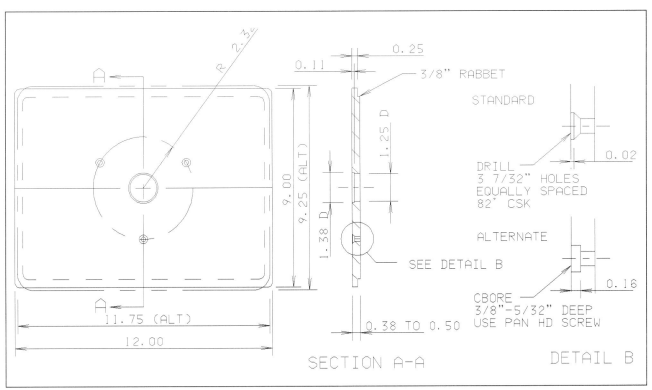

PORTER-CABLE 690 SERIES

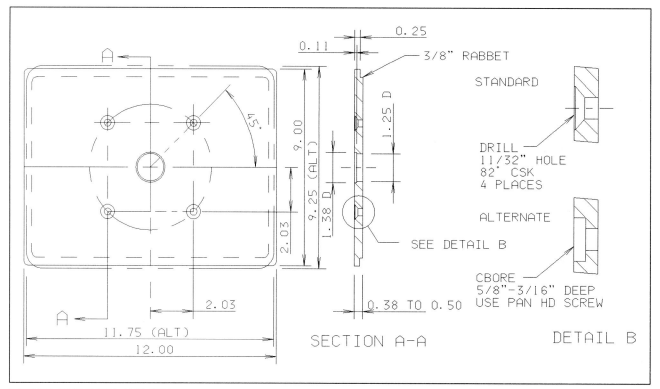

PORTER-CABLE 5718 AND 5719

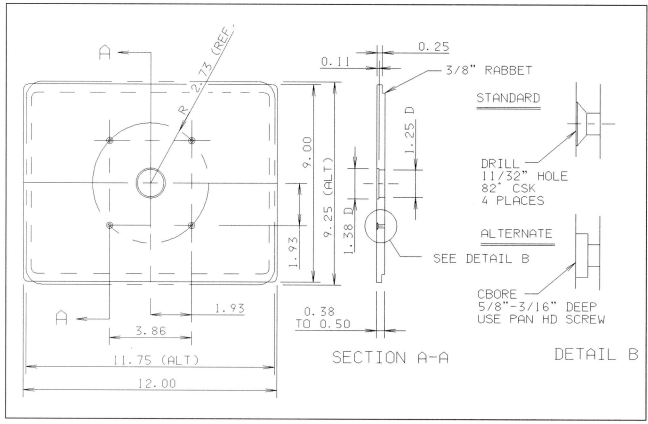

BOSCH 1601A, 16042A AND 1604A

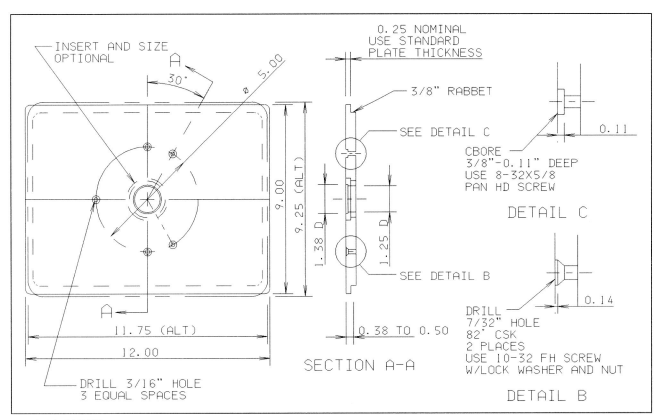

DEWALT DW 610

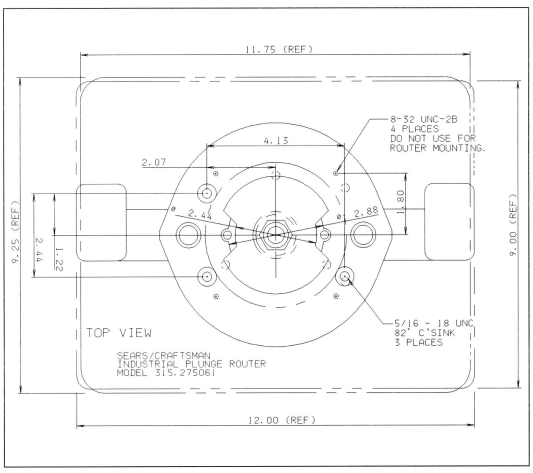

CRAFTSMAN INDUSTRIAL PLUNGE

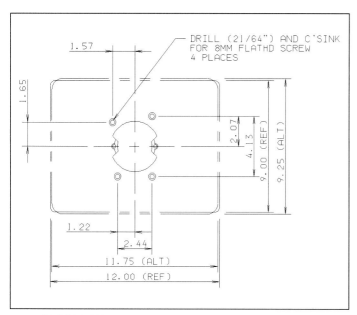

RYOBI R-600 AND RE-600

SPECIAL-APPLICATION PLATES

Some of the special-application plates covered here are simple extensions of the router plates. Others will require more cutting. They are included both as examples of techniques that can be applied to other needs not covered and because they, together with the mounted tool, offer additional capability to the router table.

Dremel

You can make an adapter plate to use the Dremel Shaper/Router and the Dremel Moto-Tool in the router table. When table-mounted, the tool is controlled from the table's on-off switches.

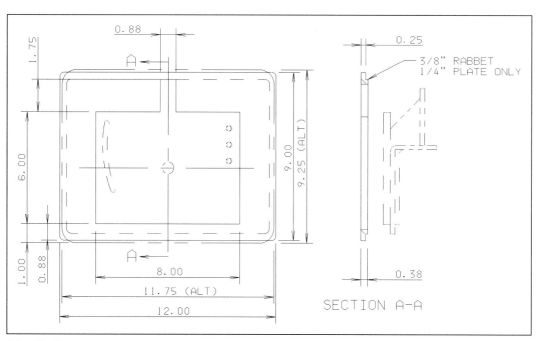

DREMEL SHAPER/ROUTER TABLE MOUNTING

DREMEL SHAPER ROUTER TABLE MOUNTING

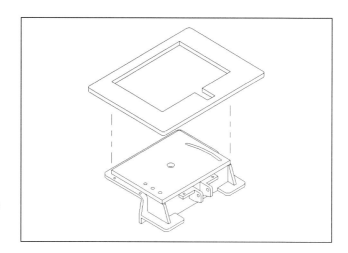

Sears BisKit

The use of a biscuit joiner can be enhanced when it's table-mounted. Dedicate an inexpensive router to this application so that you can quickly accomplish setup and teardown. To mount the BisKit, you must cut a number of pieces to pick up the required mounting surfaces and clearances. These pieces are shown below.

Porter-Cable Tru-Match

Porter-Cable's Tru-Match is designed for handheld router use and is used to cut an edge-bounding joint in solid-surface materials. Adaptation to a table-mount configuration can be done, but it's not a perfect marriage. Notwithstanding, it does work and is included here as another example of what you can do with the table and accessories like the Porter-Cable Tru-Match.

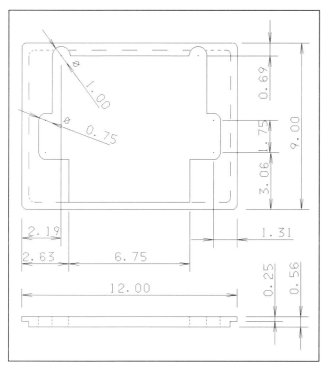

BISKIT ADAPTER PLATE

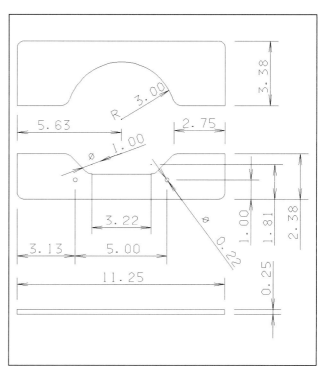

BISKIT ADAPTER PLATE

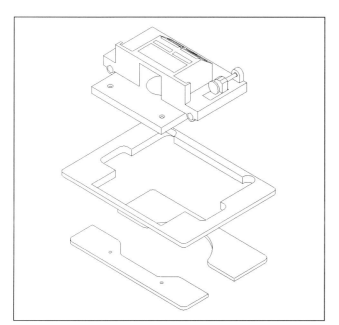

BISKIT ADAPTER PLATE

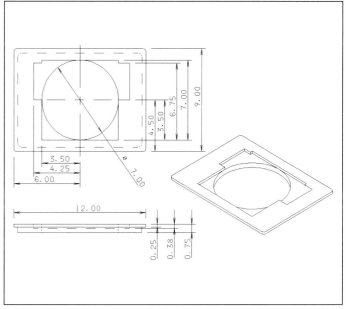

PORTER-CABLE TRU-MATCH ADAPTER PLATE

MOUNTING JIGSAWS IN A ROUTER TABLE

Most of the jigsaws have a similar base or shoe-plate design. An example is shown below.

To mount the jigsaw in the table, use the rolled edges to position and retain the jigsaw on the plate. Use wooden and/or purchased clamps to grab the sides of the shoe plate. The variations in plate design account for the differences in the particular jigsaw being used. The objective is to have an adapter-plate design that allows quick and easy attachment and removal of the jigsaw. You can make inserts similar to those used with the shop-made router plates, again allowing additional workpiece support and improved cutting quality.

The clamps used for this application can be ordered from Welliver and Sons, under their part number 15181.

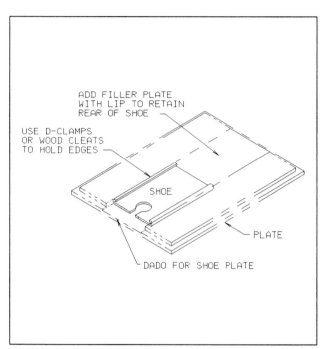

JIGSAW SHOE PLATE

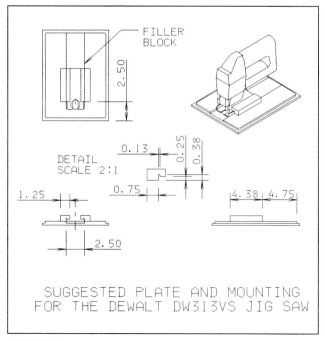

CRAFTSMAN

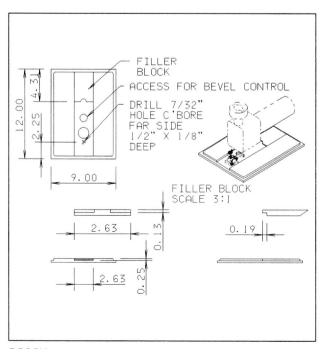

BOSCH

DEWALT

MOUNTING CIRCULAR SAWS IN A ROUTER TABLE

You can increase the functionality of the job-site router table by having the ability to do board ripping and crosscutting on-site. Other tools are normally available at the job site for these types of cutting, but when there aren't, having the capability is a real boon. The mounting of different circular saws varies more than jigsaws. The adaptation is mainly a function of the saw's plate and the method of the plate's attachment to the saw motor. Depending on the circular saw, you may need to cut away part of the router table's subtop to allow the saw to fit. The photograph at right shows the cuts made to accommodate the Bosch saw.

Two plates, shown below, are necessary to hold the Bosch saw.

In order to use a circular saw in the table, you must circumvent its primary safety feature, the trigger on-off switch. Most handheld tools allow you to set the tool in the "power on" state, however, a circular saw can only be turned on by depressing and holding the finger switch. To use the saw in the table, you need a "finger" that allows you to control the power through the table's on-off switches. I designed a plug

SUBTOP CUTAWAY
To mount certain circular saws in the job-site table, you must cutout some of the subtop. The cut here is for the Bosch saw.

that fits into the handle to depress the trigger switch. It is designed to make it extremely difficult to grasp and pick up the saw when the plug is in place. If you attempt to pick up the saw, the plug is pushed out, freeing the switch. The plug is safe only if designed

BOSCH SAW PLATES

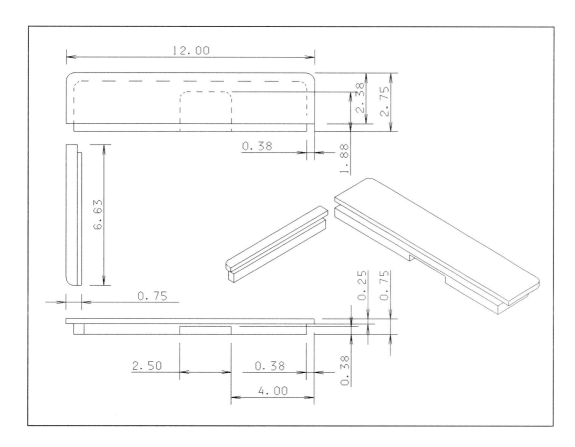

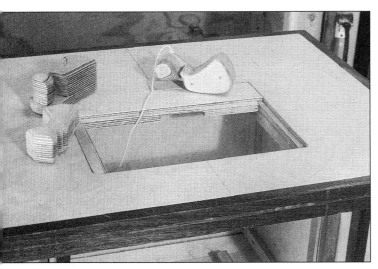

BOSCH, DEWALT AND CRAFTSMAN PLUGS
The plug required is a function of the circular saw being used. Shown here are plugs for the DeWalt the Craftsman Sawmill and the Bosch.

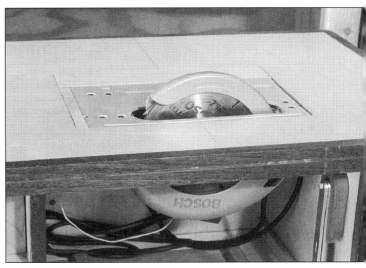

BOSCH CIRCULAR SAW
When table-mounted, the saw's on-off power is controlled from the table's switches.

and used as described. If you attach the plug to the wall of the router table with a cord, the saw cannot be removed from the table without disabling the switch's safety override. A cord also keeps the plug from being lost.

You can create a laminated wooden plug with a router and oscillating sander. To determine the shape required, cut a piece of cardboard in the shape of the hand opening. Trace the outline on two pieces of 1/4″ or 1/2″ scrap ply. Cut the pieces out and check the fit to the handle opening. Smooth out the rough edges and then bond the pieces together. Using a sander or a pattern bit, flush the second piece to the first layer. Repeat the process until the block is at least 2″ thick. Some handles, like the DeWalt or the Bosch styles, shown above, will require secondary laminations that are then glued to the primary.

The plug should fit easily into the handle opening and depress the trigger. Try to pick up the saw with the plug in place. When the plug is properly contoured and of the correct thickness, it should be difficult to lift the saw without dislodging the plug. Using screw-eyes and cord, attach the plug to the inside wall of the router table. A dowel holder for the plug on the inside wall will keep the plug out of the way when it is not being used.

BLANK PLATES

The last plate is the blank plate. When you are not routing , you can use the table as a workbench, so it's nice to have a blank plate to cover the router-plate opening. With the solid-surface top, use the piece you cut out for the opening and border it.

It won't take long to find an application for this spare plate. When you do, you can make another blank.

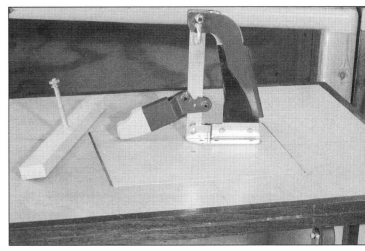

ROUTER-TABLE TOP WITH BLANK PLATE
The blank plate for the router table can be used for many applications. With the addition of a center hole, this lever clamp can be used as a powerful hold-down. The bar shown fits on the underside of the plate and extends out picking up the underside of the subtop. Also shown is an attachment to mount the lever clamp at the table's corner.

CHAPTER THREE

MAKING ROUTER-TABLE FENCES

Fences can be purchased or they can be made in the shop. In this chapter we will look at a couple of commercial fence designs and see how these fences can be adapted to the router tables. We will also learn how to combine commercial fences with commercial and shop-made components to make hybrid fences. Last but not least are the shop-made fences used for both general and specialized applications.

You can purchase commercial fences that will fit a variety of table sizes or will only fit a specific table size. Most are best used with the size range or table they were designed for. When adapting commercial fences to other tables and table sizes, take care that the features and functionality of the fence are not lost through the method of adaptation. Sometimes it is possible to add functionality to the basic fence, thereby creating a hybrid fence.

USING COMMERCIAL FENCES

The main advantage to a commercial fence is they offer machined quality and accuracy not easily duplicated with shop-made fences. Their disadvantage is they may not offer the features and functionality you want.

We'll examine two types of commercial fences. One is a general-purpose fence of a traditional design. The other is a fence system, a collection of components that together solve the total requirements for positioning and fixing the workpiece. The Rousseau fence is a good example of a traditional fence design, and the INCRA Jig Ultra is an example of a fence system.

The Rousseau Fence

The Rousseau fence is intended for use in the Rousseau router table. It consists of a cast main fence and two Baltic birch fence face plates, one on each side of the cutter opening. The base of the casting has cast bosses to position and mount the fence to the Rousseau table. In order to use the fence with the tables covered here, you must make a base adapter for the fence and cut new birch fence faces that span our table sizes.

ROUSSEAU FENCE
The Rousseau fence comes with the casting, fence faces and attachment hardware. Make new fence faces for use with the jigs and fixtures described in the next chapter.

ROUSSEAU FENCE CASTING
The Rousseau fence casting is the keystone of the hybrid fence system.

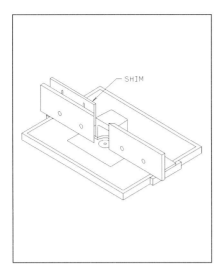

OFFSET SHIM FOR THE FENCE FACE

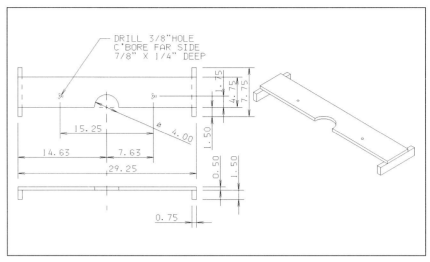

FENCE CARRIER—JOB SITE TABLE

Fortunately, these changes do not compromise the basic Rousseau design. After you make the changes, you can use a number of jigs and fixtures with the fence, offering increased functionality.

The Rousseau fence is solid. The casting is a right-angled piece with provisions for attaching it to the table or carrier and attaching fence faces to it. The center housing offers ample room for the cutter bit, and bits up to 3½″ in diameter can be used. This housing also includes provisions for a vacuum attachment for dust removal. Cast slots for attaching the fence faces allow you to open or close the individual fence faces at the cutter opening. This feature ensures a minimum fence opening for any cutter size. Since the fence casting is one piece, no alignment adjustment is required for the individual fence faces. Some router-table fences allow independent positioning of each of the fence faces. This feature is found on most shaper fences and has been carried over to some router-table fence designs. For the router, it is not a desirable feature and is best left with shaper tables. With the Rousseau style fence, if you need to offset one of the fence faces, place shims cut to the desired offset dimension between the fence casting and the fence face.

To adapt the Rousseau fence to a specific table size, construct a carrier. Make a carrier, as shown above, from flat ½″ stock long enough to span the table and attach to its pontoons. The pontoons position the fence on the table with respect to the router in both axes.

One valuable advantage of mounting the primary fence to a carrier is that two or more fence positions

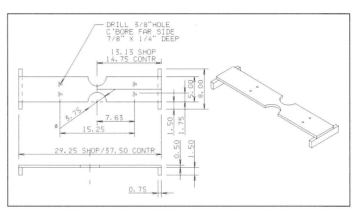

FENCE CARRIER—SHOP AND CONTRACTOR TABLES

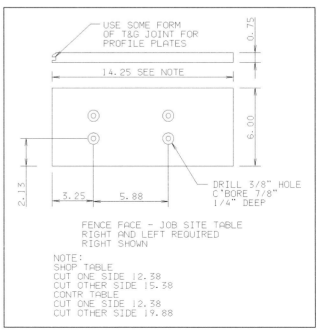

FENCE FACES

FENCE ALIGNMENT TIP

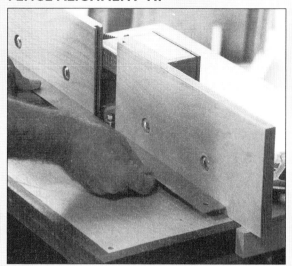

FENCE ALIGNMENT TIP
To align the fence to a bearing bit quickly and easily, place a straightedge against the fence and then push the fence back until the straightedge touches the bearing. This technique is particularly valuable when part of the workpiece surface has been cut away. For example, a dado cut in the workpiece can allow the bearing and cutter to ride into the dado if the fence is not used to keep the workpiece in place when you make the edge cut.

can be established for a particular cutting sequence. The best example of this is cutting drawer joints using a drawer-joint bit. The fence position is set to one dimension to make the horizontal cuts for the drawer fronts and backs and to an offset dimension to make the vertical cuts for the drawer sides.

Cut new faces to account for the increased height of the fence casting caused by the addition of the carrier. The height of the fence is also increased for additional vertical support and for the use of a number of jigs that are described in chapter four. With these jigs, we now have a "fence system" with the following attributes:

1. Variable-sized bit opening
2. Multiple positioning of fence-face distance from the cutter
3. Independent infeed and outfeed fence-face positioning
4. Acceptance of profile plates
5. Provisions for attaching various jigs and fixtures
6. Dust removal

INCRA Jig Ultra

As stated before, a fence system is a collection of components that together solve the total requirements for positioning and fixing the workpiece with respect to the cutter. When the INCRA Jig Ultra is properly placed and clamped to the router table, the user has complete X-Y position of the fence components and therefore the workpiece. In one dimension, the control range is 16″ and, in the other dimension, 24″. The micropositioning features and control of the Ultra fence are discussed in chapter four under "Micropositioners."

You can mount the Incra jig to a carrier similar to that used for the Rousseau fence. Orient the fence along the shorter table axis to allow the fence's maximum adjustment range of 16″. The pontoons on the carrier are used to position the fence-cutter opening with respect to the router's mounting. Independent positioning of the fence with respect to the carrier is not required since this capability is inherent in the Incra design. The router mounting is asymmetrical with respect to the table, and therefore the Incra fence is also mounted asymmetrical to the router-table center (not the bit center).

The INCRA fence system's primary fence-cutter bit opening is sized for small cutters. To use larger bits, make an add-on or auxiliary fence face. The width of the auxiliary fence determines the maximum-sized cutter that can be used. For example, if a ¾″ auxiliary fence face is used, the maximum diameter bit is 1″. If you are using a 2″-wide fence face, the maximum bit

INCRA JIG ULTRA
Because of its size, the INCRA Jig Ultra is best used with the contractor's table. If the Ultra is used extensively, consider relocating the router-plate cutout to center the Ultra fence on the table.

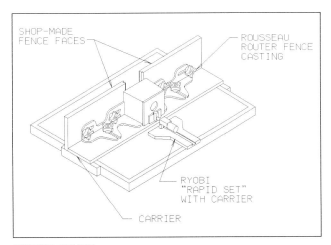

HYBRID FENCE

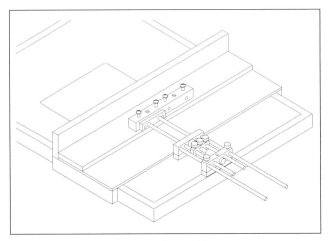

SLIDING FENCE WITH MICRO FENCE

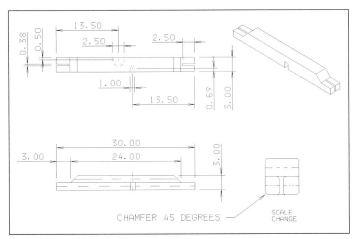

STRAIGHT LAMINATED FENCE

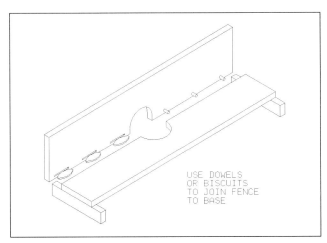

RIGHT ANGLE FENCE

diameter can be increased to 2¼″.

There are other fence systems on the market that I have seen but not used. I am sure they are worth looking at if you are in the market for a fence system to complement your router table. Smart Fence Plus and the Jointech fences are two products that come to mind.

Hybrid Fence Systems

Hybrid fence systems consist of both purchased commercial parts and shop-made parts. The hybrid fence system shown above consists of the Rousseau fence casting, the Ryobi Rapid Set Micropositioning Device and shop-made fence faces and carrier.

Another example of a hybrid fence system is the shop-made sliding fence combined with the Micro Fence circle guide. The circle guide is used as a micro-positioner for this application.

The methods of attachment and uses of the micro-positioners are covered in chapter four, "Building Router-Table Jigs and Fixtures."

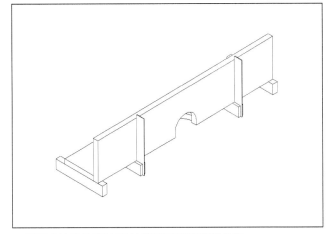

RIGHT ANGLE FENCE WITH TRY SQUARES

USING SHOP-MADE FENCES
The Straight Fence

If you have not adapted a commercial fence to your table, you should make a straight fence by laminating a number of ¾″ strips to form a block-type fence. See pages 57-59.

The Right-Angle Fence

A right-angle fence is easily constructed using ¾″ lengths of Baltic or Finnish birch. It is similar in construction to the carrier and faces of the hybrid fence. Since you won't have the casting to hold the vertical piece in its vertical position, take care to ensure that the face is truly at a right angle to the base and router-table top. Use try squares to hold and maintain the base-to-face relationship while the glue is drying. If you want to add triangular support blocks to the fence, do so after the faces have set. The blocks may not have the precision to establish the right-angle relationship.

The Sliding Fence

This sliding fence system is in reality a number of jigs and fixtures built around the sliding fence. I built the sliding fence to solve a problem I was having in using a box joint. The error in the spacing of a normal box-joint jig resulted in fifteen times the error over the length of the workpiece I was using. I needed the final pin to be an exact distance from the starting pin.

To solve this need, I developed the sliding fence. By sliding on the router-table top, the fence becomes a large miter. Sliding the fence into the cutter bit marks on the fence's face the exact location of where the cut is to be made. Using a pencil, you extend both sides of the cutting lines to the top of the fence. These lines are used to position the marked workpiece with respect to the cutter path.

The asymmetrical position of the router with respect to the table's top allows the fence to slide right to left and left to right. This allows you to locate two cutter positions. In the drawing on page 55, one position is shown for a ½″ cutter and one for a ¾″ cutter.

As with the Incra fences, this fence is normally used only with ¾″ or smaller dado and dovetail bits. Large cutters will spoil the fence for detail cutting. The sliding fence and the hybrid fence are complementary fence systems. Though either can be used for many of the cutting operations, generally the sliding fence is used for small detail work using straight and dovetail bits under ¾″, and the hybrid fence is used for the larger cutting operations like mouldings or rail-and-stile doors.

One of the beauties of this sliding fence setup is that, without any adjustment or measuring, the location of the cutter to the fence is fixed and known, and it is repeatable any time you use the fence. As discussed in chapter two, the router-to-router-plate relationship must remain fixed for this repeatability to be assured.

This repeatability allows a number of cutting operations to be done quickly and accurately. You can add a right-angle stop so duplicate cuts can be made on many workpieces. An extension can be added for longer workpieces. One frequent use of the fence and stop is to make small boxes. Review the sidebar, "Cigar Boxes."

To accommodate angled miter cuts, use an apron on the back side of the fence. Tack workpiece positioners to the apron at the required angle to secure the workpiece for the miter cuts. The fence can get in the way of some cutting operations, like cutting large

SLIDING FENCE
The sliding fence is a miter fence for the router table. It is used primarily to cut dadoes and dovetails.

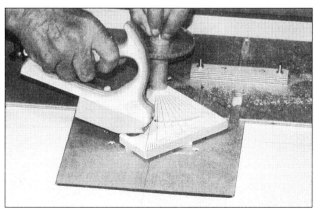

PROTRACTOR—CUTTING ARCS
The fenceless fence, a variation of the sliding fence, is ideal for cutting arcs. In this photograph, the adjustment slot for a protractor jig is being cut.

arcs. To solve this, make a sliding platform without the fence face. Clamp this fenceless fence to the router-table top to position the workpiece to the cutter. Use dowel pins for the pivot point. You can use this setup to cut a protractor, as shown on the previous page. Spacers are used to keep the workpiece level with the sliding platform.

As I used the fence, I added new cutting fixtures and holders. The first was an extension stop which replaced the right-angle stop for longer workpieces. This extension stop is secured both with a clamp and by fitting it into the sliding dovetail cut in the fence's face. For extremely accurate positioning of both the right-angle stop and the extension stop, I developed the threaded adjustment locator. Make adjustment to $1/128''$ using a 10-32 machine screw as the locator. As

MAKING CIGAR BOXES

"A woman is only a woman but a good cigar is a smoke." Whoever first said this left out the box. When you finish your last smoke, the cigar box can be used to store all your little goodies. If you don't smoke cigars or you need a different size box, you will have to make your own.

When you make small boxes, trays and dividers, use the sliding fence together with a bit that is one half thickness of the stock. The position of the right-angle stop allows all the pieces to be cut from the same bit-height setting.

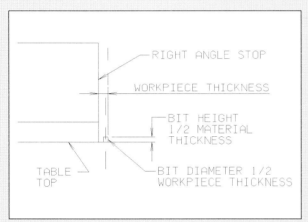

STOP AND BIT SETTINGS

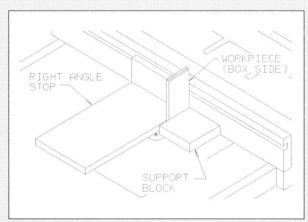

THE SIDE CUTS

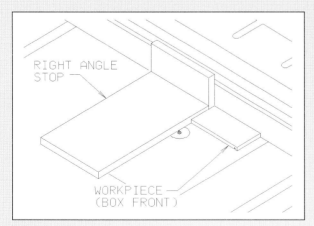

THE FRONT AND BACK CUTS

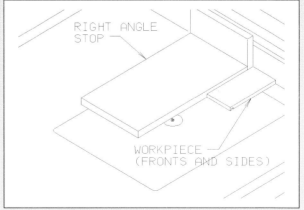

Note: The normal material for these boxes is ¼" Baltic birch ply, but the joint works well with ½" birch and even ¼" hardboard.

with most cuts, the exact dimension is not as important as the relative position of the cut to some baseline or a cut in a mating piece.

To make vertical cuts—for example, end-cut dovetails in narrow stock—I needed a way to hold the workpiece in the vertical position. The answer was to build a sliding holder. The fence already had a dovetail slot in its front face, so I used this slot to position the vertical clamp.

Finally, I added the box-joint jig. This jig will cut the waste between the pins on both workpiece ends and sides at the same time. It will handle four pieces of stock up to ½″ thick and 6″ wide. It handles any multiple of ⅛″ spacing.

The construction of these fixtures and accessories, which constitute the Special Fence System, is explained in chapter four, "Building Router-Table Jigs and Fixtures." Start with the basic sliding fence and then plan to build the add-on jigs as they are required.

BUILDING THE SLIDING FENCE

Five pieces need to be cut and assembled. For the sliding fence to work, your router-table top should be a perfect rectangle. Check your top and, if required, trim it so you have four right angles and four straight sides.

Step 1. Cut the pieces for the fence and fasten with screws only.
Later, one pontoon and the subbase can be glued to the base. Make sure the base is at a right angle to the top's side, and the fence face is at a right angle to the router-table top. Use try squares, as mentioned earlier, to maintain these relationships.

Step 2. Put a ½″ straight cutting bit in the router and set the fence on the router table.
Turn on the router and slide the fence into the cutter far enough to completely profile the cutter bit in the fence's face. Turn off the router and remove the fence.

Step 3. Using a pencil, extend the bit profile to the top of the fence. Mark the center of the cut.
If you will be using a ¼″ bit, you'll need to position the workpiece with respect to the center, not the edge. Turn the fence around and, using with a ¾″ bit, make another cut in its face. Extend the bit profile as before.

Step 4. You can now add the dovetail slot.
I never permanently attach the fence to the base since I may want to modify it (again) or replace it.

To account for the vagaries of wood fixturing, add adjustment screws to one of the fences' pontoons. Place three 10-32 or ¼-20 inserts in the pontoon arm as shown here. See the sidebar on the next page to make an insert installer.

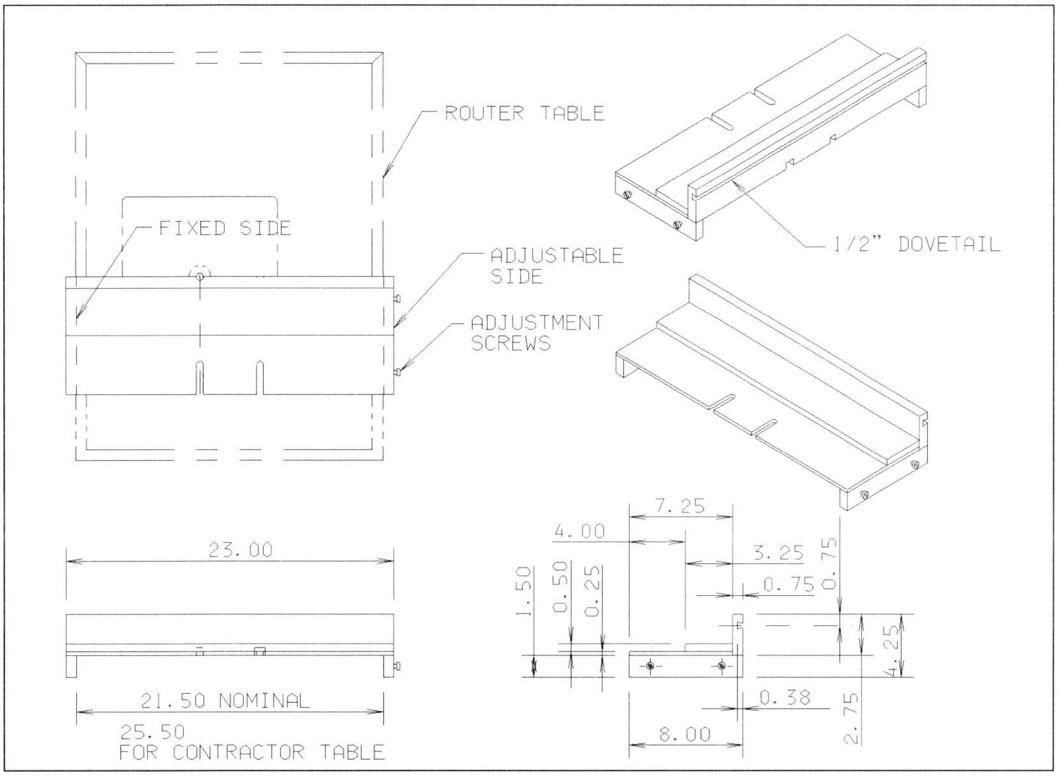

SLIDING FENCE

ALIGNING THE FENCE

To align the fence to the top, position the fence face on the top's center line, holding the fixed pontoon firmly against the top's side. Now, tighten the outer screws until they just touch the table's side. Check the fence's movement and adjustment by sliding the fence away and then up to the center line. The movement should be smooth and the fence should return to the center line without cocking. Next, adjust the center screw so it is touching the table edge and back the outer screws off by about a quarter turn ($\frac{1}{128}$" in the case of 10-32 threaded inserts). Always check the fence alignment when it is used again.

SPECIAL-FUNCTION FENCES

Special-function fences are used for special cutting operations. They don't have the range of application found with normal fences, however, when they are needed, they are valuable.

Two special-purpose fences are discussed here: the taper fence and the vertical fence.

The Taper Fence

A taper fence can be a hand addition to your router table. The taper of the fence can be cut so that for a standard vertical displacement a known horizontal displacement will be made. We have all seen road signs that indicate an approaching grade—let's say a

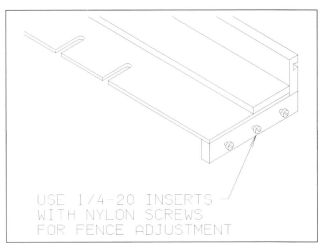

USE 1/4-20 INSERTS
WITH NYLON SCREWS
FOR FENCE ADJUSTMENT

PONTOON ARM INSERTS

7 percent grade. This means that for every mile we travel horizontally, we will travel .07 miles vertically. In other words, the 7 percent tells us the ratio of the X and Y components of the grade. This, of course, is the tangent of the angle of the grade. A 100 percent grade would be a 45° slope.

For the taper fence, the grade or tangent of the taper is used to allow the fence face to move toward or away from the cutter (in the X direction) by moving the sliding portion of the fence a corresponding distance (in the Y direction.)

The example here is a taper fence that uses a taper of 7.1°. The tangent of 7.1° is approximately 0.125

INSTALLING INSERTS

Installing threaded inserts can be a problem when you don't have the right tools. You can easily make a tool to install these inserts.

Find an eyebolt with matching threads to the

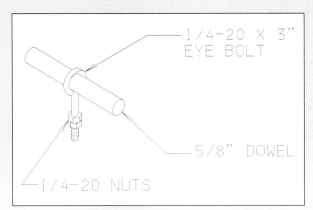

1/4-20 X 3"
EYE BOLT

5/8" DOWEL

1/4-20 NUTS

SHOP-MADE THREADED INSERT INSTALLER

insert. Using a dowel, make a handle that goes through the eye of the bolt. Screw on two nuts, jamming them about ½" up the eyebolt's threaded shaft. You now have a tool for installing the inserts.

SHOP-MADE THREADED INSERT INSTALLER

Here, a 1/4-20 X 3" eyebolt is used with a ⅝" dowel. The eye of the bolt is ⁹⁄₁₆" diameter, so you must open the eye slightly to insert the ⅝" dowel handle. Taper one end of the dowel to drive it into the eyebolt's eye. Use a pair of wrenches to cinch the nuts tight. This shop-made insert installer can be duplicated for any size insert. It is quickly made with an eyebolt, a dowel and two jam nuts.

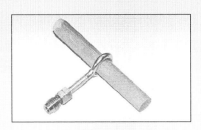

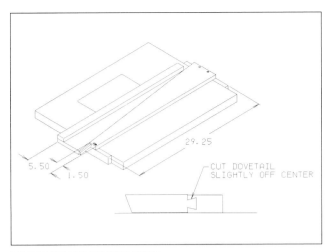

TAPER FENCE DIMENSIONS

USING THE TAPER FENCE
The taper fence is used to make spaced cuts in a workpiece. Cutting featherboards is a typical application.

or $\frac{1}{8}$. So, when you move this fence 8 units in the Y direction, it will also move 1 unit in the X direction (or perpendicular to the Y direction). If you move the fence 1″ vertically, the fence will move $\frac{1}{8}$″ toward or away from the cutter. Indexing the fence's sliding arm to the fixed arm permits adjustment of $\frac{1}{128}$″ to be made by moving the sliding arm $\frac{1}{16}$″ $(.8 \times \frac{1}{128}$″$)$.

BUILDING THE TAPER FENCE

Connect the two fence arms with a sliding dovetail. One arm is clamped to the router-table's top. The fit of the sliding dovetail will allow you to position and use the sliding arm without clamping. The dovetail is cut slightly off-center so that the sliding arm will not bind on the top. The fence assembly fits on the top in a manner similar to all the fences that have carriers and pontoons.

You can make the fence with other taper angles allowing either finer or courser movement away or toward the cutter. Since the complete fence can be moved with respect to the cutter, I have opted for the rather fine adjustment offered by the 12.5 percent slope or taper.

The taper fence, in conjunction with a saber saw mounted in the router table, is frequently used to cut featherboards. Cut the featherboard slots from the center out to ensure the firmest edge of the featherboard is riding against the fence. Make the cuts in pairs, turning the workpiece over, for each fence setting. The taper fence can also be used in conjunction with a normal fence to control the normal fence's position with respect to the cutter.

The Vertical-Miter Fence

The vertical-miter fence was developed for the shop table to handle large stock, for example, to cut the rails and stiles for doors or to make vertical end cuts. The fence is used with the special miter gauge when making end cuts.

BUILDING THE VERTICAL-MITER FENCE

The router fence is made from strips of plywood glued together. These strips are cut oversize and later trimmed with a saw. This massive fence is designed to support the router's vertical-miter attachment and other accessory fixtures. The construction is straightforward, but take care to maintain the squareness of the piece.

1. The final width of the fence is 4″, so cut the strips about 4½″ wide to allow the necessary leeway when gluing and clamping.
2. Glue the strips in pairs, forming a bottom half and a top half. Before gluing the bottom half, dress one strip to about 4¼″ wide. This board will be used as the reference for the final trimming to the required width. To make sure that the edges of this board are parallel, tack a known straightedge to this strip, and then, with this straightedge against the fence, cut the other side, remove the straightedge, turn the board and cut to the 4¼″ width. You now have a board with parallel sides 4¼″ wide.
3. Use this same method to cut the fence to its final width, except that the previously dressed

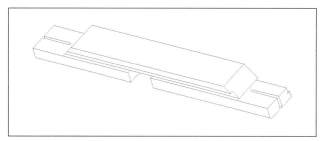

VERTICAL MITER FENCE

board replaces the straightedge.

4. Glue the two bottom pieces together offset from each other, as shown in the figure opposite, top. Note that the board with the exposed edge is also offset on the other side. This will result in a dado when the fence is finished. This dado will be used as the miter slot for the router miter. It's because of the router miter that we are going to all this trouble with the fence.

5. Before gluing the upper and lower halves together, cut the slots for the clamps and cut out the router-bit clearance hole.

6. If you want 45° chamfers for the top half, cut them now. Their purpose is to give your hand a little more room when clamping the fence and to keep your knuckles from getting too skinned up.

7. After gluing the top and bottom halves together, you are ready to trim the fence to its final width. Not that, as shown in the figure opposite, middle, the fence and cut are set to leave a ⅜"-deep slot or dado. This dado can be dressed up later, so don't worry too much about being exactly on the mark.

8. Make the first cut as shown, with the edge of the previously dressed board riding against the fence.

9. Turn the board over and cut to the 4" width.

10. Clamp the fence to the router-table top with C-clamps. When it is not possible to use C-clamps because of interference with the vertical miter, you can make simple cheat-type fence clamps.

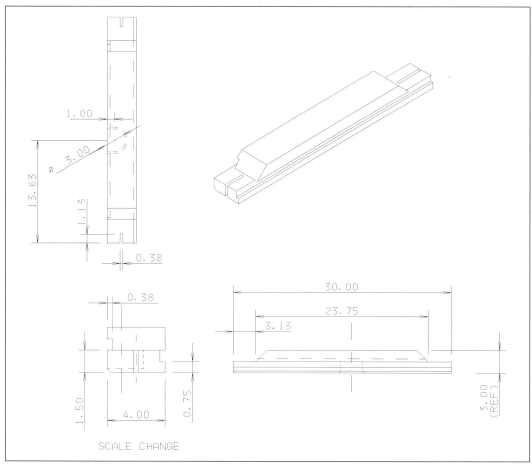

DIMENSIONED DRAWING—ROUTER VERTICAL MITER FENCE

The Vertical Miter

Conceptually, the vertical miter is similar to a saw miter turned 90°. Think of the vertical-miter fence with its miter slot as the table surface of a table saw. The router bit replaces the saw blade in this analogy. The vertical miter can hold workpieces up to 11″ wide. The workpiece is positioned both against the fence and the handle/miter fence and then clamped against the miter bar using the horizontal quick-release clamp. Additionally, the workpiece should be clamped to the fence with C-clamps.

Many of the edge-forming cuts made with the vertical miter are complementary cuts. When you use a lock-miter cutter or a drawer-joint bit, one cut is made with the workpiece held horizontally, and the mating piece is cut while held in the vertical position. Since the special miter holds the workpiece above the actual router-table surface by the thickness of the clamping plate, it is necessary to clamp the complementary vertical workpiece this same distance off the table surface. The easiest way to do this is to have a strip of the material used for the special miter's clamping plate available as a spacer to hold the workpiece up when it is clamped in position to the vertical miter. Don't let the workpiece drag the spacer into the router bit.

BUILDING THE VERTICAL MITER

The vertical miter is a box that rides on the vertical-miter fence. The basic box is made with Baltic birch MDF. The handle/miter fence, miter bars and the clamp base are made from Baltic birch. Use either a box joint or dovetails to attach the clamp base to the handle at a right angle. The finished assembly should slide easily without rocking on the vertical-miter fence. To keep the miter bar against the vertical-miter fence, attach a strip of hardwood at the end. This strip will limit the width of the workpiece. I used the quick-release straight-line clamp available from Woodcraft.

You will need a number of push blocks and related aids when using your router table and fences. Some of them can be purchased. All of them can be made. A number of them are described in *Build Your Own Mobile Power Tool Centers* (Betterway Books, 1995).

Profile Plates

Profile plates are the router table's equivalent of a saw table's zero-insert plates. They serve the same purpose, reduction of chipping and additional workpiece

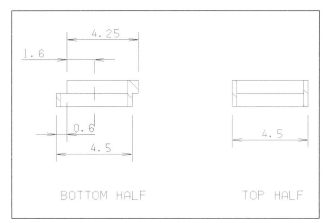

OFFSET EDGE

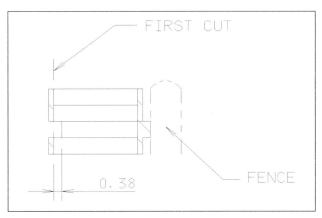

TRIMMING THE FENCE

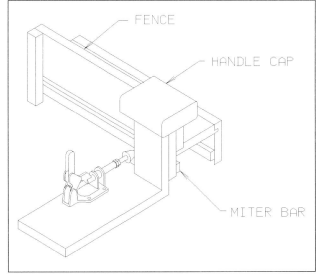

VERTICAL MITER

support. You must design the fence to accommodate and retain the plates.

The fence faces used with the Rousseau casting have 45° miters on the sides that meet at the fence's center. These miter cuts can be used to hold a profile

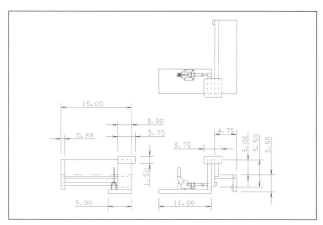

VERTICAL MITER

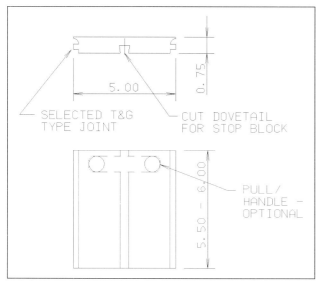

VERTICAL MITER FENCE
The vertical miter fence is a special-purpose fence used to make vertical cuts in large workpieces.

HYBRID FENCE PROFILE PLATES

plate. A tongue-and-groove mating makes a more positive attachment. I used my rail-and-stile cutters for this attachment.

To make the plate, use the same ¾" stock used for the fence faces. Cut the plate to the 5" dimension so that it is both retained and supported by the center housing of the casting. The profile can be cut one of two ways. For both methods, first establish the fence position with respect to the cutter. In the example here, the fence and the cutter height are set for cutting lock-miter joints in ²³⁄₃₂" stock. The drawing shows an optional handle cutout. This handle makes it a little easier to reposition the profile plates.

For the first method, lower the blank profile plate on to the cutter until it touches the router table. Fasten a backing board to the profile plate for safety and control. Before you cut the actual profile, cut away most of the material with a jigsaw or band saw. This step is mandatory for bits that have bearings or other noncutting tops.

The other way to cut the profile opening is to start with the cutter inside the housing and slide the complete fence into the rotating bit.

Step 1. Establish the fence position and cutter height.

Step 2. Clamp stop blocks at the rear of the fence carrier or pontoons.

Step 3. Slide the fence forward until the cutter is totally within the fence housing. Make sure the bit cannot touch any of the housing sides.

Step 4. Place the profile plate and its backing board into position.

Step 5. Slide the fence into the bit until it hits the stop blocks.

For fences other than the hybrid fence, you must first modify the fence to accept profile plates.

Cutting out an opening allows mating profile plates to be made that are positionally registered and retained by the tongue-and-groove joint, dado in the fence and the rabbet in the plate. Cut these plates by lowering the plate into the cutter. Use the backing board as we did in the first method when you cut the profile.

The profile plate does not need to be a true profile. A simple cutout with a jigsaw offers the support needed for the workpiece without the need for special cutting.

You can now use the true profile plates, unlike the simple type shown, to set the fence and cutter height

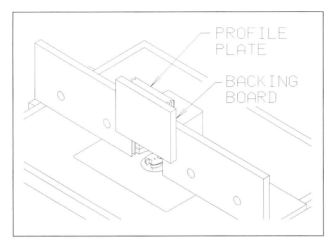

BACKING BOARD

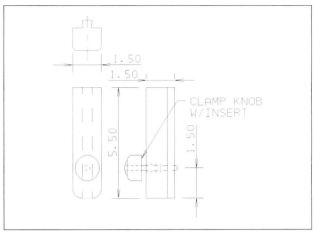

HEIGHT CONTROL STOP

for subsequent cutting. Before you turn the router on for these subsequent cuts, reestablish the fence and the height of the bit carefully to ensure the bit won't bind.

You can add a height-control stop if you cut a dovetail slot in the profile plate. This is a stop, not a clamp, and is used to ensure the cutter does not lift the workpiece as it is being cut. The elevation of the stop is adjustable for varying workpiece thicknesses. Use it with wide workpieces, but remove it for the narrow workpieces since it will interfere with other jigs.

The sidebar, "Building Router-Bit Boxes," shows how these features were developed and how they work together.

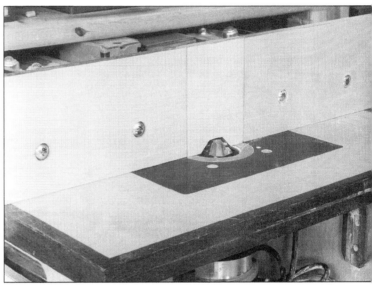

PROFILE PLATE WITH HEIGHT-CONTROL STOP
A height-control stop can be added to the profile plates for further workpiece control. This stop keeps the cutter bit from raising the workpiece.

SIMPLE PROFILE PLATE
The simplest form of a profile plate is made by cutting an opening for the bit with a jigsaw. Though not a true profile, it offers full support of the workpiece.

BUILDING ROUTER-BIT BOXES

The router-bit boxes shown here are the ones I build and sell through some of the local tool and woodworking shops. I have learned and use a number of techniques and aids to build these boxes.

ROUTER-BIT BOXES
I used the jigs and fixtures described in chapter four for the joinery used in the display stand. Use the hybrid fence and the combination miter with the Freud drawer-joint bit to cut the boxes. Set the bit's height and distance from the fence where both the horizontal and the vertical pieces can be cut with the same settings.

MEASURING THE TRIAL CUT
When the fence is in place before the proper insert opening has been selected, we see Charybdis in all her glory. (See page 91.) The bit box is only 3⅝" high and its sides can quickly be swallowed up in this maelstrom. The easiest way to measure the bit height is to measure the uncut lip. The stock is 0.46" wide and the lip is 0.05", therefore the height of the bit is 0.41". Note that a complete pass of the trial workpiece is not necessary to check the bit height.

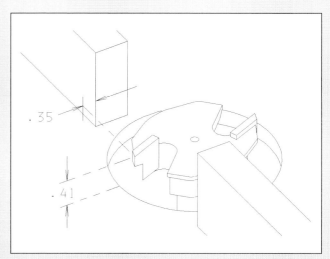

FREUD DRAWER BIT
The drawing shows dimensions used for the required setting. Try to get close using a scale and then make a trial cut. Using the trial workpiece, measure the cut offset to determine the incremental change needed. Use the router's elevation scale to adjust the height and a micropositioner to move the fence into position.

FIRST SETUP

The combination miter only partially protects the workpiece. When you cut the box fronts and backs (the horizontal cuts), the cutter bit will try to pull the workpiece in, resulting in an uneven edge.

UNEVEN EDGE

The sides (the vertical pieces) are worse. The end being cut is unsupported and will flap like a springboard after the fat lady has taken the plunge.

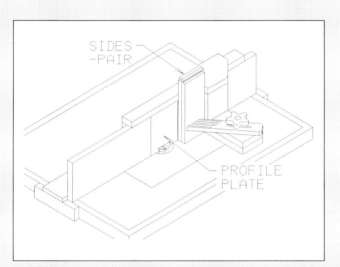

SIDE PAIRS

The outboard side acts as a stiffener and vibration damper. This is a trick or technique, however you want to look at it, that can be used in many cutting operations. If the workpiece doesn't have a mate, cut one and use it as a backing board. One other trick you may want to consider is making a scribe cut on the verticals. For the verticals, this is normally a cross-grain cut and, depending on the quality of the wood and the router bit, there can be some splintering. Use an X-Acto knife with a ubiquitous #11 blade to score along the line that represents the top of the cut. This should eliminate the splintering.

Do the setup with representative workpieces. When the first box pieces are properly cut, clamp them together as a box and do a final check on the dimensions.

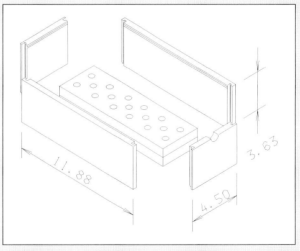

EXPLODED VIEW OF THE LARGE BIT BOX

From time to time, you will see router-bit boxes from companies like Woodcraft for around twenty dollars. You will probably spend three or four hours on your first boxes. It will give you a good idea of what your time is worth.

BUILDING ROUTER-BIT BOXES, CONTINUED

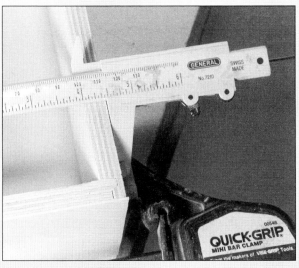

VERTICAL CHATTER

Both problems are partially corrected by using a profile plate. The plate will support the horizontal piece so it is not pulled by the cutter and the vertical piece will be supported to within 1″ of the cut. This is still only a partial solution. We find that the fronts and backs will now be slightly lifted by the cutter, resulting in a spoiled joint. With the sides, the vertical cuts, the springboard effect will still cause some chatter, though much less than previously.

To fix the lifting, add a stop to the profile plate. This stop does not exert downward pressure on the workpiece, but it does keep the workpiece from being lifted by the cutter. Use this stop when the workpiece is wider than 3″. For narrower pieces, use the combination miter with the stop removed. Normally, narrow pieces aren't wide enough to lift enough to spoil the joint.

To eliminate the last bit of chatter when you cut the verticals, mount the box sides in pairs in the combination miter.

CLAMPED TRIAL BOX

A trial box is not as important as trial drawers. The outside dimensions of a drawer, particularly its width, are critical.

I normally cut the fronts and backs with a very slight lip (rabbet). After the drawer or box has been glued, this lip is sanded away. With the lip as shown here, the blank is cut at 4⁹⁄₁₆″ for the required 4½″ wide face. The sides will normally be cut ³⁄₃₂″ to ⅛″ shorter than the desired depth of the drawer. After these dimensions have been verified, using the trial box, cut all the sides and fronts for the drawers/boxes you will be making.

My bit boxes are sold as both "plains" and "fancies." The fancies have mock dovetails or splines to gussy them up. These cuts are made using the 45° cradle.

FORTY-FIVE-DEGREE CRADLE

Mock dovetails or spline joints can be an attractive addition to any box. Planes for building and using the jig shown here appear in chapter four.

DUST CONTROL

Getting rid of router dust is either easy or hard to do. The level of difficulty depends on the type of cutting and the style of fence. Plate inserts and profile plates also affect the ease of dust removal.

Plate inserts prevent a lot of dust from going down onto the router cavity. Profile plates block a lot of the dust from entering the router-bit cavity. The only place left for the dust to go is out the cut space, and normally it will pack the cut space. For most cutting, it is better not to block the free movement of the dust. Accumulated dust will cause heat buildup and, in some cases, can keep the router bit from being freed after the cut is made. This form of dust buildup happens most often when I cut bind dovetails. The dust cannot escape to the sides, it won't go down due to the cut geometry and the upward air pressure caused by the router motor and/or a plate insert so it can only go out the passage made by the cutter. This passage will quickly fill with packed dust. Since this is a blind cut, the result is that the router bit is trapped. The only way out is to pull the workpiece out with power on. The workpiece is moving the wrong way with respect to the cutter-bit rotation and special care must be taken to keep the workpiece from wandering away from the fence.

Now that you have your fences, it's time to start building the basic jigs and fixtures to complete your system.

VACUUM HOOKUP FOR THE JOB-SITE TABLE
This small, one-gallon vacuum attached to the hybrid fence works well with the job-site table.

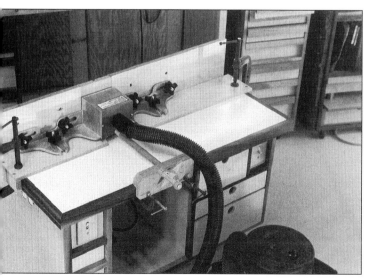

VACUUM HOOKUP FOR THE CONTRACTOR'S TABLE
A complete hybrid fence system consists of the fence components, a micropositioner and a method for dust removal. This five-gallon shop vacuum will keep the work center clean.

VACUUM ADAPTER PLATES
Both vacuum hose size and the micropositioners attachment will dictate the actual design of the coupler plate.

CHAPTER FOUR

BUILDING ROUTER-TABLE JIGS & FIXTURES

Jigs are devices used to maintain mechanically the correct positional relationship between the workpiece and the tool (Merriam Webster's Collegiate Dictionary, Tenth Edition, 1993). Fixtures are things that fix, i.e., hold steady, the workpiece to maintain this positional relationship. A clamp is an example of a fixture, and a saw's miter gauge is an example of a jig. A miter equipped with a clamp is a jig and a fixture. If your jigs and fixtures are well designed, they will allow safe and accurate cuts.

When designing jigs, first take a look at its definition: A jig positions. Start the process by holding the workpiece in the required position with respect to the cutter and then think about what must be done to maintain this relationship. Next, figure out how you are going to hold it in this position when you do the actual cutting.

Many jigs are built as *soft tooling*, which means the jig is built for only a few cutting operations and then it will be discarded. Another case of soft tooling is when the jig or parts or the jig are consumed during the cutting operation. *Hard tooling* is building the jig to perform its task over and over again. The saw's miter is hard tooling. It is also starting to be general tooling. General purpose is that the miter's relationship to the cutter (saw blade) and therefore the workpiece's relationship to the cutter can be changed. The miter is a good example of how far a tool should go in search of generality. Having one miter instead of forty-five (a ninety, considering the complementary cuts) is certainly preferred. Designing a miter that will also cut tenons is probably a waste. It would be overly complicated or difficult to use. Jigs should be designed to do one task well. Doing it well means it's easy to use, sets up quickly and doesn't take up a lot of shop space when it is not being used. Hard tooling jigs are jigs that

you plan to be using frequently or at least often enough that rebuilding the jig each time you need it is more time consuming than building a permanent reusable jig. In order for the jig to be usable, it must be well constructed and accurate. Cuts made with the jig must be repeatable each time it is used. Repeatable here means that if it is designed to make 45° cuts, then it must make a 45° cut every time. If it makes 43° cuts, you are not going to be happy with the results.

Few of us waste money on the schlock tools often found on the bargain counter. We also normally don't buy ugly-looking tools. Apply the same rules to the tools you build. Give your tools some panache. You'll like using them and will treat them better. Like Rodney Dangerfield, a couple of boards nailed together get no respect. And after you have kicked them around on the shop floor between uses, they could ruin an expensive workpiece.

Start the jig-design process by making your jig soft. See what is good and what is not so good about its design. If it's an important tool, repeat the process a few times until all of the bugs are worked out and then make a hard version. If you have made numerous versions of a similar soft jig, make a hard jig. Sometimes you will find a general solution that will warrant a hard version. The featherboard bar, described later in the chapter, is an example of this design process.

Before building the specific jigs and fixtures, let's examine some general techniques.

MATERIALS

Use the best material available to build your own jigs and fixtures. Working with metal, particularly tool steel, is outside the scope of this book (and the tools and abilities of the author). Some of you may have the resources for metal cutting and may want to make truly hardened jigs. For the rest of us, we will stick with the two materials I am most familiar with: 14-layer birch ply and MDF (medium density fiberboard). MDF is stable and flat, and it cuts well, but it is heavy and can only be purchased in 4′ × 8′ sheets. Certain plastics can be used to make jigs, but like the MDF, they are heavy and normally come in large sheets. These plastics are also expensive. An exception with regard to the sheet size is the Ultra High Molecular Weight (UHMW) sheets sold by companies like Woodcraft. You can buy 4″ × 48″ strips of varying thicknesses. Like the other plastics, it is still expensive.

When you get the to the chapters on building router tables, you will see that I recommend using ¾″ Finnish birch for the case material and ¼″ and ½″ Finnish or Baltic birch for the drawers and related items. Finnish Birch is of a better quality and more expensive than Baltic birch, and, unlike Baltic birch, is available in 4′ × 8′ sheets.

Build your jigs with the material left over from your router table. For part thicknesses other than the standard ones, you will need to do glue-ups from the standard sizes.

GLUE-UPS

When gluing pieces together, always start by cutting the individual pieces slightly oversized, that is, ¼″ to ⅜″ larger than the final dimension.

After applying the glue, clamp the pieces so that you leave a clear reference edge to position against the saw's fence or miter when you trim the piece to the required size. See the example at right.

A similar technique is used to cut a jig to its required edge relationships. For example, if one face of a jig must be perpendicular to a reference edge, use this edge to cut the perpendicular edge.

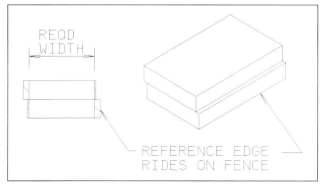

EXAMPLE OF A GLUE-UP

JIG ASSEMBLY

Position the components of the jig during its assembly with care. The required relationships must be accurately maintained. Dowels make good locator pins during this assembly process. You can also use screws, but make sure they don't end up where you will later be cutting. A try square can be a useful jig to hold the pieces while you drill the dowel holes or attach the screws. In the picture shown here, the clamped square ensures the proper positioning of the added piece.

You can also use this technique when gluing drawers and even cases together. Use a couple of framing squares as a try square for carcass assembly.

The all-steel try squares sold as engineer's squares are very good for this application. They are durable and clean easily. When you use them for glue-ups, they can end up covered with glue residue. Keep their edges clean for the next time you use them.

CLAMPED TRY SQUARE
Clamp a try square to a jig assembly while the glue is setting to ensure the positional relationship between the parts is maintained.

CLAMPED CARCASS
Using framing squares apply the clamped-try-square technique to the gluing of the carcasses. This picture shows the gluing of the subassembly of the shop table.

FIXTURES

Fixtures must be fixed. If you use a backing board to position and fix the workpiece, you must attach the backing board to the workpiece. You can do this in a number of ways. Here are my thoughts on the more common methods you might try:

1. Nails/Screws. I have found that the best way to use mechanical fasteners is to predrill pilot holes for the fastener, clamp the fixture to the workpiece and then attach. I usually use 18-gauge nails that are $1/8''$ to $1/4''$ longer than the width of the backing board. If possible, use a hidden surface of the workpiece. If this isn't practical, don't worry; the resultant holes are easy to fill. Using a $1/16''$ bit, drill pilot holes in the backing board. Place the backing board in position and then tap the nails into the workpiece.

2. Toothpicks. Toothpicks are a simple variation of nails or dowels. I buy round birch toothpicks at the local supermarket. These toothpicks have a $3/32$-square-inch cross section at their center. Drill a $3/32''$ pilot hole through the backing board into the workpiece. Tap in the toothpick to attach the two boards. Use the toothpicks as locating pins for cutting sequences that require the removal and subsequent reattachment of the backing board. For many work-pieces, you can use the toothpick to fill the hole left from this operation.

3. Dowels. Dowels are an extension of toothpicks. Use them as locating pins to reattach the backing board or some new fixturing.

4. Hot Glue. I don't recommend hot glue for this application, because it can be difficult to find balance between a reliable, easily removable bond and the overly fast bonding that results from too much glue. Accurate positioning can also be a problem.

5. Double-backed tape. Thank goodness for double-backed tape. I use it all the time and find it very reliable. Just make sure that the surfaces being attached are clean. Sometimes I end up attaching the sawdust on the workpiece to the sawdust on the backing board—not what I had in mind.

6. Clamps. C-clamps or hand screws are fine if you can find a way to use them. For most setups, they will get in the way and can't be used. Don't use the quick-grip style for clamping your fixtures. They are not designed for this type of use.

Tip—Have you ever noticed how hard it can be to hold the workpiece and the backing board and the C-clamp and the C-clamp thumbscrew together for clamping? Use your quick-grip clamp to position the boards and then, with two hands, set the C-clamp.

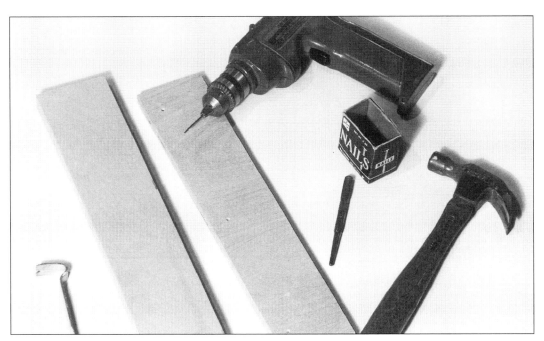

USING NAILS TO FIX BACKING BOARDS
Although they leave small holes in the workpiece, use small nails to quickly and accurately attach backing boards. The nails should be placed so as to not interfere with the router base or other surfaces.

USING TOOTHPICKS TO FIX BACKING BOARDS

Use toothpicks as small dowels for an effective way of fixing a workpiece to its jig. Shown here is a piece of Avonite being attached to the turntable for cutting. Since the toothpicks can be pushed through the holes in the workpiece, the workpiece can be turned over for cutting on the far side without loss of the registration.

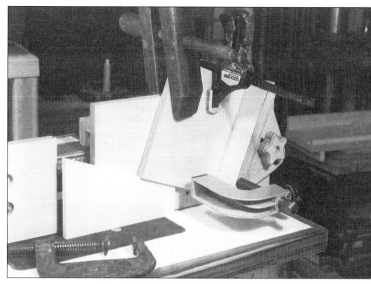

C-CLAMP AND QUICK-GRIP CLAMP

Sometimes we need three hands. When you need to set a C-clamp or hand screw, use a quick-grip type clamp to hold the pieces in place. Here, the tenon jig is being clamped to a nonstandard angle. The quick-grip clamp holds the position so the positive clamp can be set using two hands.

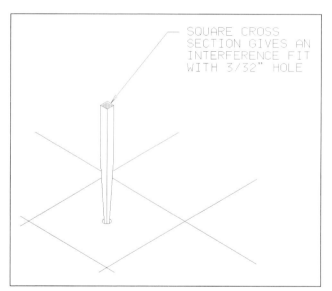

SQUARE CROSS
SECTION GIVES AN
INTERFERENCE FIT
WITH 3/32" HOLE

TOOTHPICK CROSS-SECTION

FEATHERBOARDS IN USE

Using featherboards and push blocks allow for safer and cleaner cuts.

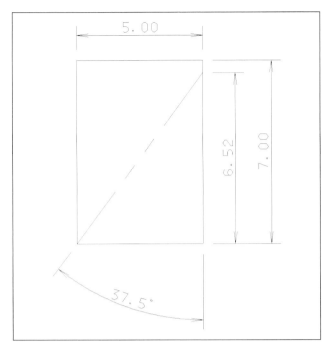

TANGENT EXAMPLE—RATIO OF THE TWO LEGS

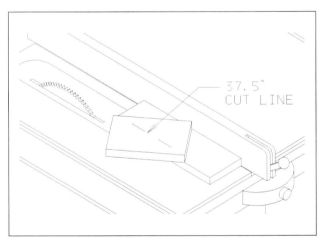

CUTTING THE 37.5° ANGLE—TACKED BOARD

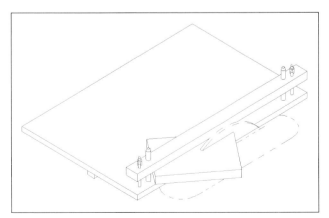

CUTTING THE 37.5° ANGLE—CUTOFF BOARD

LAYOUT AND MEASUREMENT TOOLS

In chapter one, we discussed the importance of good layout and measurement tools. Here we will discuss how to use them.

For tool construction, the absolute dimensions do not normally have the importance that they do in case construction. It is not overly important how long a table saw's miter bar is. What is important is that the miter is accurately aligned to the miter slot and the saw blade. The same is true for your router-table jigs. Jigs are designed and built to maintain positional relationships. Use measurements to check these relationships and specifically to lay out angles. Although you can use a protractor to lay out angles, the tangent is more accurate. The tangent of an angle is the ratio of the two legs forming the angle. Look up the tangent of the angle and then lay in the longest possible legs that form the required angle on the workpiece. The following example is artificial, but it illustrates the steps nicely.

Let's form a 90° triangle with one side at a 37.5° angle to the base.

Determine the tangent of 37.5°, using a scientific calculator or a book of trigonometric functions. The tangent is 0.767. Our board is 5″×7″, so use the 5″ dimension for the length of one leg. Since the tangent is the ratio of the two legs, we can find the length of the other leg by dividing 5″ by 0.767. So the length of the other leg is 6.52″. Mark this length on the 7″ side. Connect the 6.52″ mark to the corner of the 5″ leg. This line is a 37.5° angle to the base. To cut the line, either use a cutoff board or tack a board to the workpiece parallel to the cutting line and use the saw's fence. I set the fence to the width of the board and align the board's edge to the cutting line.

Note that the longer the legs, the more accurate the result. So for layouts with short legs (less than 5″), a protractor is probably accurate enough. An error of ¹⁄₁₆″ has a greater effect on a 2″ leg than on a 20″ leg. Otherwise, the only safe method is a measured layout. Another concern with most shop protractors is that their placement on the workpiece is often a problem. (There is a very elegant protractor that solves this problem. It won the 1988 Gold Metal Award for new inventions in Geneva. I have one but can never remember how to use it.)

The protractor, used in the miter/bevel jig, shown opposite, top, is laid out using the tangent of the angle

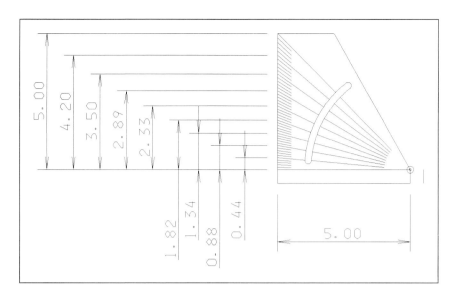

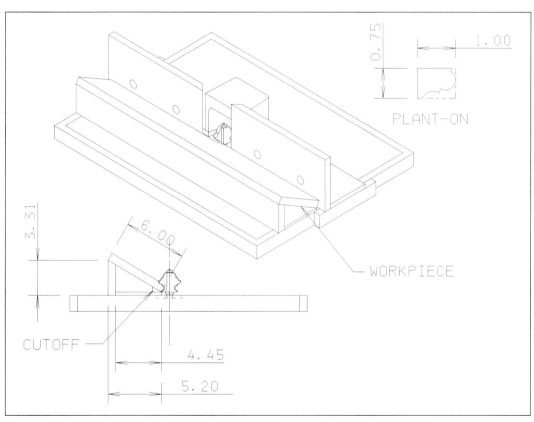

to calculate the location of the angle lines drawn on the workpiece. The dimensions shown are used to lay in the lines every 5°. The 1° steps are determined the same way.

You can use the tangent calculation to build the jig to cut this plant-on. The jig used to position the workpiece is a strip of wood as long as the workpiece and cut with a 37° miter at a height of 3.31″. Hold the workpiece at a 37° angle and use a multiform cutter to cut the edge. After the edge is formed, cut

the 1″ strip from the workpiece blank. The workpiece must be at least 6″ wide to work in the setup shown.

The bench rule is the best scale to use to make the measurements for longer legs, however, bench rules can move or slip. A solution is to make a bench-rule hook. Similar in concept and use to the tape-measure hook, the bench-rule hook holds the rules against the workpiece edge. The sidebar, "Bench-Rule Hook," on the next page shows how to make the hook.

BENCH-RULE HOOK

A hook for your bench rule can be made quickly and easily. You will use it all the time. The bench-rule hook is a simple T-square, an adjustable rule and a valuable layout tool.

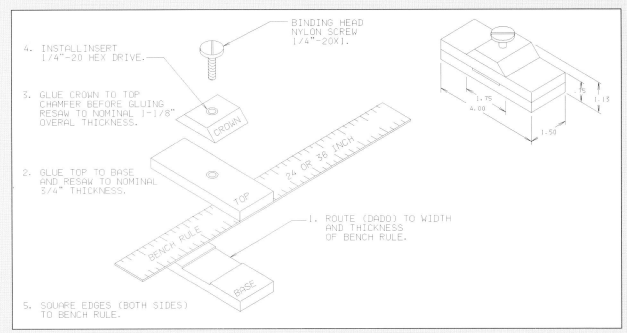

BENCH-RULE HOOK

Using the Bench-Rule Hook

Imagine a series of holes need to be drilled on 4″ centers with the first hole 2½″ from the workpiece edge. Set the hook at 22½″, place it on the workpiece and mark off the hole centers at 20″, 16″, 12″, etc. This is easier than marking at 2½″, 6½″, 10½″, etc., especially if the edge distance to the first hole had been 2.65″.

When the box or case depth is less than the length of your framing square's leg, laying out dimensions is an awkward task. With the hook, merely adjust your rule to the case depth.

Always keep in mind that the hook is set to something other than zero (0″). Normally, it is placed at the 1″ mark. A point 18″ from the edge of the workpiece will read 19″. I have cut a lot of oversized pieces that made me feel pretty dumb when I realized what I had done.

Making the Bench-Rule Hook

Step 1. Cut the base and top strips over-sized. They will be 1½″ × 4″ × ¼″ after gluing and trimming. See step 3.

Step 2. Cut the dado in the base. The dado width and depth are the width and thickness of your bench rule.

Step 3. Glue the top to the base. When the glue has dried and set, resaw to a thickness of ¾″.

Step 4. Cut and glue the crown to the top/base assembly. Make sure you cut the bevels before gluing.

Step 5. Install the 1/4″-20 insert into the crown.

Step 6. Slide the rule into the hook until one end is just under the binding screw, then clamp. Place the rule on the table saw's miter to trim the edge of the hook. Reverse the hook on the rule and repeat the process to trim the other side.

The hook faces are now perpendicular to the bench rule.

MITERS

A router table's primary jig is its fence. You also need a jig for the miter cuts. These miters are normally cut at a right angle to the fence's primary axis. Although many router tables include a miter slot, I prefer to reference this cut off the fence. Edge cuts are one of the most common cuts made with the router and often require a miter to make them. The need for a miter jig is normally a function of the size of the workpiece. Larger workpieces can be cut using only the fence to maintain the positional relationship.

Two styles of miter jigs are shown on the next page. One is used to hold the workpiece in a horizontal position. Its use is primarily for end edge cuts. The combination miter can hold the workpiece in either a horizontal or a vertical position.

The miter guide bar shown in the top left drawing on the next page is a piece of ¾″ × 3¾″ × 15¾″ stock. This guide bar rides the fence. The workpiece positions under the bar and is held by both a fixed and a sliding clamp. (Glue a strip of router pad to the clamping surface of the sliding clamp.) Hold and squeeze the grips to pull the clamp against the workpiece. While maintaining the grip pressure with one hand, tighten the knobs with the other hand. This clamping is an aid to cutting, because if the fence opening is wider than the workpiece, the workpiece will probably slip when you try to take a big cut out of it.

The combination vertical/horizontal miter has a guide bar long enough to bridge the fence opening. By bridging the fence opening there is no possibility of the miter jumping or getting hung up at the transition between the two fence faces. The fence in this case is the hybrid (modified Rousseau) fence. For the laminate fences previously discussed, the guide bar is as long as needed for stability. Make the right-angle miter from pieces of ¾″ ply which are glued or screwed together. During the assembly, be sure the vertical is vertical and the horizontal miter face will be perpendicular to the fence. This miter assembly is then fastened to the guide bar.

The cap and filler give a smooth grip for your hand to hold and push along the fence. Earlier, I tried a handle for this style miter and found the handle acted as a lever, cocking the miter and workpiece. The cap solves this problem by keeping the force vectors in line with the cut.

The addition of a featherboard helps fixture a vertical workpiece. When the workpiece is horizontal, the featherboard can be pulled back and turned out of the way.

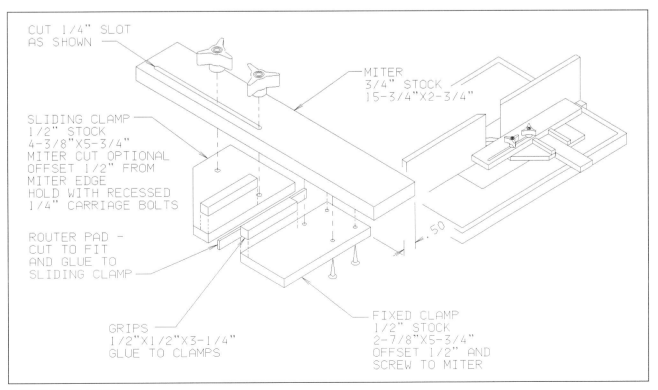

CUT 1/4" SLOT
AS SHOWN

MITER
3/4" STOCK
15-3/4"X2-3/4"

SLIDING CLAMP
1/2" STOCK
4-3/8"X5-3/4"
MITER CUT OPTIONAL
OFFSET 1/2" FROM
MITER EDGE
HOLD WITH RECESSED
1/4" CARRIAGE BOLTS

ROUTER PAD -
CUT TO FIT
AND GLUE TO
SLIDING CLAMP

.50

GRIPS
1/2"X1/2"X3-1/4"
GLUE TO CLAMPS

FIXED CLAMP
1/2" STOCK
2-7/8"X5-3/4"
OFFSET 1/2" AND
SCREW TO MITER

HORIZONTAL MITER

USING A HORIZONTAL MITER
The horizontal miter is used like a backing board, riding the fence while holding the workpiece. Note the scallop cutout on the top of the miter. Use this cutout as an inspection hole to check that the workpiece is against the fence.

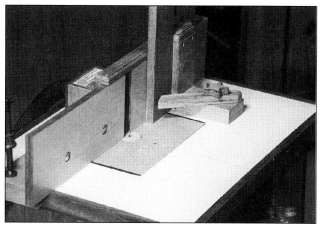

USING A COMBINATION MITER
The combination miter can hold the workpiece for both horizontal and vertical cuts. Here, the workpiece is held in a vertical position.

COMBINATION MITER

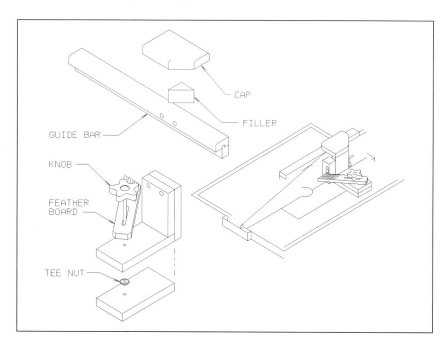

CAP

FILLER

GUIDE BAR

KNOB

FEATHER
BOARD

TEE NUT

COMBINATION MITER

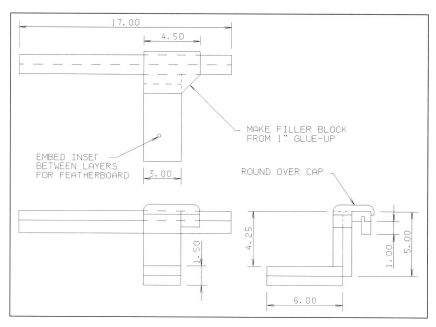

17.00

4.50

MAKE FILLER BLOCK
FROM 1" GLUE-UP

EMBED INSET
BETWEEN LAYERS
FOR FEATHERBOARD

3.00

ROUND OVER CAP

1.50

4.25

1.00

5.00

6.00

SLIDING-FENCE JIGS
The Right-Angle Stop

Before using the sliding fence, you need a stop. The stop is a simple right-angle fixture that is clamped in position on the sliding fence. A box joint is probably the best joint for connecting the two pieces. Just make sure to form an exact right angle and that the resulting assembly is at a right angle to the fence face. To use the stop, position the marked workpiece against the fence, and then slide the stop up to the workpiece's edge, and clamp the stop to the fence. When sliding the workpiece into the cutter, place your hands on the fence and use your fingers to hold the workpiece against both the fence and the stop. If you are making a cut at the edge of the workpiece, you will need to use a hold-down. The eraser end of a pencil makes a good hold-down for small pieces.

One of the nice features about the sliding fence is that, when you have completed the cut, the cutter bit is under the fence, protecting you and the workpiece. You should never drag the fence back while the router is on and the workpiece is still positioned. Position the workpiece and the stop, turn the router on and slide over the bit to make the cut. Now, turn the router off and remove the workpiece, leaving the fence over the router bit.

The Extension Stop

To use the extension stop, you must cut a dovetail slot in the fence. Make the dovetail cuts in the extension stop bar at the same time. Cut a number of extra bars (you can also cut a longer bar). The extra length or pieces will be used for some of the other tools. By cutting them all now you have only one final setup to make. The fit of the sliding dovetail should be loose enough that there is no binding and the bar easily slides in the fence's dovetail slot. To cut the dovetail bar, clamp the sliding fence to the top. Cut both sides, working toward the center by moving the fence, until you have the fit you want. Now, cut the dado in the stop's arm and fasten it to the bar. What you will end up with is a small T-square. Pin the arm to the bar with ⅛″ or ³⁄₁₆″ dowels. Use the extension stop when the workpiece's edge-to-cutter distance is greater than the length of the fence.

The Vertical-Miter Clamp

The vertical-miter clamp used with the sliding fence is a valuable jig. Use it to cut tenons and sliding

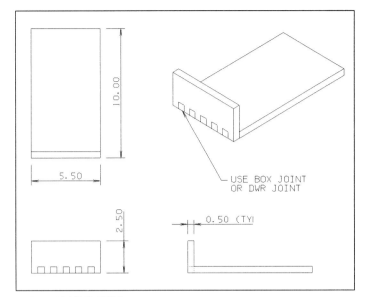

RIGHT ANGLE STOP

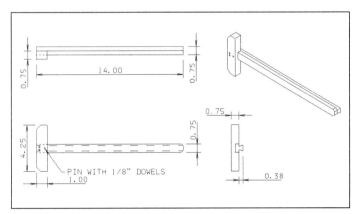

EXTENSION STOP

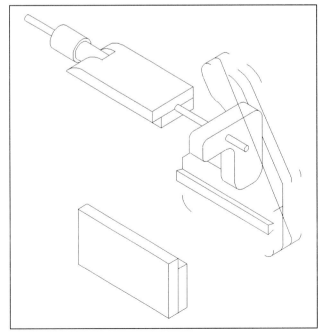

VERTICAL CLAMP

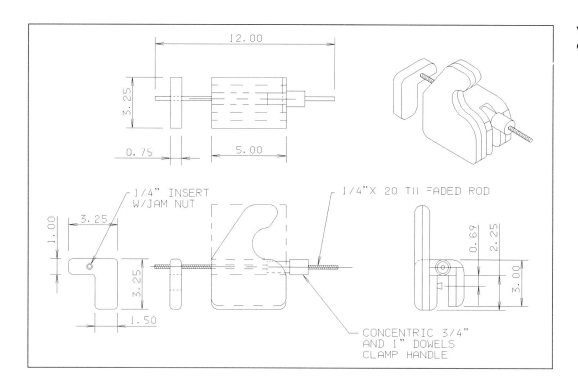

VERTICAL CLAMP

dovetails in small workpieces. The clamping screw is intended to hold the piece steady during the cut. It is not a clamp that totally immobilizes the workpiece.

FEATHERBOARDS

The featherboards are basically all the same. Use ½″ oak for the featherboards. You can cut the feathers with a handsaw, but I prefer to use the jigsaw mounted in the router table with the taper fence. Make two cuts with each fence setting. You can eyeball the cuts or use one of the position jigs discussed later in this chapter. If you have a thin kerf saw blade less than ³⁄₃₂″, you can use the table saw to cut featherboards.

There is nothing magic about the 25 equal spaces; just make sure the fingers are thin enough so they are flexible and thick enough so they won't break the first time you use the board. If you have a 1″ belt sander, you can thin a thick finger by sliding the featherboard into the turning belt. It sands quickly, so don't lean on it too much.

The featherboard must be long enough for some cuts to pick up a clamping edge and reach the workpiece. Use a clamping unit that fits on the table edge. A C-clamp also works well and is faster. A 19½″ featherboard will reach the work on any of the tables. Its problem is its length. The mechanical advantage of the 19½″ lever arm works against the desired retaining force. It works best clamped close to the workpiece.

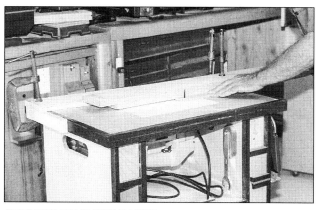

CUTTING FEATHERBOARDS
You always need extra featherboards. Cut the feathers with a jigsaw mounted in the table and the taper jig.

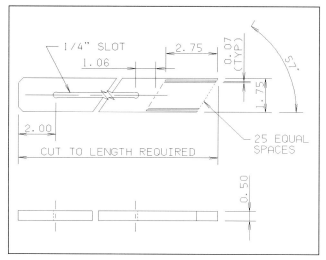

FEATHERBOARD

Block Featherboard

If you need multiple featherboards, use the block featherboard. This block featherboard is made from a laminated fence. The fence is the right length and has the mass and bulk to support multiple featherboards. Clamp the block to the table and then individually clamp the featherboards.

CUTTING DOVETAILS AND SPLINES

Mock dovetails and finger splines can often add a nice touch to a box or drawer. This 45° cradle jig allows the cuts to be made in a simple and straightforward manner. Use a dovetail bit for the mock dovetails and a straight bit for the splines. Use a stop block to hold the box's position when cutting its four corners. Reposition the stop block and repeat the cutting.

You can easily adapt the original INCRA Jig to the cradle and use it to position the box for each series of cuts.

Screw the INCRA Jig to a glue-up cut to a 45° angle. Use dowel pins to attach the jig and angle block to the cradle. The jig and block unit can be removed when not in use. The unit doesn't need screws or glue to hold it in place. Make the block thick enough so that the unit doesn't rock when installed.

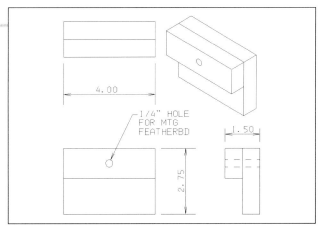

FEATHERBOARD CLAMPS

BLOCK FEATHERBOARD

Use several featherboards with large workpieces. The block featherboard shown here was adapted from a laminated fence. Small blocks at each end elevate the assembly so the individual featherboards don't bind on the router-table top.

45° CRADLE

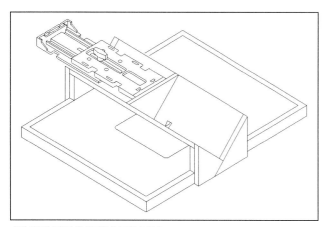

45° CRADLE WITH INCRA JIG

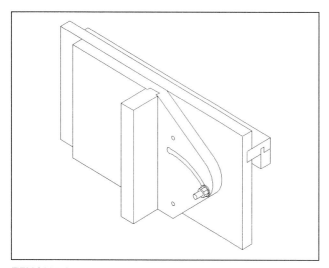

TENON JIG—ISOMETRIC DRAWING

TENON JIG

You can build a tenon jig for your router table similar to the saw-tenon jig described in *Build Your Own Mobile Power Tool Centers* (Betterway Books, 1995). The basic design is shown below left.

A variation is the reversible or complementary tenon jig. This jig allows the fence position to remain fixed for cutting either side of the tenon.

CLAMPING AND POSITIONING

For most of the cutting discussed so far, the fence must be in the correct position relative to the workpiece. A number of commercial positioners/adjusters are available for this purpose, including the INCRA Jig Ultra, the Micro Fence Circle Jig Attachment and the Ryobi Rapid Set Micropositioning Device. The INCRA Jig Ultra was designed for router tables. (It is also available as part of a table-saw fence system.) The Micro Fence Circle Jig Attachment was designed for handheld router use and adapts well to the table application. Ryobi's Rapid Set was designed for the BT3000 Table Saw System but, like the INCRA, can be used with the router table.

The INCRA Jig Ultra is both an absolute and a relative positioner. The Micro Fence and the Ryobi are relative positioners. Where you are doesn't matter, but if you want to move a little closer or a little farther

TENON JIG— BASE

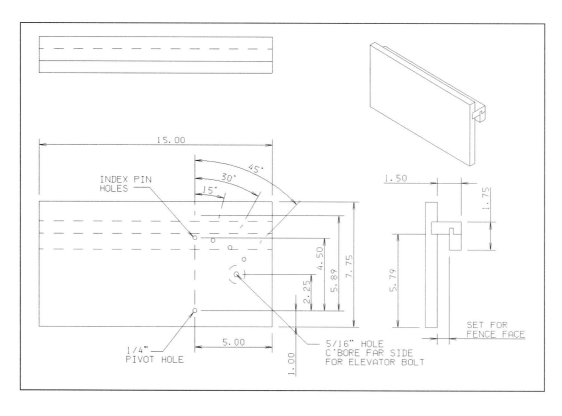

away, a relative positioner will get you there. When I use a micropositioner, I am most interested in the relative change. The various aids built into the table will get you close and then you use a positioner to get it exact. The positioners make incremental changes. The INCRA Jig Ultra and the Micro Fence allow you to make changes as small as 0.001″. The Ryobi can be positioned to $\frac{1}{128}$″. The INCRA Jig Ultra is a complete system that mounts to your table. It was covered in chapter three, "Building Router-Table

Fences." To use the Micro Fence Circle Jig Attachment or the Ryobi Rapid Set, you must build a device to attach them to the fence and table.

The INCRA Jig Ultra

Use the Ultra as a system. That's the way it was designed and that's the way it works best. There is absolutely nothing wrong in knowing absolutely where you are.

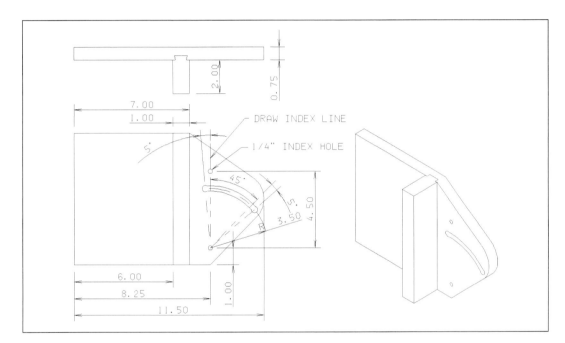

**TENON JIG—
CARRIAGE**

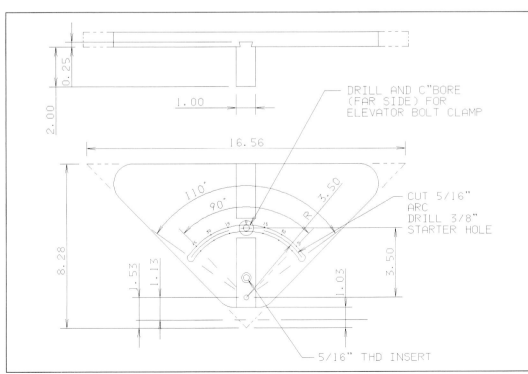

**REVERSIBLE
TENONING JIG**

The Micro Fence Circle Jig Attachment

The Micro Fence Circle Jig Attachment attaches easily to the fences or, as will be seen later, to the planer/circle cutter. Since the Circle Jig Attachment is designed for routers, the fence won't need additional clamps. It is designed to handle circles up to a 24″ radius, so you can position the fence anywhere on the two router-table tops covered in chapter three. The same is true when it is used with the planner/circle cutting jig. It is also easily stored when not in use.

The interface coupler of the Micro Fence Circle Jig Attachment is router type and model specific. It is the mounting dimensions of the Micro Fence interface coupler that are used for attaching the Circle Jig to the sliding fence. The one shown here is for the Porter-Cable 690.

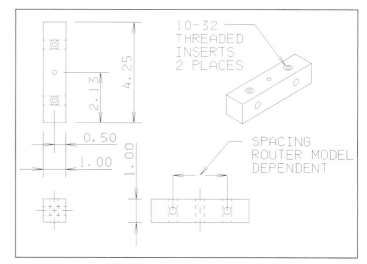

MICRO FENCE COUPLER

The Ryobi Rapid Set Micropositioning Device

The Ryobi Rapid Set Micropositioning Device is the smallest and therefore the easiest to store. It is also easy to adapt for use with the router table. This adaptation requires the making of couplers for attachment to the fence and to the table. For the BT3000 Table Saw System, it hooks to the saw fence and attaches to an extruded channel for positioning on the table. This attachment method is copied for the router table attachments. Add a pick-up bracket to the sliding fence to mate with the hook and cut a wood channel to simulate the saw's channel. The Rapid Set is attached to one end of the wood channel and the other end of the channel is clamped to the table top, as shown below in the illustration. If desired, the channel can

be calibrated to the table so that it can be clamped close to the required fence distance. Having gotten close, the micropositioner is then used for the final adjustment.

The Ryobi positioner has a 1⅜″ adjustment range. It uses a 5/16-16 LH thread lead screw for the adjustment. Sixteen threads per inch allows ¹⁄₁₆″ movement for each revolution of the positioner knob. The knob is marked in ¹⁄₆₄″ increments (a quarter turn) and can be interpolated to a ¹⁄₁₂₈″ change. The INCRA Jig Ultra uses a ¼″ lead screw with 32 threads per inch. It is marked in ¹⁄₃₂″ increments and has a ¼″ adjustment range. The primary jig has an adjustment range of 16″ or 24″ in ¹⁄₃₂″ increments. The Micro Fence micrometer dial is the easiest to read. It is marked in 0.001″ increments. Since it uses a 7/16-20 lead screw, one

RYOBI COUPLER

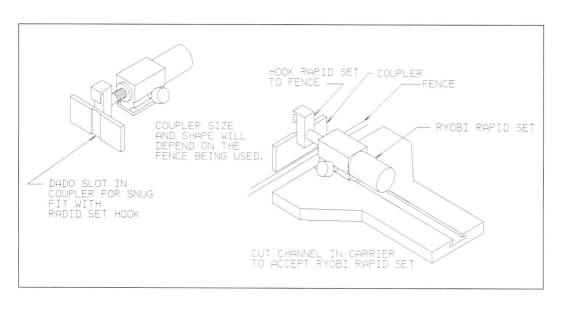

revolution of the dial will move the fence 0.050″. The micrometer adjustment range is about 1″. Total adjustment of the Circle Cutting Jig is 24″.

Shop-made Positioning Devices

To make your own positioning device, you need a lead screw of known pitch and some way to attach the screw to your fence. Use a 16- or 32-thread-per-inch screw if you like working with fractions and a 20-thread-per-inch if you want to work with decimals. My advice is to go with the decimals. You will want to remove a whisker or increase a tad to the cut in the workpiece. The best advice for measuring tads and whiskers is the dial caliper. They all read in 0.001″ increments. Some also have a metric and a fractional scale (¹⁄₆₄″), but most don't.

The adjustment locator is the simplest shop-made positioner. It clamps to the sliding fence and is used to locate the right-angle stop. Make the threaded adjustment locator from the exact bar stock cut for the sliding-fence accessories. Drill a 10-32 tap hole and cut the tap. If you don't have the drill and tap, you can use an insert. Thread a 10-32 machine screw into the block and put two nuts at the end of the screw.

To use the adjustment locator, clamp it next to the stop and turn the screw until the nut touches the stop. Now move the stop and turn the screw to make the adjustment. Each complete revolution of the screw is ¹⁄₃₂″. A half turn is ¹⁄₆₄″ and a quarter turn is ¹⁄₁₂₈″.

The next positioner in this evolution was the nudger. After the nudger came the threaded adjuster.

Wood Thread Micropositioner

The wood thread is cut with the Beall wood threader. I use the 1″ and ¾″ cutter with good results. Both cut 6 threads per inch. Use couplers of the type shown on the next page, top, to attach the wood thread to the table and the fence. These designs use axle pegs which allow for quick and easy mounting and removal of the jig. The drawings detail the parts used for control and connection to the sliding fence. Similar connections can be used for the hybrid fence.

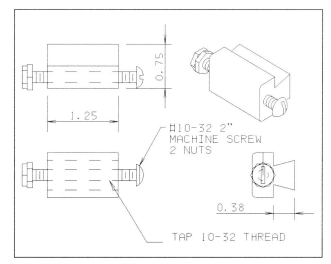

ADJUSTMENT LOCATOR

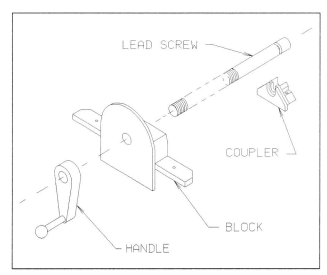

THREADED ADJUSTER—EXPLODED

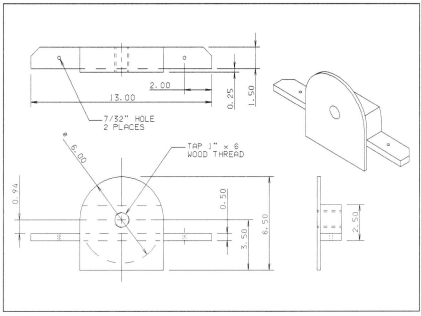

THREADED ADJUSTER—BLOCK

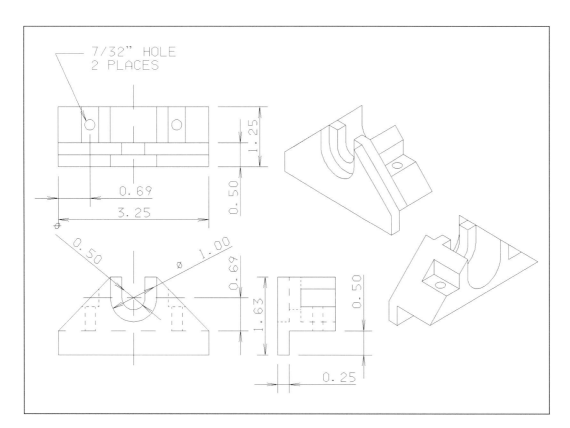

THREADED ADJUSTER— COUPLER

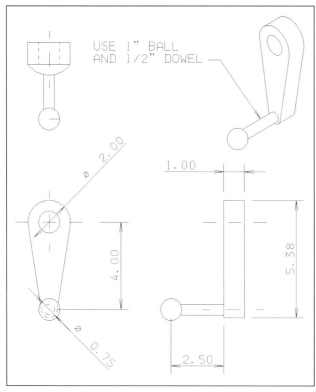

THREADED ADJUSTER—HANDLE

THREADED ADJUSTER—PATTERN

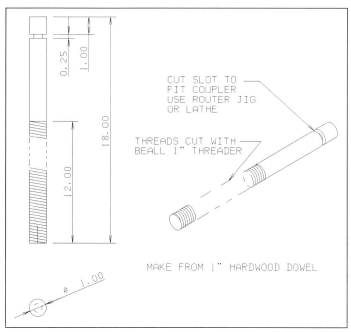

CUT SLOT TO
FIT COUPLER
USE ROUTER JIG
OR LATHE

THREADS CUT WITH
BEALL 1" THREADER

MAKE FROM 1" HARDWOOD DOWEL

THREADED ADJUSTER—SCREW

THE PLANING AND DADO JIG

The planing and dado jig was first described in my first book *The Next Step—the Building of a Professional Home Workshop*. It is particularly useful for doing blind dadoes and mill work. This jig is really a simple X-Y table. To move in the X direction, you move the stock and to move in the Y direction, you move the router.

The carrier for the router is its base plate. As a result, the jig is quickly set up and put into operation. It is better for planing than a belt sander and good for cutting out recessed areas. This jig is also valuable for making spaced dado cuts in, for example, a bookcase side.

I normally use a plunge router with this jig. With the router mounted on an acrylic plate, the workpiece and work area are clearly visible. Be sure the workpiece is flat and level. Special clamping or fixing is often required to ensure the workpiece moves only where it is supposed to. The photographs on the next page show some of the solutions I have used.

When it is time to cut circles, the planing jig shows its versatility.

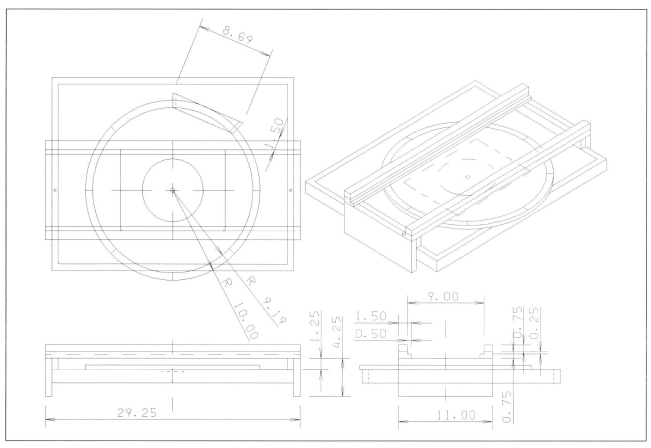

PLANING AND DADO JIG

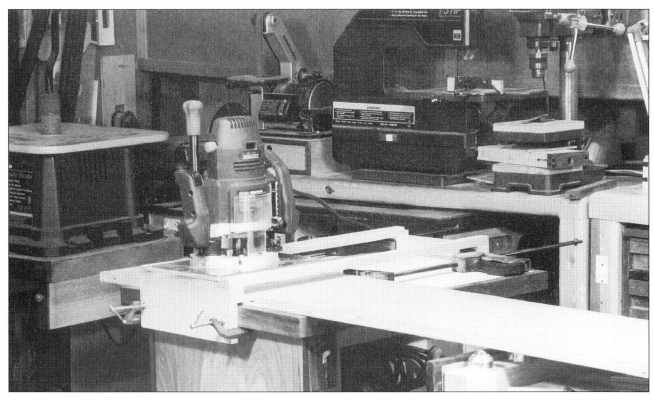

CUTTING SPACED DADOES WITH A DADO JIG
Spaced crosscut dadoes are cut in this case side. Note the use of the spreader
clamps to retain the workpiece while the cut is made.

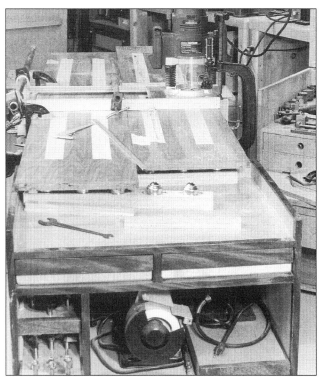

**CUTTING BOOKCASE SIDE SUPPORT STATIONS AND
OTHER BOOKCASE SIDE**
Another example of crosscutting is shown here. Both sides of
the bookcase are cut with one setup.

CUTTING BOOKCASE SIDE HOLD-DOWN
To cut the vertical channels for the bookcase shelf standards,
clamp the router and slide the bookcase side through the
cutter. Boards clamped to the front of the jig ensure the
bookcase side does not rise up as it passes the cutter.

CIRCLE-CUTTING TURNTABLE

To cut circles with the planing jig, make a turntable that mounts in the table's plate cutout. First make a plate to fit the router-plate opening. Use ½″ stock, as with all the plates, but don't rabbet the plate's edges. The plate's surface will be ¼″ above the table's surface. Cut a 6″-diameter hole in the plate. Now, cut a 6″-diameter circle to fit in the hole cut in the plate. This circle is the bearing pivot for the turntable.

Again using ½″ stock, cut a 20″-diameter circle to make the actual turntable. The jigsaw is probably the easiest to use, but you can also use a band or table saw to cut out the circle blank. Fasten the 6″ bearing circle to the turntable and set it in the plate. The blank should turn freely but not wobble on its bearing pivot.

Using the planing and dado fixture to hold the router, trim the turntable to the 20″ diameter. The setup for this cutting operation is shown above. Clamp the turntable so it's stationary, turn the router on, and slide the router along the planing jig until you reach the 20″ circle line. Now clamp the router in place and unclamp the turntable. Turn the turntable against the router-bit rotation to trim the edge. This sequence assumes you cut the turntable blank to within 1/32″ of the 20″ line. If you didn't cut this close, you will have to cut off the high (long diameter) spots and work your way in by taking small cutting steps until you reach the final diameter. Large bites, larger than 1/32″, can result in a very energetic lazy Susan. The Micro Fence Circle Cutting Jig offers the greatest control.

Duplicate the adapter coupler designed for the sliding fence and mount it on the bottom of the router plate. When the router is mounted in the table, the coupler is out of the way and doesn't interfere with the router's use. When the router and plate are used in the planing and dado jig, the coupler is there to set up and attach the circle jig.

The circle jig's trammel point is fixed to the planing jig. With all of the knurled screws firmly locked in position, you can cut the turntable to its final diameter by dialing-in 0.01″ (1/100) cutting steps. Start the cutting at the circle blank's high point, turn the circle one complete revolution and then dial-in another 0.01″ step and repeat the turning of the blank for complete revolution. Step and repeat to the final dimension.

The turntable has a hardwood border. I did this because I didn't have a piece of ½″ stock large enough

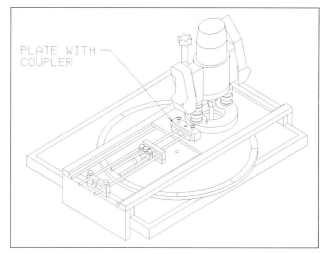

PLATE AND COUPLER

for the circle piece. I tried to make do with an 18″-diameter turntable and found that it was too small to hold and control. The edge of the turntable must overhand the table edge enough so it can be held and rotated. Cutting this outer ring gave me the opportunity to use the circle cutter right away. Make the concentric nesting border piece by cutting eight ¾″ × 1½″ segments to form an octagon. Connect the segments of the octagon with tongue-and-groove joints or just glue the end cuts together. This is not a strong joint but it won't matter once it's glued to the circle piece. Fasten this border with toothpicks at each segment to the turntable and cut it to form a circular ring. Cut the inside diameter first to a depth of ⅜″ to form a rabbet. Use toothpick dowels to hold the octagon ring to the turntable for the inside cutting. When doing inside cuts, turn the table clockwise to feed fresh wood into the cutter. Now, cut a ⅜″ rabbet in the turntable to allow the pieces to be nested and joined. After the glue has set, cut the outer circle. Use a saw to trim the octagon into a circular shape before doing the final router cutting.

The turntable must not wobble when you do nested rings. Make sure the circle hole in the plate and the circle mounted to the turntable are a tight fit.

SHOOTING AND MITER BOARDS
Shooting Boards

From time to time, the need to do repetitive cuts with the router will occur. The shooting board shown on the next page was made for, of all things, cutting parts for Roman catapults. At Christmastime, I sell the catapults both as kits and finished models. For this

This model of a medieval catapult is made using straight and mitered lapped dadoes. All the cuts can be made with the sliding fence or with a special adaptation of the sliding fence.

quasi-production work, I need to be able to make the cut pieces quickly and accurately. Looking at the model in the photograph you can see that there are a number of mitered dadoes.

I constructed the shooting board so all the catapult's pieces could be cut with one setup. For some of the pieces, I need to use a second dado, reposition the pieces on the board and then make a second pass with the shooting board.

Miter Cutting

We previously discussed using one side of the sliding fence for doing miter cuts. When large workpieces must be accommodated, construct a special-purpose shooting board. The one shown on this page is made from ¼″ hardboard. Cut the base with the selected bit to determine the router-bit path. Now, lay in the workpiece's required position with respect to this cutter path. Glue or tack the positioning strips to the hardboard base to hold the workpiece. If you tack them in, you can change them for other cuts or if you make a mistake in your layout.

The Adjustable Miter

If you want a general-purpose miter like the one on your saw, make an adjustable miter. The adjustable

SHOOTING BOARD ON ROUTER TABLE
A special adaptation of the sliding fence is the shooting board shown here. The individual pieces are first cut to length using the table saw's shooting board shown in the upper right of the picture. These individual pieces are then placed on the router table's shooting board which is cradled and positioned by the tacked-on fixtures. The required mitered dado is then cut. This type of fixturing can be extended to numerous designs of limited production.

miter is simply a pivot board that can be rotated to the required setting and then clamped to the cutting board. Use the method described in the protractor example to lay in degree marks. This cutting board can be used for end cutting or internal cuts.

You won't have the flexibility you have with your table saw to do compound miters using the router table. A limited number of edge-cutting operations at some arbitrary bevel angle are possible. To do this type of cutting, use the protractor made in the tangent example earlier.

MAKING TEMPLATES

We have already made some templates (the opening for the router plate, for example). With the various pattern bits available and the manufactured template guides that fit most routers, templates are not the chore they once were. Notwithstanding, they still demand some care and some calculation in their development. Often, you must make intermediate tools, i.e., cutting jigs, that are then used to make the final tool.

Templates are most often needed for inlays, such as the router plate. Fitted jewelry boxes, electrical plates and instrument cases are all examples of projects requiring templates. Templates are also needed to duplicate edge patterns for cathedral doors, corners, handle openings and repetitive shapes used in a design.

The applications for templates are endless. Many templates are applications for using the router as a handheld tool. The size of the workpiece, how the workpiece is retained and your need to see the cutting action that will decide if it is a table or a handheld application. If the workpiece must be elevated in order to make the cut, turning it over and using the router table is often easier.

The application will also determine the size of the template. The workpiece must be retained to the pattern, the pattern itself must be retained when the router is handheld and there must be a surface for the router base or the table to ride on. The router bit and the size of the template guides determine how thick the template should be. A typical template bit was shown in chapter two.

Looking at the making of cover plates for electrical parts, we will see examples of both using the router alone and using it mounted in the router table when using templates.

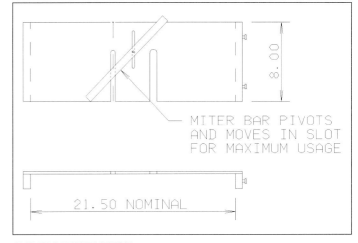

SLIDING FENCE MITER

Jigs for Making Cover Plates

Hardwood receptacle and switch cover plates add a professional look to computer and entertainment centers. Often, when building these centers the cover plates used must be of a nonstandard size or made with nonstandard cutout arrays. The designer touch can be added to kitchens and bathrooms with custom plates. The jigs shown on page 88 will cover a variety of your cutting needs.

You first need a set of pattern templates for the various receptacles. Use purchased plates to start the pattern-making process. Using the cover plate mounting holes, fasten the plate to the template blank and trace the opening outline. Remove the plate and then drill as much of the material as possible from the template blank. Reattach the cover plate, using a standoff to raise it at least 1/4″ above the pattern surface. Put a pattern bit in your router and, using the cover plate as the pattern, trim the edges to the plate opening. You can't use your router to cut the switch opening for a switch plate. Drill the top and bottom of the switch opening and then chisel away the bridging material.

You should have a pattern now for each of the shapes you will be cutting. Cut the cover blank oversized from 1/4″ stock. Attach the pattern to the cover blank, cut the cover holes and sharpen the corners with a file or chisel. Now, cut the plate to its final dimensions, slightly larger than the standard cover plate. Use your router (with or without a jig) to recess the back, leaving about a 1/8″ border of uncut material remaining around the recess.

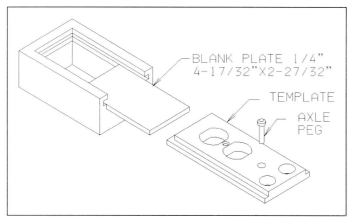

SWITCH PLATE 28

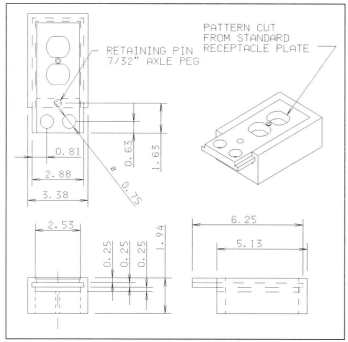

ELEVATION VIEW

The jig shown above is designed for use with either a handheld router or with the router mounted in the table. The box height was chosen to allow a standard pattern bit to be used for all the cutting. Since the pattern-bit bearing is 1″ from the end of the bit, the bearing surface must be 1″ from depth of the recess. The box sides are the bearing surface and the box bottom (or top, depending on how you look at it) are the surface the router base will ride on. Take a look at the elevation view, above, of the pattern box to see what this all means.

The pattern box is designed to accept a variety of receptacle and switch patterns. Cut the cover blank to its final size $\frac{1}{4}″ \times 4\frac{17}{32}″ \times 2\frac{27}{32}″$ and slide it into

the box. Slide the selected pattern in above it. Retain both in the box with a dowel pin or axle peg. Use one surface of the box to cut the openings and the other surface to cut the recess. Use the finger holes in the pattern piece to pull the pattern out of the box.

Corner Cutting

Use this corner jig to cut corners on the router plate. Individual jigs must be made for each required corner radius. Make the jig large enough so it can be clamped to the workpiece and to the router table. Glue edge guides to the pattern to position the workpiece.

To make the pattern, lay in the radius with a compass and then sand to that line using a 1″ belt sander. Normally this method works fine to form the corner. To be more exact, however, cut an intermediate tool. After reading the following "how to" description, you will probably opt for the sander. I do.

This two-step sequence requires first the making of a female pattern and then, using this pattern, cutting the final corner pattern. This method also requires the use of template guide bushings and being able to drill the required diameter hole in the female pattern. The example here is making a $\frac{3}{8}″$-radius corner jig. This is the jig used for the router plate.

1. Using a $\frac{1}{2}″$ bit and a template guide bushing with a $\frac{21}{32}″$ inside diameter and a $\frac{3}{4}″$ outside diameter, the hole in the intermediate pattern must have a diameter of $2[\frac{3}{8}″ + \frac{1}{2}″ + \frac{1}{2}(\frac{3}{4}″ - \frac{1}{2}″)] = 2″$. These are all standard sizes, so making the final pattern won't be a problem. The radius of the required hole is the sum of the required corner radius ($\frac{3}{8}″$), the diameter of the pattern bit ($\frac{1}{2}″$), half the difference between the guide bushing outer diameter ($\frac{3}{4}″$), and the diameter of the pattern bit ($\frac{1}{2}″$). So the radius is 1″, and the required diameter is 2″.
2. Cut the intermediate pattern board as a square or rectangle. Lay in the circle's center and center lines somewhere near the center of the pattern blank and drill the 2″ hole.
3. Accurately position the intermediate pattern on the final pattern board. The center of the hole in the intermediate pattern board is offset from the center point of the $\frac{3}{8}″$ radius by $\frac{1}{8}″$. Use the center lines previously drawn to aid in positioning the pieces.
4. Cut the radius.

Corner jigs like the ones shown here are quick and easy to use. Although they can be used with the router table, they are best cut using a handheld router with a ½" pattern bit.

You can also fit a circular piece to your template. Drill a ¾" hole in the template blank. Cut a ¾" dowel and glue it to the hole. Now, cut along the tangent lines to form the final template shape. This method works best for templates with a large radius. Instead of using a dowel to form the circle, use a circle cutter in your drill press.

Handles

Handles like those shown in the photograph at right are cut using a template pattern.

This pattern can be used with the router handheld or table-mounted. To make the pattern, start by drilling the holes for the internal radii of the handle. As with corner jigs, the external radii can be shaped or you can use the two-step sequence. The resultant pattern looks like this.

After the drawer front has been cut, use a roundover bit to smooth and round the edges.

Wine Rack Cradles

A similar template was made for cutting the cradles used in the wine rack on the next page.

The template holds a cradle pair. The front cradle has 1½" diameter cutouts for the bottle neck and the rear cradle has 3" diameter cutouts for the bottle base. Some wine racks I build hold four bottles to a row

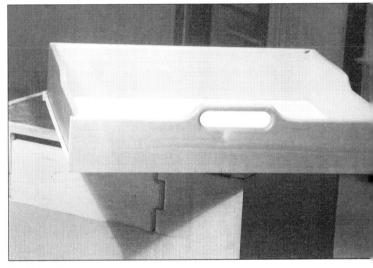

DRAWER HANDLES
Make drawer handles of the type shown here either on the table or with a handheld router. The size of the drawer face normally determines which method is best.

and some hold five. The template was made for the five-bottle type with spacer blocks being added when the four-bottle version is being cut. The handles for holding the pattern jig are also the knobs used to clamp the workpiece into the jig. Polycarbonate shields keep fingers away from the pattern bit.

When cutting the cradles, it is normally best to cut the "wrong way" at the top of the right-hand

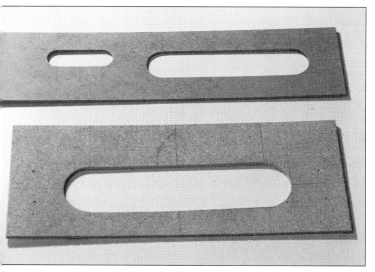

HANDLE PATTERN
The patterns used to cut handles are the same for both router-table use and the handheld router.

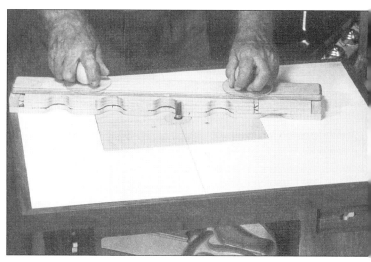

WINE RACK
All the joinery for these wine-rack pieces were cut using the router table with the sliding fence. The wine-bottle cradles were cut using a pattern jig.

transition. The chances of the workpiece splintering are too great coming into the transition from left to right.

Sometimes the template bit bearing is used to set the radius of the inside corners. If you want to form a corner like the one shown above, right, glue fillets into the corners to give the additional material required for the finished shape. These fillets should be cut with the grain parallel to the hypotenuse of the triangular piece. Use a corner template for the outside cut and the 1⅛″ pattern bit for the inside corner.

RULES OF THE ROAD

A table router, like any other stationary tool, has certain rules that are best followed.

Within reason, you can make most cuts with your router and router table. The important thing is not to push it. If the workpiece cannot be adequately secured or if inordinate amounts of material must be removed in one pass, find other tools for the necessary cutting. Let the size of the workpiece dictate whether to use your router in the table or to make the workpiece the table.

Using a router, as it is designed to be used, the hands and fingers are protected from the cutter by the fact that they are being used to hold on to the router. When the router is mounted in a table, both the bit and the fingers are exposed. (A number of shields or guards have been designed for use with router tables. I personally have never found any of

WINE-RACK PATTERN JIG IN USE
This pattern jig has been designed to hold both a front and a rear cradle. The individual cradles are clamped in place with the ball handles. The Lexan guards won't stop the router bit, but they do keep your fingers out of the router-bit path.

them to be satisfactory for their intended use. At best they offer some degree of false security, and at worse they are actually dangerous.) All of them I have tried I have ended up throwing away. I, further, don't like the idea of throwing some of my fingers away. For this reason, I will not make what I consider a dangerous cut. I want neither to ruin the workpiece nor the fingers that are holding the workpiece. To keep the cut from being dangerous or uncontrollable, take the time to understand how the cut should be made and how the workpiece should be held to make the cut.

1. Don't position the workpiece between the fence and the cutter. This is like being between Scylla and Charybdis. Charybdis, a whirlpool off the Sicilian coast (Strait of Messina) is across from Scylla, a rock on the Italian coast. This particular rock and hard spot were personified by the Greeks as a nymph that changed into a sea monster. A sea monster that caused great harm to ships sailing between its jaws. Think of Charybdis as the rotating router bit and Scylla as the fence. Don't place the workpiece between the jaws of this monster. Keep both the cutter and the fence on the right side of the workpiece. See the drawings below. If the workpiece is trapped between the fence and the router bit, the workpiece will be forced to move right, away from the fence and into the cutter. The hands holding the workpiece will also be moved into the cutter.

2. Try to make the cut so the router bit is turning into the workpiece. The simple rule for handheld routers is *inside clockwise, outside counterclockwise*. For the table-mounted router, the rule is complemented (the inverted flat earth). The "try" of this rule is for normal cutting. Sometimes the workpiece grain or the required symmetry will dictate breaking the rule. The important thing to remember is that you are breaking the rule, so take special care when making the cut. If you cut the wrong way with some bits, they will grab the workpiece and toss it across the shop floor. Be

careful, you're on a one-way street going the wrong way.

3. Make and use the featherboards and push blocks that are described here and in my book *Build Your Own Mobile Power Tool Centers* (Betterway Books, 1995). Build these aids so they are easily installed and used and keep them accessible. When we get lazy and try to do the quick-and-dirty cut, we get in trouble.

4. Don't cut off more than you or the router bit can chew. Don't use the router to remove inordinate amounts of wood, especially in a single pass. Take the time to use the table saw or the band saw to remove the majority of the material prior to using the router for defining the edges. If the router bit is used, plan for multiple passes. Be more aggressive on the first cuts and then fine-tune to the final profile.

SAFETY EQUIPMENT

The two primary pieces of safety equipment you need are eye protection and ear protection. The best eye protection is a face shield. I wear prescription glasses for close work and have safety glasses made from polycarbonate. These are the best lenses. This will give you an idea of how good they are: Safety glass will break when shot with a $\frac{1}{4}''$ steel ball at about 100 ft./sec.; plastic will break about 120 ft./sec.; and polycarbonate will *never* break. Whether prescription or plano, opt for the polycarbonate. The same is true

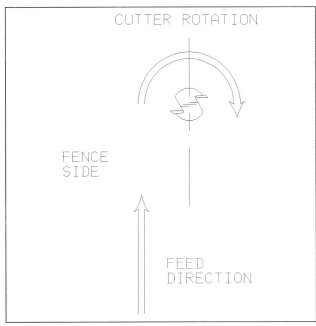

CUTTING DIAGRAM—HANDHELD

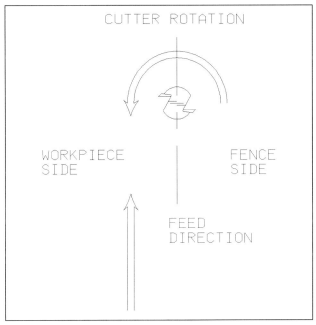

CUTTING DIAGRAM—TABLE MOUNTED

with the face-shield material.

I have mixed feelings about ear protection. I want to protect my hearing, so if I am going to be doing repetitive production-type cutting, I wear the muffs. Most of my cutting is on and off—new setups, new cuts. For this type of cutting, I want to be able to hear the router and any vibration that may be occurring. It's like driving your car, when the engine starts making funny noises—something is not right. You will want to stop and see what the problem is. Don't let your ear protectors hide these problems.

TABLE RECEPTACLES

Each of the router stations has a switched receptacle. Normally this receptacle powers a shop vac. Whenever the router is turned on, so is the vac. It's disconcerting sometimes to throw the switch to make a cut and to hear behind you the sound of the vacuum turning on. You will get used to it after a while.

When using the vacuum for cleaning up, turn the router off at its switch and use the table switches to control power to the vacuum. The vacuum's power switch is always at the other end of the hose from you and usually is not as easy to get to as the table's switches.

Our router table can be used in a number of ways. To start with, it is a workbench. It can also be used as a table saw or jigsaw table. Of course, first and foremost, it is a router table.

The next chapters describe how to build three styles of router tables. Review each of the table's characteristics before deciding which table type best fits your needs. It may be a combination of the designs shown.

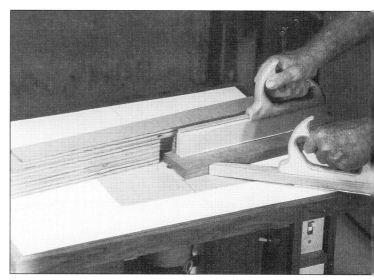

HANDHELD FEATHERBOARD AND PUSH BLOCK
For even the simplest cuts, always keep your fingers and hands away from the bit. This handheld featherboard and push-block hold-down allow for safe cutting.

USING THE TABLE AS A WORKBENCH
For some cutting, whether with a hand saw or a trim router as shown here, you need a vise and a work surface. When you round over the finger pulls in this drawer front, the lever clamp is the vise and the router-table top is the work surface.

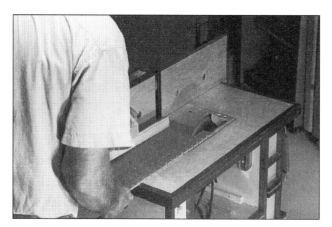

USING THE TABLE AS A TABLE SAW
When you need to rip boards, at the job site, a mounted circular saw is beneficial. For crosscutting, use the sliding fence.

USING THE TABLE FOR JIGSAW CUTTING
Cut out the push-block handles easily by using the jigsaw in the router table. Cut the concave surfaces first with a drill.

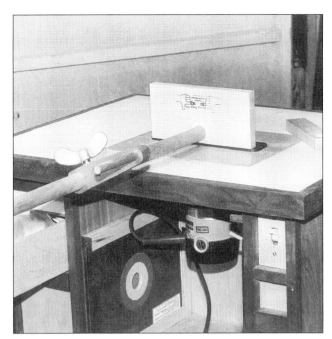

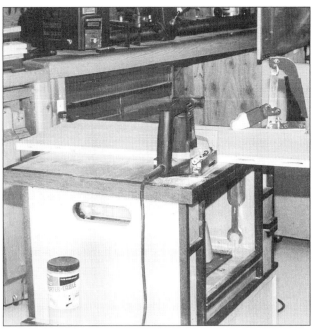

USING THE TABLE FOR THREADING

Add a couple of ³⁄₁₆″ holes and a threader can be attached to the table. Here, it would appear J.R. Beall is giving a thumbs-down to J.R. McPherson's adaptation of the threader. It really works fine and sets up quickly. Here, the threaded screw for a micropositioner is being cut.

USING THE TABLE FOR PLATE JOINERY

The router table makes a good surface for cutting biscuit slots, but remember, the reference edge/face is down.

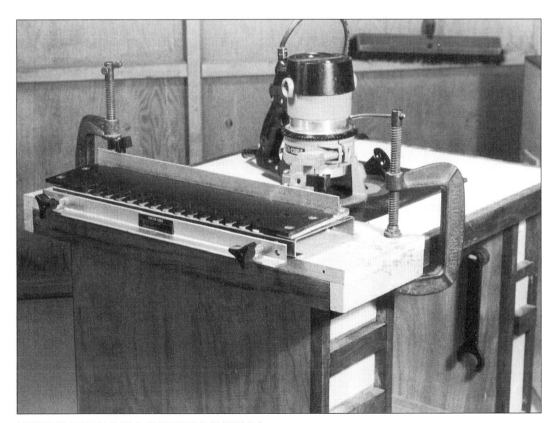

USING THE TABLE FOR CUTTING DOVETAILS

Since all your router tools and bits are at the router table, this is the logical location for cutting dovetails. The table height allows the cutting of fronts and sides up to 36″ in length.

CHAPTER FIVE

THE JOB-SITE ROUTER TABLE

Take your table to the work. The job-site router table is your portable router workstation. Portability may mean moving it from one corner of the garage or shop to another corner, or it may mean loading the table on your truck and driving to the current job site. If you can get away with it, you can bring it into the house while you are remodeling the kitchen or bathroom. The table is designed not only as a router table but also as a table saw and a jigsaw table.

All the routers and all the various jigs and fixturing previously described can be used with this table. The weight of the table is, of course, a function of the type of router used and the tools stored in its drawers and compartments. When I have the Porter-Cable 3¼-hp router mounted, which weighs about 15 pounds, and the center compartment loaded with drill motors, batteries and a charger, my table weighs 100 pounds. I can easily carry it around the shop and to the truck. I made the wheeled base box for the longer distances. This base box gives me additional storage space and a platform for the table. For other applications, the table's platform is a set of legs.

JOB-SITE ROUTER TABLE

TABLE ANATOMY

The base box is simple—three sides, a top and a bottom. It holds a large slide-mounted drawer which in turn can hold the sliding fence, the modified Rousseau fence, a jig and a circular saw, along with some miscellaneous bits and pieces stuck in the corners. Sometimes the legs fit in the box and sometimes they don't. There comes a point where making the box (or the table for that matter) any bigger defeats the whole idea of a portable work center. The box is designed to be longer than the length of the table so the drawer can hold the fences. The height of the box puts the height of the router table at 34½". I want a work surface, especially for the router, to be on what's considered the low side. I like being on top of what I'm doing, not acting as a spectator on the sidelines. When making a cut, I want to see where everything is, including my fingers. All my mobile workstations are the same height so they can be used with and support one another.

The size of the router table itself is also taken from the other workstations. The top surface is my standard 21½" × 27¾". All the jigs and fixtures are compatible with these dimensions. These dimensions also set the size of the storage drawers. The space needed for the router is determined by the size of the largest router that will be used in the station. The large routers, the Porter-Cable model 7518 3¼ hp, the Craftsman industrial 3½ hp plunge and the Ryobi RE-600 3½ hp plunge, all fit the allocated space. If you use a plunge router, either make the center box/drawer smaller or remove it during router usage.

There are a number of options for what is stored in the drawers. One drawer space is reserved for the power switch box. This box is designed so it can be located in either the upper right or upper left corner under the tabletop. By allowing the relocation of the power switches to either side of the table, a shortcoming in the shop table design is answered. As will be seen, the shop router table has fixed two-point switch control. There are some cutting sequences using this table where having the switches on the side where one is working would be better. To correct this drawback, the movable switch box was developed. The contractor table, described in chapter seven, has four-corner power control. There is also a modification to the shop table described in the next chapter that adds three-point power control.

For the remaining drawer spaces there are drawings and pictures of suggested uses of this space. I use the complementary switch box space to store the Micro Fence. It's a good fit for the space available. For one of the bottom locations, I have a router-bit drawer, and on the other side I store layout and measuring tools. Storing a trim router or router accessories are other examples of how these drawers can be used. The center drawer or pullout box normally is only loaded when I am going on-site. The most frequent use is for the drawer to hold the cordless drill

motors, the batteries and drills.

Miter chop saws have replaced most of the table saws that used to appear at job sites. Notwithstanding, having a table-type available can be of benefit. It is for this reason that there are provisions included for the mounting of a circular saw. It is not an ideal marriage but it works. The circular saw model type will dictate the elegance of the solution. As with routers, some models are more amenable to this application than others.

Jigsaw mounting is easily accomplished and makes a worthwhile addition to any router table.

Before doing any cutting, take a long look at your shop and tools to see if these tables have the right space allocations and dimensions for your needs. Three basic designs are covered in this book, and you can easily combine and blend their features.

Height is an important parameter and is easily changed. None of the NBA players who are also woodworkers would like the height I have chosen. The table height should be a function of the height of other tables in your shop and your height.

To change the height, you can change the layout of the design, you can use larger or smaller wheels on the box and you can use elevator blocks both to mount the wheels and to place the router table on its supporting surface. The legs will be mounted with wood cleats on the bottom of the table. These cleats can either rest on the top of the wheeled box or they can be set in recesses cut in the box's top. This will vary the height by up to ¾". Finally, of course, the legs can be of any reasonable height. The same is true of the router table's top. It can be of any reasonable size.

Materials

I recommend using ¾" birch plywood sheets for the primary construction. You can use Finnish birch, Baltic birch or shop birch. Finnish birch is the best and naturally the most expensive. Next comes Baltic in both price and quality. Although shop birch is the cheapest, it will offer no problems in cutting or in strength. My personal opinion is the shop birch finishes the best and makes the most attractive case. The Finnish and Baltic birch veneer layers show very little pattern or contrast, and the cases tend to look a little bland. Shop birch, however, is not well suited for building fence, jigs and fixtures. The unused parts of the shop birch will end up as scrap. A table made

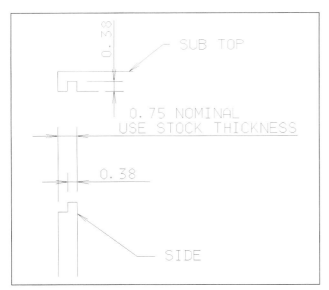

ALTERNATE JOINT

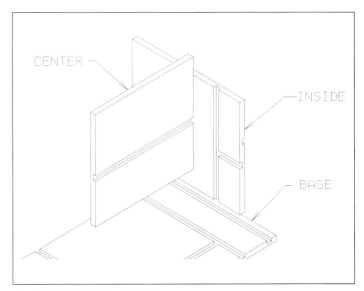

CENTER, INSIDE AND BASE

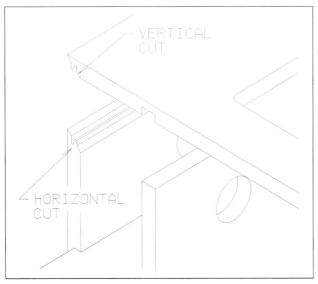

CORNER SUB-TOP

BUILDING THE ROUTER-TABLE CASE

Once you have selected and purchased the material, cut out the various pieces. If you are using a solid-surface material like Avonite for the router-table top, don't cut out the piece marked *top*. This piece will be used for a natural birch top or for a top covered with a plastic laminate. As described in chapter two, the ½″ solid-surface material is bonded to ½″ birch ply.

You may use different joints than those shown here. If you do, make sure you follow through and change all the affected parts. At the beginning of the book, I suggested that you study the drawings. Please take a close look at the rest of the drawings in this chapter now.

When you buy plywood sheets these days, especially plywood coming from Europe, you never know how thick it is going to be. With the ¾″ stock, you can find a variance of ¹⁄₁₆″ from sheet to sheet. Since you will be working with one sheet, this won't be a problem, but what *will* be a problem is that I have assumed that all ¾″ sheets are three-quarters of an inch thick and all saw blades have a ⅛″ kerf. The ⅛″ kerf assumption won't cause any problems but the ¾″ thickness assumption can and does. Normally, if you use a ¾″ dado setup in your saw or a ¾″ dado bit in your router, the resultant dado will be too wide. I have found that for all of my cutting of the European birch, I have been using the ¹¹⁄₁₆″ dado setup with my Forrest dado blades and have been using an undersized router dado bit made by Onsrud for dado cutting with the router. When using the shop birch, I

from of the various birch sheets should outlast the builder.

The Finnish birch and the shop birch both come in 4′ × 8′ sheets. The Finnish birch grain pattern runs along the 4′ axis, whereas the shop birch grain runs along the 8′ axis. Cutting diagrams for both grain orientations are given later in this chapter. Baltic birch comes only in 5′ × 5′ sheets.

Each of the sheets has been laid out so straight ripping cuts can break them into more manageable sizes. I also attempted to grade or nest the parts to allow the largest possible leftover pieces of unused stock.

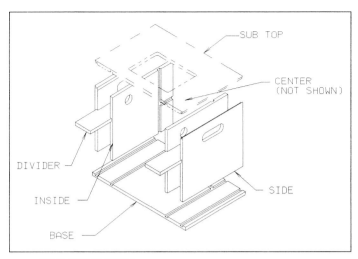

EXPLODED VIEW

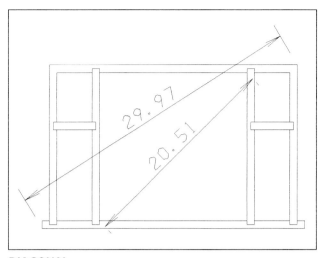

DIAGONAL

have been using a normal ¾″ setup. I think the problem is that 20mm European plywood stock is too thick to sell in the U.S., so we get the undersized 18mm stuff.

To overcome this problem to a degree, the job-site case is designed to be symmetrical. Choose a reference edge—the piece's center line is best—and then stay consistent. Make sure either the parts are cut to the dimensions shown or adjusted to the dimensions of the actual piece. Now flip the workpiece and make the symmetrical cut. The fence that you are flipping against can be either the saw fence or a router fence.

In many cases, cuts are shown being made on the router table when in reality it is easier and faster to make the cut with a table saw. Since this is a router-table book, I wanted to show as many examples as possible of router cuts. There are also, cases where, a simpler joint could be used. I tend to use the making of shop furniture as a learning experience. Try using the joints and methods that you will be using for the cabinets and furniture that is going into someone's home. You can't beat the production shop on price, so beat them on quality and uniqueness.

The catch-22 is that you may not have a router table. That's why you bought this book. There is only one joint in the basic job-site table that requires using a router table—the lock-miter joint used to connect the subtop to the sides. If you don't have a router table yet, or the lock-miter bit, use the alternate joint for the top-to-side connection. Note that the sides are ⅜″ shorter when using this joint. The following joint is used in the construction of the shop table and is described in some detail in chapter seven.

After you cut the pieces, the case is ready for gluing. Before doing the actual gluing, do a dry assembly to check the fit and to determine what clamping is needed. For this dry run, go through the following sequence without actually gluing. Do perform the clamping so you can check the square and level. The compartment shelf and its door will be glued in later. After the case has been clamped, but not glued, check the shelf fit. Once you're sure of the fit, repeat the following sequence, this time using glue.

Step 1. Set the base on a low surface with the base edges overhanging the support surface so there is space for clamping.
Use a moderately strong cardboard box or something like an Workmate bench set to its low height for this low working surface. Try to have the surface level at least in one axis.

Step 2. Apply glue to base and mating pieces.

Step 3. Set mating pieces to base.
Start by joining the center with one inside piece and the base, then add the other inside piece and the sides.

Step 4. Glue and set top on the sides, the center and insides.

Step 5. Glue and slide dividers into position.

Step 6. Clamp vertically and lightly clamp the dividers.

Step 7. Clean off the excess glue.
Make sure that the drawer tunnels are free and clear of any glue buildup for easy drawer movement.

Step 8. Check the square and level.
The diagonals are shown above. If they are not equal, use a clamp along the longer one to bring the case into square.

Step 9. After the case has dried and set, cut and glue on the hardwood trim strips.
Hold off the rear center strips until the compartment door has been fitted.

Step 10. Make the top and its plate.
Follow the procedure outlined in chapter three.

Step 11. Position the top on the case and use the router-plate opening as a pattern to trim the subtop opening.

The first drawer to make is the switch box drawer. The drawer must fit either the right or left opening, so if the openings are not identical in size, make the box so it fits the smaller opening.

TRIMMING THE CASE

Use ¾″ × ¾″ hardwood strips to trim the case. Use the same type wood you used for the router-table top borders.

CUTTING DIAGRAMS

Use these diagrams for planning the cuts. Mark the pieces with their name and major dimensions.

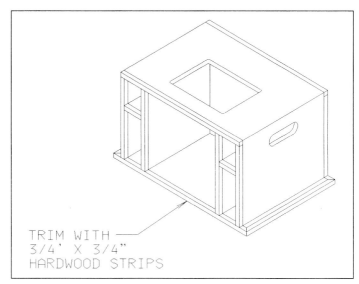

TRIM WITH
3/4' X 3/4"
HARDWOOD STRIPS

TRIMMING THE CASE

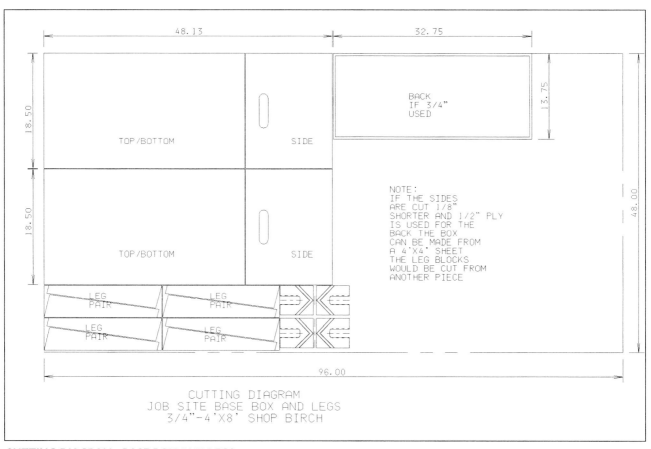

CUTTING DIAGRAM—BASE BOX AND LEGS

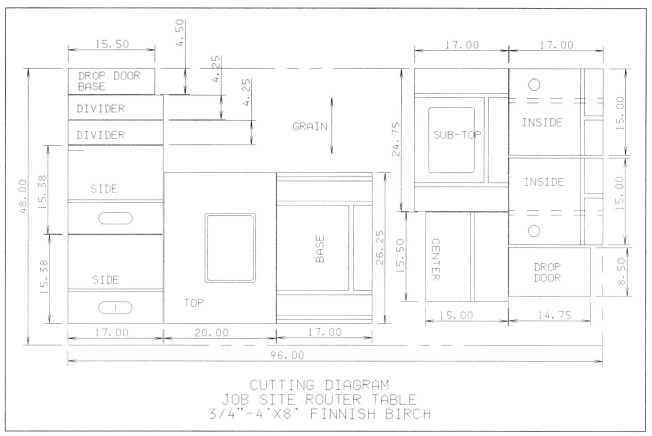

CUTTING DIAGRAM—JOB SITE ROUTER TABLE, 4′×8′

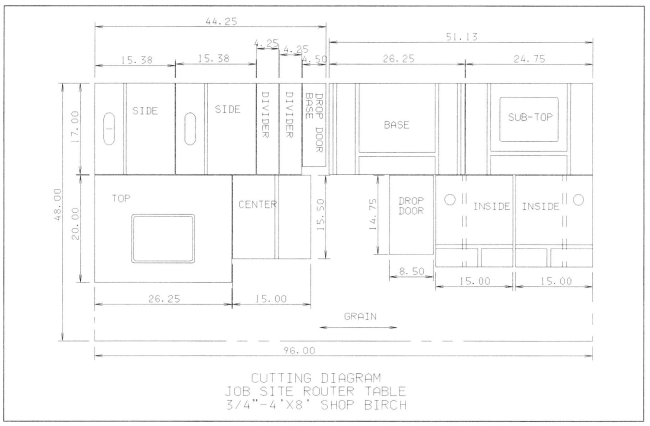

JOB SITE ROUTER TABLE, 4′×8′

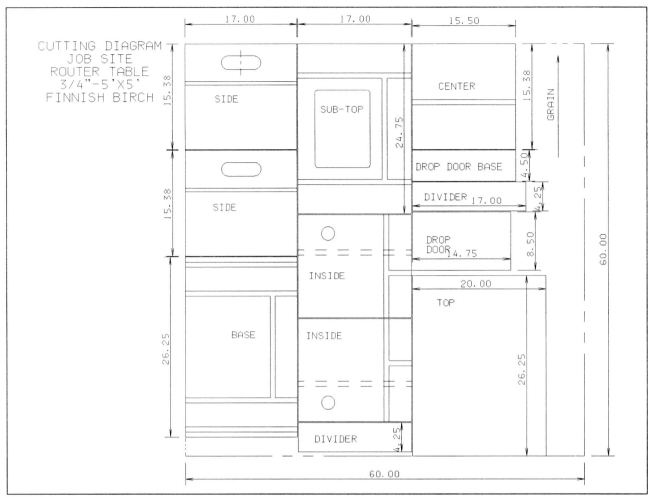

CUTTING DIAGRAM—JOB SITE ROUTER TABLE, 5′×5′

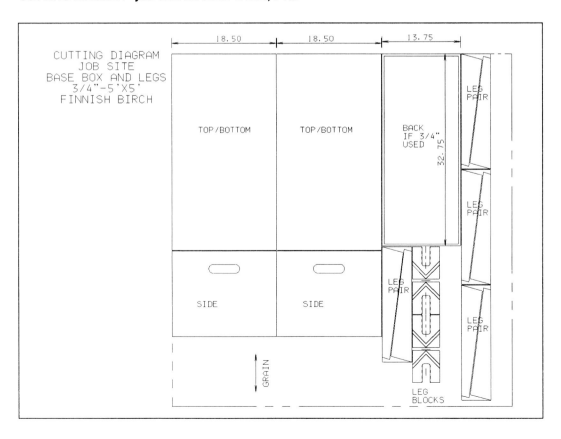

**CUTTING
DIAGRAM—
BASE BOX AND
LEGS, 5′×5′**

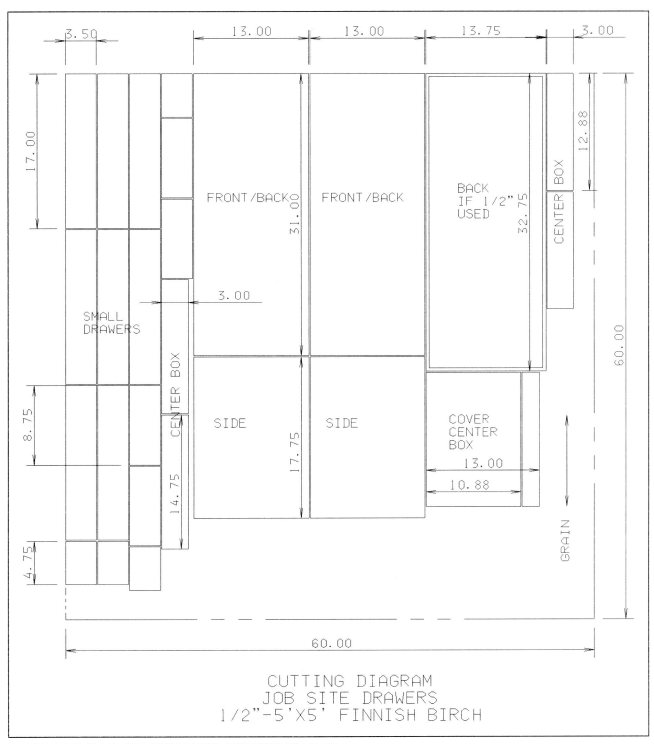

CUTTING DIAGRAM
JOB SITE DRAWERS
1/2"-5'X5' FINNISH BIRCH

CUTTING DIAGRAM—JOB SITE ROUTER DRAWERS, ½″ × 5′ × 5′

DETAILED DIMENSIONED DRAWINGS

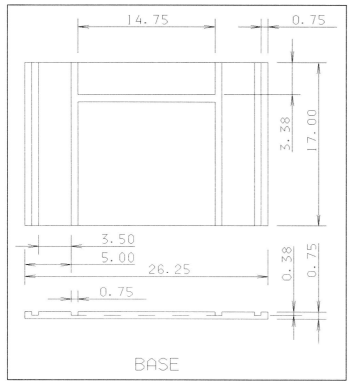

BASE

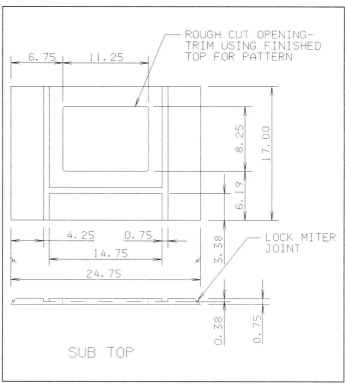

SUB-TOP

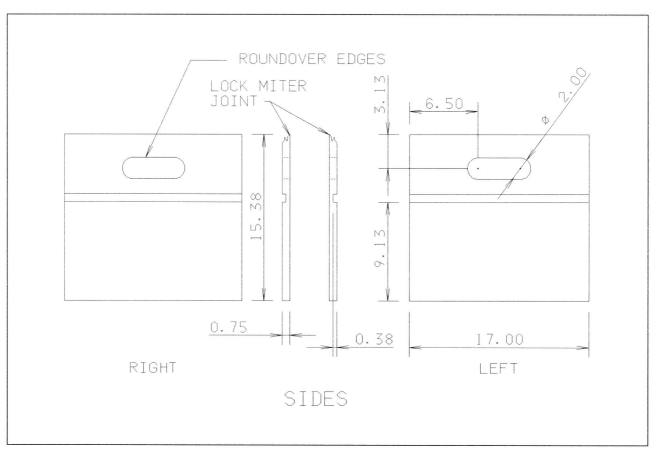

SIDES

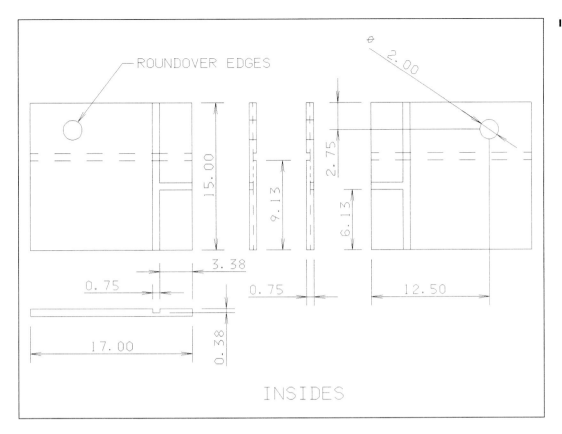

ROUNDOVER EDGES

ø 2.00

INSIDES

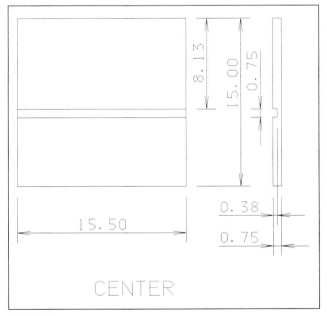

CENTER

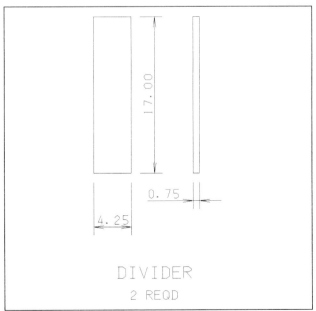

DIVIDER
2 REQD

INSIDES

CENTER

DIVIDER

CLAMP HOLDERS

The clamp holders can hold four or five C-clamps in the space under the compartment. Check the size of your C-clamps to determine if your clamps will fit side by side as shown or if you need to change the block dimensions. The block dimensions are a function of the inside dimensions of the C-clamp. My 4″ clamps just make it by the skin of their skinny skin teeth. You may have to opt for one center-mounted holder. Glue up two pieces of ¾″ scrap to form the 1½″ block. The front locking bar has a ¼″ insert or T-nut threaded to a carriage bolt protruding from the center of the block. The lock bar screws onto the carriage bolt until it is tight and blocks the C-clamps. It's a big wing nut.

CUTTING AND FITTING THE COMPARTMENT DOOR AND SHELF

The important part of the compartment is its door. When hinged down, this door makes a super tool tray to keep the junk off the top of the table. I keep a handheld featherboard and some pushers in the compartment so they are quickly accessible. The door is held in the horizontal position by a support hinge mounted at one end.

Here's a case of using the router to make a hinge when a couple of strap hinges would certainly do the

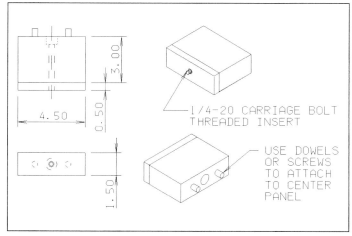

CLAMP HOLDER

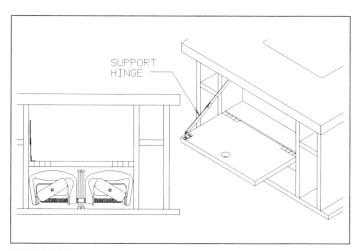

REAR VIEW

SUPPORT HINGE

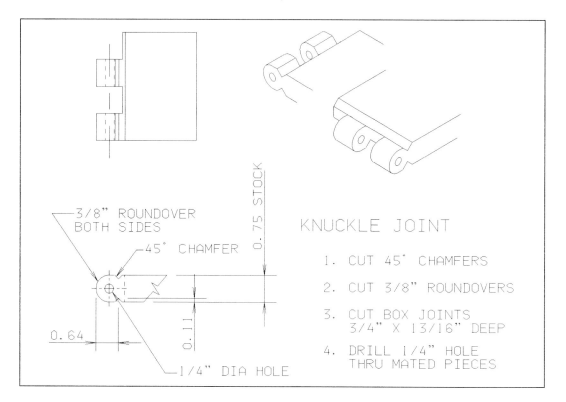

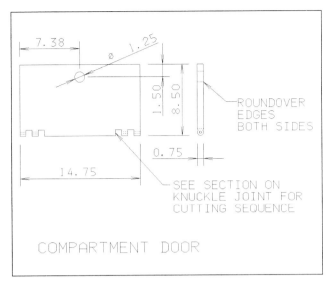

COMPARTMENT DOOR

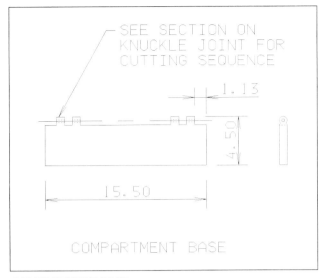

COMPARTMENT BASE

trick. Anybody can screw on a couple of hinges. Your table can have a bona fide old-world knuckle-joint hinge that you have made with your own router. We will go through the steps here but it may be easier to cut the hinge after you have completed most of your table and made a fence.

If you haven't cut the pieces yet, cut them now.

Step 1. Cut the 45° chamfer on both sides of both pieces.

Step 2. Cut the ⅜″ roundover on both sides on both pieces.

Step 3. Cut the box joints using either the router or saw.

Note that the depth of the cut is ¹³⁄₁₆″. This extra depth keeps the pins from binding when the door is hinged.

The number of knuckles on each end of the shelf and door depends on the length of the ¼″ drill that is used to drill the hinge pin holes. The drill I use comes from Beall and is 6″ long with 4″ flutes. It only comes with a ½″ shaft, so it must be used in a drill press. The drilling of the hole should be done with a drill press so the ½″ shaft shouldn't be a problem. Spade drill bits won't work when using birch plywood; the bit wanders all over the place. The extra long (12″) bradpoint drill bits also wander too much. I have not tried the 10″ length bradpoint bits but I think they should work for this application. A standard 4″ drill bit, a little less than 3″ of flutes, can be used for drilling through four knuckles total, two in each piece.

Step 4. Mate and clamp the pieces to the drill-press fence and drill one end.

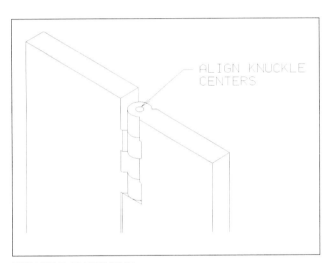

KNUCKLE ALIGNMENT

DRILL PRESS

The hinge pin hole for the knuckle joint requires accurate alignment and drilling. A drill press using a 4″ to 6″ bit is best.

Make sure the pieces are positioned correctly so the hole is drilled in the center of the knuckle. There will be a gap between the two pieces as shown in the illustration. Pin the two pieces together with a dowel, turn the pair over and drill the other hinge pin hole.

Step 5. Fit the assembly to the case and then cut and glue on a trim piece.

Step 6. Fasten the shelf to the center with screws.

Step 7. Attach the support hinge.

Step 8. Cut and glue the remaining trim to the case.

MAKING THE SWITCH BOX

To make the switch box, you will need

- Two 20-amp 3-way switches
- One male receptacle
- One 20-amp double-outlet receptacle
- One 20-amp single receptacle

The only part you may have trouble finding is the male receptacle. I use either the Sylvania Flanged Inlet Outlet, part number 5278-FI or the Bryant Nylon Cup Male Base, part number 5278. They are probably not available at your local home improvement center but can be found or ordered from any contractor electrical supply outlet.

Build the box from ½" birch ply. The top, bottom and one side of the box are permanently attached with

glue. The other side, which is removable, is secured with screws. The electrical receptacles are mounted flush to the sides. Note that one of the receptacles is switch controlled whereas the other half is powered whenever the table is powered. This allows, for example, the shop vac to turn on whenever the router is turned on. It also allows switch control of the vac when it is used to clean the table.

The female receptacles attach from the inside surface of the sides and the male receptacle attaches from the outside surface. Use wood screws to fasten the 3-way switches to the ends of the box. The spacer blocks, located at each end, are needed to pick up the center-to-center spacing of the switch's mounting holes. Wire the box using the wiring schematic. Allow yourself some slack in the wire so it can all be wired together and checked out in an open configuration. Use 14-gauge (14/3 AWG) wire for the connections. The box is large enough to hold a reasonable amount of slack wire. Make sure the ground is carried to each switch and outlet.

Use ¼" plywood stock to make the switch cover plates. Cut to fit the box end and then cut out the switch-toggle opening. Drilling the ends is the easiest way to make the opening. Drill ³⁄₁₆" holes for the mounting screws. Recess the back of the plate so the switch can mount flush. Use your router with the switch plate on a router pad to hog out the recess or use the jig described in chapter four. Rout the inside to about a ⅛" depth leaving a ³⁄₁₆" border. When

SWITCH BOX

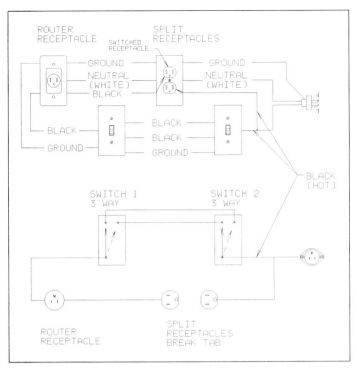

ELECTRICAL DIAGRAM

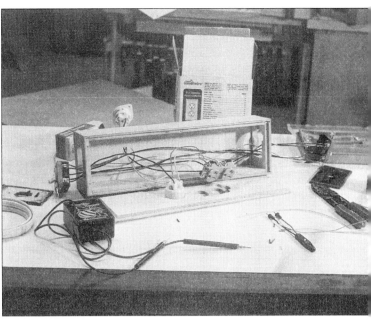

SWITCH BOX WIRING
The removable side provides good access for the wiring of the switches and receptacles. Do a continuity check of the wiring before checking with normal power.

you're done, make sure the switch-toggle opening doesn't bind the switch.

Now, if you make a simple fence, you have a router table you can use for the rest of the cutting.

MAKING THE DRAWERS

All the drawers use ½″ Finnish or Baltic birch with ¼″ tempered hardboard backs. Of the four corner types I have shown, my preference is the lock-miter joint, because the tops, bottoms and sides can be cut to the size of the opening. Another advantage is once the router bit height and the fence positions have been established, you don't have to change them when making the horizontal or vertical cuts. This is a real time-saver. Using the drawer-joint bit is almost the same except that the sides are shorter than the actual depth of the drawer. Unless you made the box-joint jig described in *Build Your Own Mobile Power Tool Centers* (Betterway Books, 1995) for either the saw or the router table, making box joints takes longer to cut and all that cutting can get boring. The same is true for the dovetail joint. The dovetail joint can also cause tear-outs with the plywood, even the Finnish birch.

If you use a box joint or dovetail corner joint and then use a dado or rabbet cut to hold the back (bottom), the slot will show from the front. For this reason, I started building and gluing the box sides

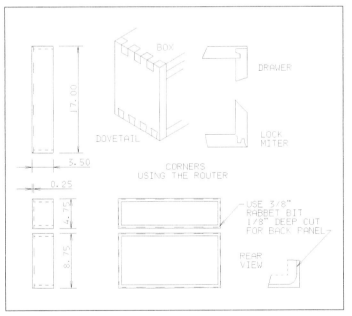

DRAWERS

together first and then rabbeting the back with a ⅜″ rabbeting bit. Set the bit's height for the thickness of the hardboard plus a tad.

I now use this method for most of my drawers and boxes, since I find it simpler to do. Cut the hardboard back to the opening size, round its corners and then glue it in place.

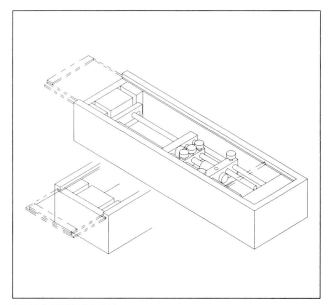

MICRO FENCE BOX

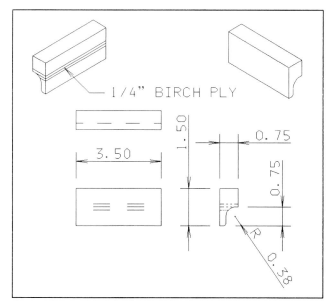

DRAWER PULLS

Pulls and Drawer Retainers

Any number or types of knob can be used with the drawers. Shown above, right, is a simple and effective pull made from $3/4'' \times 1\frac{1}{2}''$ stock. Start by cutting a strip of stock long enough so all the required pulls can be cut from the stock after it is formed. A variation is to use $3/4''$ strips left over from cutting the case trim strips. I often have strips too narrow to do much with. One use is to sandwich a strip of $1/4''$ ply with the thin stock to form a laminate. Use this laminate to then cut the $3/4'' \times 1\frac{1}{2}''$ strip. It's an attractive pull and goes will with the table.

When cutting out the actual blank, I normally cut out most of the waste on the saw and then finish with a $3/8''$ core box bit. Sand the strip smooth before cutting off the individual pulls.

A retainer like the Stanley Mini Bolt works well to hold the boxes in the case. One per box is best.

Building Bit Drawers

Even if you go ahead and cut the drawer sides, including the corner joint, you may want to hold up gluing them together until you have worked out what is going in them. Another option is to go ahead and glue up one of the boxes and then use it to try out various ideas. The glued boxes can always be used for router bits or measuring tools since these modifications are add-ons to the basic box and require no internal cutting to the box itself.

The basic box is configured into a router-bit box by adding a couple of pieces to hold router bits. It's

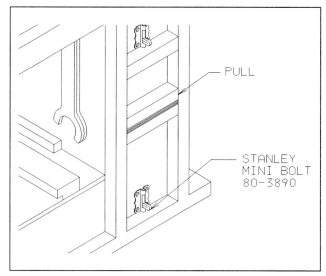

MINI BOLT/PULL

simple and effective. Dowel pivots allow the top bar to rotate so bits can be removed. A stop block ensures that the bar doesn't rotate too far.

Make a strip 1″ wide by gluing up $1/4''$ and $3/4''$ birch or two $1/2''$ strips cut to a final length of $16'' \times 2''$ wide. Cut the strips slightly oversized so they can be trimmed after gluing. Glue a $1/2'' \times 1/2''$ stop block to the back of the bar. This stop block keeps the bar from turning too far which in turn keeps the bits from spilling on the floor. Drill holes in the resultant bar on $1\frac{3}{8}''$ centers to hold the bits. Try to find a 13mm or $33/64''$ drill bit to drill these holes so your router bits will fit easily into them.

For your $1/4''$ router bits, make inserts from $1/2''$

dowel stock with a $^{17}/_{64}$" center hole. Put the inserts into the holes drilled for the ½" bits. For the larger diameter bits, set a 45° plate on the bottom of the box. You won't be able to use all the holes in the plate but go ahead and drill them anyway. They add flexibility. Drill the holes in the box ends and the top bar for the dowel pivots. Chamfer one end of each dowel pivot to aid in positioning them through the box and picking up the hole in the bit bar.

Layout and Measuring Tool Drawers

The basic box is configured for the layout and measuring tools by making a removable plate that sits in the box at a 15° angle. This bias allows the tools to stay in place when the box is upright or on its side. As you can see in the photograph, with the use of magnets and ¼" divider strips, the 8" × 16" plate can hold a complete set of measuring tools. The strips and magnets hold the tools in place so, like the router bits,

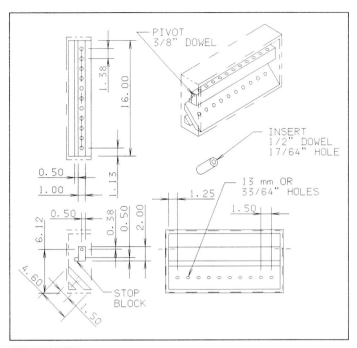

BIT DRAWER

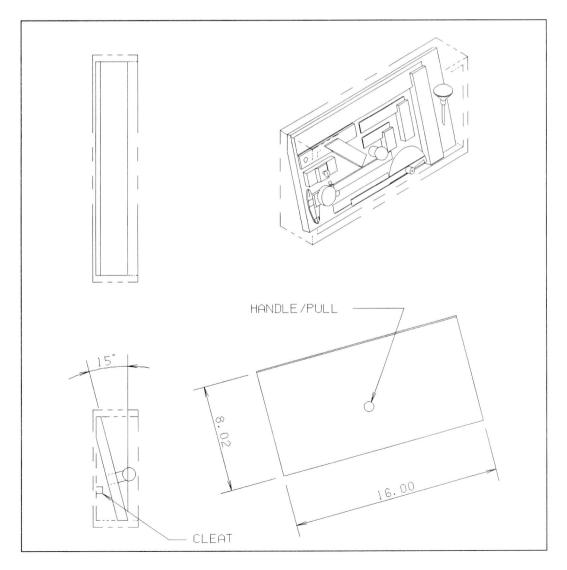

DRAWER MEASUREMENT TOOLS

they won't spill on the floor.

A handle in the center of the plate lets you lift it out and set it on the box for bench top use. A cleat glued to the box back sets the plate at an easy angle for use and also keeps the plate from sliding back into the box.

Other potential uses of the boxes are the storing of a trim router and its accessories, a jigsaw or the router's accessories. The top of the drawer will need to be cut for most jigsaws to fit.

Look at the photographs to get some ideas for the storage of your tools.

TABLE DRAWERS
The drawer configurations for the job-site table are shown here.

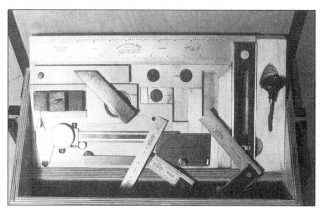

MEASUREMENT TOOLS
This set of measurement tools just fits in the available space. The fitted strips and magnets keep the tools in place when the drawer is in the upright position.

CENTER DRAWER
The center drawer can be fitted to store a variety of items. Here, the drawer is used to hold a small drill motor, maintenance tools, a mirror, two shim plates and some axle pegs. Axle pegs tend to get lost so have extra ones available.

BASE BOX DRAWER
The base box drawer can hold tools or fixtures. The drawer shown here holds the sliding fence, the hybrid fence and the table legs. Only one leg shows in the photograph.

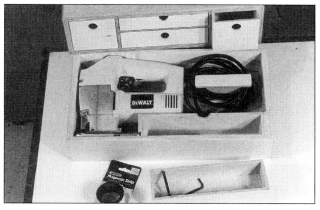

CUSTOM DRAWERS
Many custom drawer configurations are possible. Here is a bottom drawer fitted for a jigsaw and a top drawer used as a chest. Tape adhesive-backed magnetic strips to the bottom of small drawers to keep things like allen wrenches and jigsaw blades in place.

CUSTOM DRAWERS
One drawer here is fitted for a trim router and its accessories, including bits. Above it, a top drawer is used to store standard router bits. This top drawer has two slide-out trays, one of which can be seen in the photograph.

CUSTOM DRAWERS
This is another variation of a drawer fitted to hold a jigsaw. Note the material cut from the top. Cut this clearance recess before the box is glued together.

MINIATURES
A designer table like this one is ideal for doing miniatures and models. With a Dremel Moto-Tool and shaper/router table attachment, all sorts of small pieces can be formed. The model shown is a representation of a corner computer cabinet. The 1:6 scale allows ⅛″ stock to be used for full-size ¾″ material.

The Center Box Drawer

The center box drawer serves more than one purpose. First it is a storage box. It also serves as a holder for the router, as a place to put the table's cover plate, as a dust baffle, and finally as a safety step for the router. When the table is being moved, the router, attached to its plate, is stored and held by the slide bars on the box's top. When the router is being used, the cover plate is stored here. Lifting the box cover will help contain the router dust and chips to the cavity. If you

got away with taking the table into the house, the lid will help minimize the cutting mess. If the router motor is turned on before it is clamped to its base, the box will serve as a safety stop. This can happen.

Both of the plunge routers discussed are too high to be stored on the box. Since the routers do fit when being used in the table, I suggest leaving the box height as shown in the previous diagrams. Cutting it down will limit what can be stored in it.

Build the box using ½″ birch ply. The cover can be

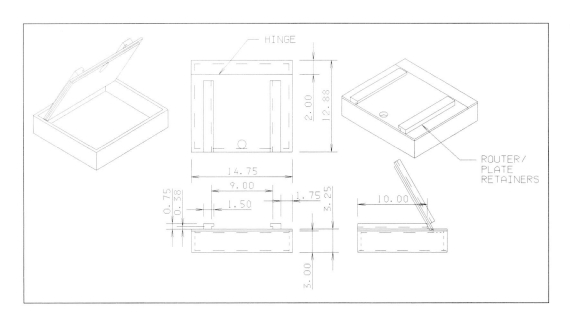

CENTER BOX

either ½″ ply with a rabbeted edge or ¼″. Build the box using any of the methods previously described and then cut the cover. If you do it as shown on page 107 in the drawing, cut the cover a little long (13″ or more) so it can be rabbeted and then the two pieces cut from the larger single piece. The rabbet is only required for the ½″ ply. I used three Soss 100 Invisible Hinges. If you use this type of hinge and a ¼″ cover, glue a ¼″ thickener to the cover on both sides of the hinge line for the Soss hinge mortises.

Screw from the inside or glue the router plate retainers to the top of the cover. Use your plate as a template for positioning the retainers. Drill a finger pull in the cover as shown on page 109. You can also add a pull handle.

The box is held in place with runners screwed to the table's inside walls. If the runner length is kept to about 10½″, you can pull the box part way out and open the cover while the box is still retained in the table. Also, if you mount your wrenches on the inside wall, keep them high enough so as not to interfere with the opening of the box's cover.

ROUTER-TABLE TOP

Use the instructions in chapter two to build the style top you have selected.

BUILDING THE WHEELED BASE BOX

Building the wheeled base box is a straightforward affair. Its size is based on what it will store and the height necessary to place the router-table top at the

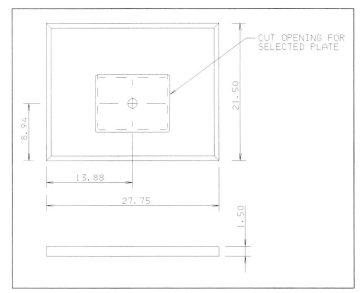

JOB SITE TABLE TOP

nominal 34½″. Making the box higher is an easy way to raise the height of the table.

If you make legs for the table, these legs will be retained by cleats fastened to the table's base. You can make cutouts on the top of the box to accept the cleats. With this arrangement the table will not slide around on the wheeled box, and the height of the combined units will be the planned 34½″.

Make the back from either ½″ or ¾″ stock, whichever material is most readily available. Naturally the box is slightly heavier with the ¾″ back. Since the back acts as a shear panel, its thickness makes little difference in the resultant strength.

Use the backing board previously described when

you cut the lock-miter joints. Cut handles in the sides for lifting and pulling the box. Use a ³/₁₆″ or ¼″ round-over bit to smooth the handle openings both on the inside surface and on the outside of the box before gluing the box together.

Use good quality casters for your box. The wheels should be at least 3″, with one pair fixed and the other pair the locking-swivel type. A 16″ full-extension slide is best for the drawer.

If you use shop birch to build the box, trim the face edges with a hardwood trim. This box, during its life, will take a lot of knocks and bumps. Don't use tape to cover the edges. If you use Finnish or Baltic birch, the 14 layers of ply make an attractive edge and do not need to be covered or protected.

The drawer is made from ½″ birch. Its dimensions are critical since it is slide mounted. Standard slides require a + 0″/¹/₁₆″ space between the box side and the drawer side. Holding to these tolerances with a large drawer can sometimes be a problem. The drawer can end up either too wide or too narrow. Wide is the hardest to fix.

TROUBLESHOOTING PROBLEM DRAWERS

To correct a drawer that is too wide, cut a dado channel in one or both sides of the drawer allowing the drawer slide half to be recessed. If you have to go very deep, more than a ¹/₁₆″, the width of the channel must be wider than the width of the box-side slide half. The half attached to the box wall will start to interfere with the drawer side.

When the drawer is too narrow, use washers or veneer strips to increase the width dimension. Edge-bonding tape works well for this fix. The tape won't move after you apply heat, and it will be hidden by the slide.

Look at the lock-miter bit diagram to review what happens when the lock-miter bit height is slightly off. If the bit is too low, you can sand away the corner and maybe do some shimming. If the bit is too high, you have to cut the channel to bring the dimension into tolerance. This is a more difficult fix.

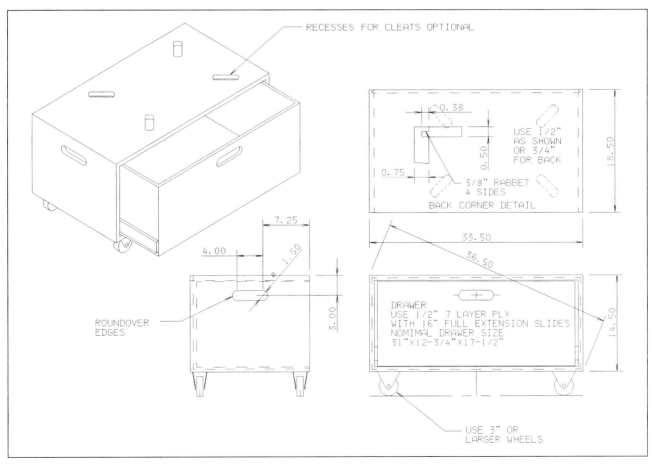

BASE BOX

MAKING THE LEGS

Those of us who enjoy elegant solutions to inelegant problems will enjoy making the legs. The rest of you can purchase legs or forget about them altogether. If you do not build or buy legs for your table, the planning and cutting sequences can still be worthwhile to review.

All too often in building, we think of the finished part and not how to get there. I hate to think of how many times I have made three or four setups and cuts and then, when ready for the final cut, realized I didn't have enough wood left to hold the piece to make that final cut. A similar problem is making the same setup time and time again in order to make the part. A little preplanning can go a long way.

The construction of the legs illustrates how you can make a large number of cuts and pieces with a minimum number of individual setups. Jim Tolpin wrote a good book entitled *Measure Twice, Cut Once* (Betterway Books, 1995). I have kidded Jim about this title since most woodworkers want to get as many cuts as possible from one setup (measurement). Cutting doesn't take long but layout and setup normally does.

Use the same setup to cut equivalent leg parts. There are four legs so you can make at least four cuts for each setup.

Step 1. Cut the leg-pair blanks and the cleat-block blanks from ¾″ birch plywood.

Step 2. Cut the cutting board.

Step 3. Position and fix the cutting board to one of the leg-pair blanks and cut the taper.
Repeat for the remaining leg-pair blanks. You now have eight leg halves.

Step 4. Position and fix the cutting board to a tapered leg and cut a horizontal lock-miter joint.
Note that the leg pairs must be matched. After cutting the first leg, hold an uncut leg to it and mark the location of the miter cut for the complementary vertical cut. Now, position and fix the cutting board to the uncut leg and make the vertical cut. Repeat for the remaining three leg pairs.

Step 5. Make the top and bottom compound miter cuts in the four leg pairs.
For one leg of the pair, set the saw's miter fence at 15° and, for the other leg half, set the miter fence at 7½°. Set the saw blade for a 7½° miter. Make all of the top 15° cuts using a stop block on the fence and then make the 7½° cuts. Now, cut the bottoms using the same procedure.

Step 6. Drill a 1½″ hole for each cleat block in the cleat-block blank (2 holes per blank).

Step 7. Cut out the waste in each block with a jigsaw or band saw.

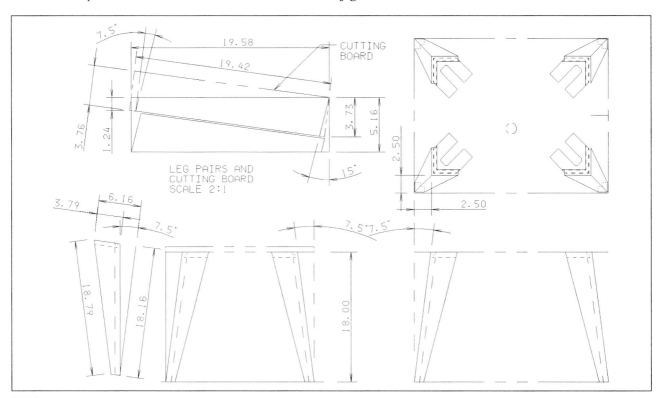

LEG PAIRS AND
CUTTING BOARD
SCALE 2:1

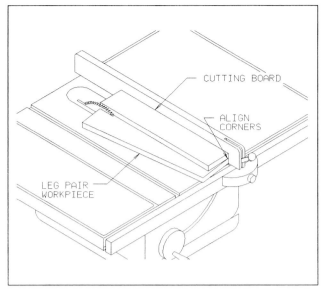

LEG SAW CUT

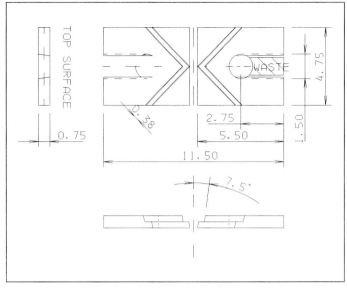

LEG BLOCK DOVETAIL

Step 8. Cut the inside edges on the blocks within a large (I use a ¾″ bit) 7° dovetail bit.
One fence setting is used for this cutting. First, cut the inside left edge with the block's right edge against the fence, then, using the 1½″ hold as a starting position, cut the other inside edge. Turn the block around and repeat. Repeat for the second block.

Step 9. Cut the dovetail cleats by edging the cleat strip with the dovetail bit.
Start with an oversized strip and work your way in to a snug fit with the cleat block.

Step 10. Cut the compound miters in the block blanks to form the actual blocks.
Work from both sides of the saw blade for these cuts.

Step 11. Cut the dadoes and rabbets in the legs and cleat blocks the same way you cut the compound miters on the leg ends and the blocks.
You can do this on the router table using a bevel-miter fixture, but the table saw is better. Watch workpiece orientation to make sure you are cutting the right side and angle. The saw arbor is still at 7½°. The dadoes and rabbets are parallel to the end cuts.

Step 12. Glue and clamp each leg pair together with a block.

Step 13. Using the finished leg as the pattern and locator, mark the cleat locations on the bottom of the table base.
Position the outer leg corner as shown on the drawing. Fasten the cleats to the table's base with #10 wood screws. Place the router table on the wheeled box when you slide on the legs.

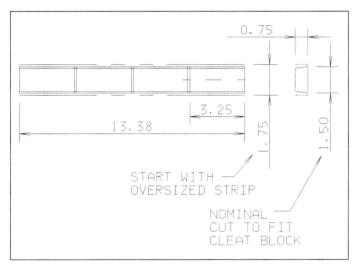

LEG BLOCK

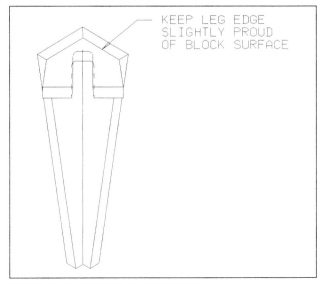

LEG BLOCK—ISOMETRIC DRAWING

CHAPTER SIX

THE SHOP ROUTER TABLE

The shop table was my first real router-table workstation. Its design has withstood the test of time. The first version was described in my book *The Next Step—The Building of a Professional Home Workshop*. An updated version with new fixtures and the sliding fence was then presented in *Build Your Own Mobile Power Tool Centers* (Betterway Books, 1995).

The shop table here is similar to that one. The differences are the router-plate size, the on-off power control and the addition of the drop-leaf shelf. This version accepts the Rousseau and Woodhaven router plates, neither of which were available when *Build Your Own . . .* was written. The third on-off switch makes the table easier to use from either side and, since the shop table is smaller than the contractor's table, it only needs 3-way power control to ensure quick and easy access to a switch from any side of the table. The drop-leaf shelf proved its value on the job-site table.

TABLE ANATOMY

This design will handle any table routing application. It has self-contained storage as opposed to the base box used as the job-site table's primary storage. The height of the unit is a function of the user and the other table in the shop. For many of the larger routing jobs, companion tables of the same height can be used as infeed and outfeed surfaces. All the stations in my shop are the same height as the table saw. This is the $34\frac{1}{2}''$ height specified in the drawings.

The lower portion of the table is laid out so the space above the bottom drawer can store a dovetail jig, a fenceless fence and the sliding fence. This space can also hold the earlier model INCRA Jig. Unfortu-

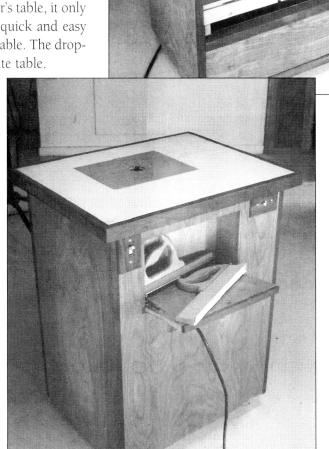

TABLE UPDATES— THIRD POWER SWITCH AND DROP-LEAF SHELF

nately, the INCRA Jig Ultra is too large to fit anywhere.

The other jigs and fixtures hang or store wherever I can find the space. As you can see in some of the photographs, the sides of the tables are festooned with push blocks, clamps, fences and small jigs.

JIGS AND FIXTURES

Some of the jigs and fixtures for the shop table covered in *Build Your Own Mobile Power Tool Centers* have been left out here. You may want to review that book for additional ideas.

BUILDING THE SHOP ROUTER TABLE

The construction of the shop table is similar to the job-site table. The primary joint is the alternate joint in chapter five. This strong joint can be cut either on the table saw or with a router, although the table saw is probably better. Take care if the stock used to build the table is significantly undersized. The shop birch I buy is close to a true ¾" thickness whereas the Finnish birch normally is closer to ¹¹/₁₆". Try to reference off of common edges where possible when making the cuts. Also watch the depth of the dadoes.

COMPANION TABLE

A companion table to handle the overflow and to support router cutting is a handy addition. The table shown here has additional bit storage, storage for other routers, and two roller bars to support large workpieces.

GROWING FESTOONS

As your shop table ages, you will notice a growth of festoons. Like any vertical surface in the shop, the sides of the tables are used for that always-needed additional storage space.

The Carcass

Cut and mark the carcass pieces from ¾″ birch. Cutting diagrams are given for 4′×8′ Finnish or shop birch and for 5′×5′ Baltic birch. You must cut the internal electrical openings for this table before assembly. You won't be able to get to them later.

The detailed drawings are shown above. Note that a larger router-table top can easily be accommodated without changing any of the case construction. The 34½″ height assumes a 2″ wheel which has a height of 2⅝″. Larger diameter wheels will raise the unit's height.

The build sequence is similar to the job-site table, except a subassembly carcass is glued together first and then, as a completed assembly, the subassembly is glued to the remaining parts.

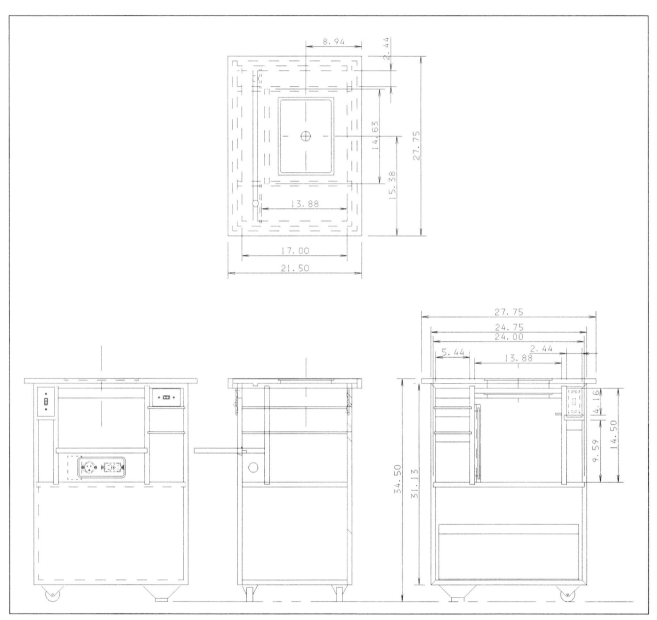

SHOP TABLE OUTLINE AND DIMENSION DRAWING

SHOP TABLE CUTTING DIAGRAM—4′ × 8′ SHOP BIRCH

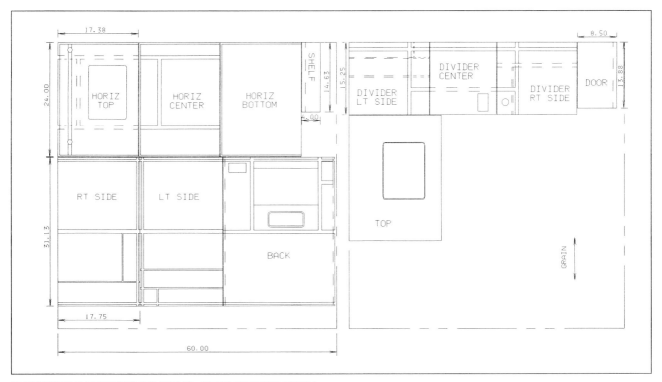

SHOP TABLE CUTTING DIAGRAM—5′ × 5′ FINNISH BIRCH

SHOP TABLE BACK

CUTOUT TO FIT
SWITCH OR
SWITCH BOX
2 PLACES

5.81

2.81

7.63

31.13

2.75

6.00

15.13

0.88

CUTOUT FOR
RECP AND
MALE PLUG

3/8" RABBET
1/4" DEEP

0.75

0.38

9.88   7.25

24.00

0.38

SHOP TABLE SIDES

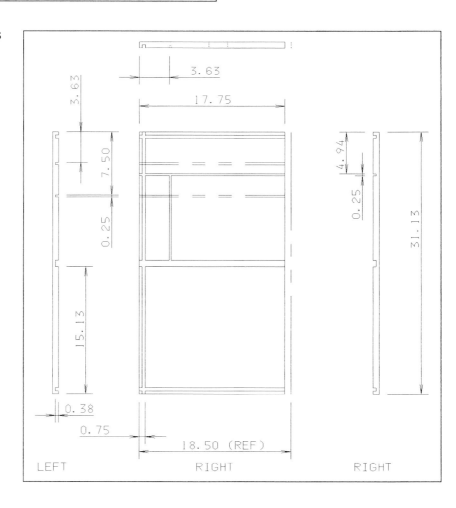

3.63

3.63

17.75

7.50

4.94

0.25

31.13

0.25

15.13

0.38

0.75

18.50 (REF)

LEFT   RIGHT   RIGHT

SHOP TABLE HORIZONTALS

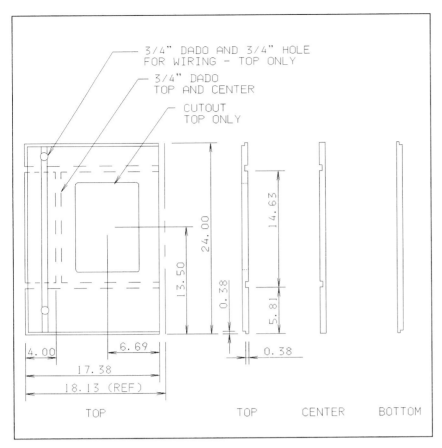

3/4" DADO AND 3/4" HOLE
FOR WIRING – TOP ONLY

3/4" DADO
TOP AND CENTER

CUTOUT
TOP ONLY

TOP   TOP   CENTER   BOTTOM

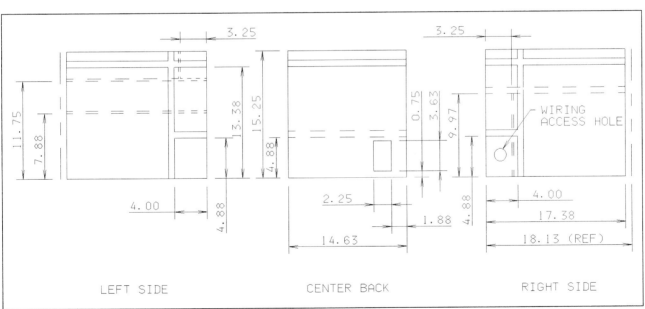

WIRING
ACCESS HOLE

LEFT SIDE   CENTER BACK   RIGHT SIDE

SHOP TABLE DIVIDERS

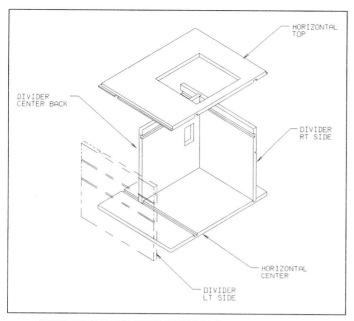

SHOP TABLE SUBASSEMBLY ASSEMBLY

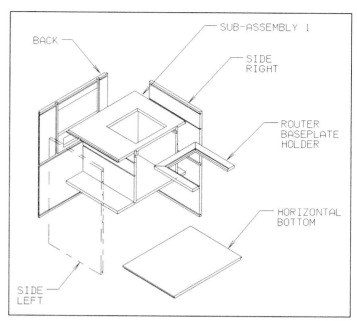

SHOP TABLE CARCASS ASSEMBLY

SHOP-TABLE SUBASSEMBLY

Step 1. Cut and mark the pieces.

Step 2. Check the layout.

Step 3. Cut the rabbets.

Step 4. Cut the dadoes.

If you cut the dadoes on the saw, cut the corresponding dado in each piece before cutting the next dado.

Step 5. Cut the openings for the electrical connections.

The runners used to support the sliding fence/INCRA Jig, fenceless fence and dovetail fixture can be done later.

Step 6. Do a dry assembly and check the fit.

Sand and clean the pieces before gluing them. Tight joints get tighter when the glue has been applied.

Step 7. Glue and clamp the subassembly.

Although the back is not glued on at this time, use it as a jig pattern to position and fit the subassembly and particularly to position the edges of the subassembly that will fit into the dadoes in the station's back.

When the glue has set, assemble the remaining pieces. Most glue manufacturers recommend waiting 24 hours. I really don't know what the circadian rhythms of glue are but I am willing to sometimes wait 24 minutes before proceeding to the next step.

SHOP-TABLE CARCASS ASSEMBLY

Step 1. Place the subassembly onto the back.

Step 2. Position the sides onto the back and the subassembly.

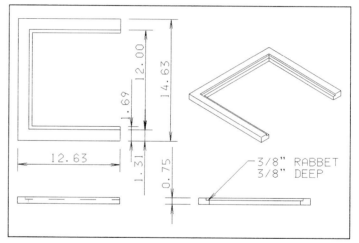

ROUTER HOLDER

Step 3. Slide in the bottom horizontal.

Step 4. Slide in the router base plate holder.

The router holder fits under the top and stores the router and base plate. Cut strips from ¾″ ply scrap.

Step 5. Cut the ¼″ drawer dividers and slide them into their respective dado slots.

No glue is needed since they will be held captive by the trim strips.

Step 6. Glue on the trim strips.

Step 7. Attach the wheels and blocks or four wheels.

If you use the wheels and blocks, you move the table like a wheelbarrow. Having four wheels, two fixed and two swivel, makes moving the table easier. It also means the table can move when being used.

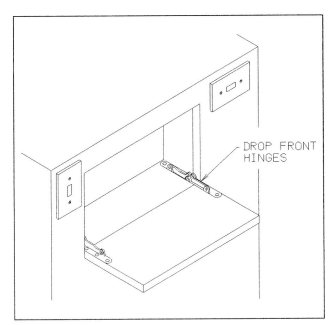

SHOP TABLE DROP DOOR

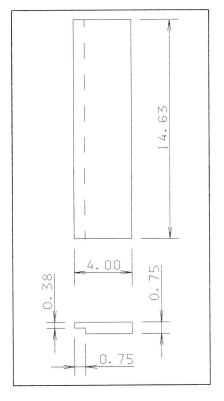

SHOP TABLE SHELF

Fitting Drop Door

The drop door is similar to the drop drawer on the job-site table. Instead of a knuckle-joint hinge, this design uses either butler hinges or the drop-door hinge found on secretaries. I use this design in computer furniture for the keyboard drawer. When the drawer is closed, the drawer front has no visible opening or gap, and when it's open, the front lies flat in the horizontal position.

Since in this application it is not a drawer, you need to cut away some material on the table's back piece, as shown in the drawing on page 122. Don't permanently attach the base until the wiring is completed. In fact, it won't hurt if the base and door are never permanently attached.

As mentioned earlier, the lower compartment is designed to hold either the sliding fence or the Incra fence, and a dovetail jig, the fenceless fence and a drawer. Use a pair of runners to allow the fixtures to slide in above the drawer. The setup described here is for either the 18″ INCRA Fence System or sliding fence and the Sears or Porter-Cable size 12″ Dovetail Jig Template.

Both the INCRA fence and the dovetail jig are attached to base plates which in turn are used to clamp the fixtures to the router-table top. These base plates are cut to a length that allows the fixture to slide into the station as a drawer. For the most economical use of space, turn the dovetail fixture upside down and put it in first.

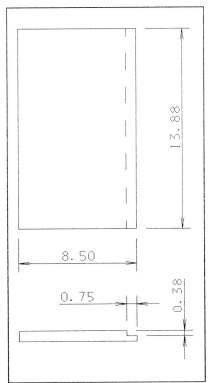

SHOP TABLE DROP DOOR DETAIL

GLUING THE TRIM STRIPS
When gluing the trim strips to the case, use spring clamps to position and hold the strips in place. As you can see, the one-gallon glue container was traded in for a more manageable size.

Cover-Plate Holder

The cover-plate holder fits on the left side of the cavity. As you can see in the drawing, the width of the holder is 1″. This width, which is accomplished by using some ¼″ shim stock with the ¾″ stock, is to allow a slight offset from the side, so your fingers can get hold of the plate when you want to take it out.

Switch-Plate Cover

The front switch plate is shop-made to fit the opening in the carcass. Cut a piece of ¼″ plywood to fit the opening and then, using your router, cut away from the back enough material so the switch can be mounted. Look at the jig described in chapter five.

The other switch plates are standards. You can buy them or make them. If you use a contrasting wood for the trim, making the switch-cover plates from this same contrasting stock can be attractive.

Collet-Wrench Peg

If the collet wrenches have holes in their handles, they can hang on the right side of the router cavity. This mounting is shown on the next page. The spacer is used to strengthen the peg and to hold the wrenches away from the case side so you can get your fingers around them. If your wrenches don't have holes, use strong magnets (Master Magnetics, Inc., part number 07001) and a ledge for them to rest on.

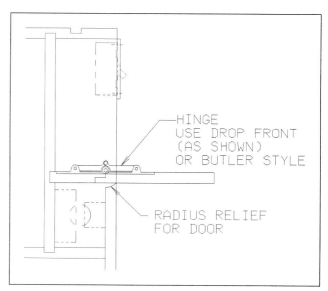

SHOP TABLE DROP DOOR/SHELF HINGE DETAIL

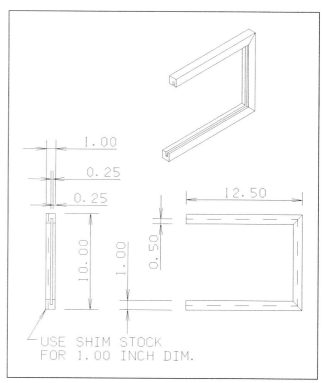

COVER PLATE HOLDER

Wiring the Shop Table

Power the shop table by plugging an extension cord into the power panel. Use a male receptacle to connect the extension cord to the station. The wiring box is located below the drop door on the back of the station. This cavity is also used as the primary electrical junction box for the station. It ensures all wiring is covered and only accessible with removal of the power panel.

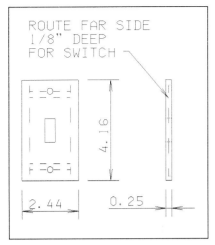

SWITCH PLATE

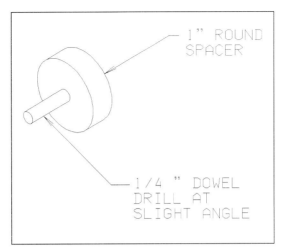

COLLET WRENCH PEG

Follow the schematic shown here for the wiring connections. On-off power to the router is controlled through any of the three switches located at the front and back of the router-table, which allows it to be used from any side. If you're not familiar with wiring household circuits, have someone who is check your work. Wire the circuit in an exposed configuration and check it before buttoning everything up. Be sure enough slack is in the wiring to make changes or repairs.

Remember, a wooden workstation has no grounding provisions. A grounded circuit is mandatory to bring power to the station. Make sure the ground circuit is completed by wiring the ground wire to all the receptacles.

The wiring terminations go in the space below the drop drawer. Mount the Sylvania or Bryant male connector and the dual receptacle in the power panel. Break the tab on the receptacle so one of the receptacles can be controlled from the table's switches. The other receptacle is powered whenever the table is powered, i.e., when the extension cord is plugged in.

Building the Router-Table Top

Select the material for the top. The top shown here uses a plastic laminate on a birch substrate. Follow the steps outlined in chapter two to build the top.

Drawers

The small drawers on the left side of the shop table are made using the cigar-box joint. (See the sidebar "Cigar Boxes" on page 54). This joint is used to maximize the storage capacity of the drawers. Measure the openings and cut to fit. The opening below the switch

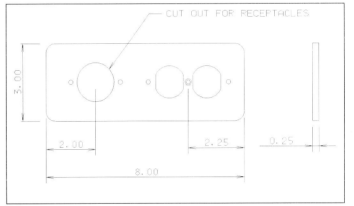

POWER PANEL

SHOP-TABLE WIRING
The wire runs for the shop table are straightforward and easy to lay-in. Keep enough slack in the wiring so repairs or changes can be made. The slack shown here works fine and causes no problem in closing the covers.

on the right side houses the custom router-bit storage drawer. The plans here show the drawer laid out for ¼″ bits. Note that the top left drawer and the router-bit drawer are not as deep as the other drawers. This space is used for the rear left on-off switch and wiring.

A collection of cigar boxes and trays to fit the left-hand drawers are shown on the next page. I use the cutter tray for ½″ bits. The lift handle in the center of the tray is a dowel topped with a wooden ball.

The lower drawer can be built as a chest of drawers. This handy configuration allows you to pull the chest out and set it on one of the other workstations when you use your router table.

Plan for growth and flexibility when you make these boxes. Remember, you will forever be buying some new bit or gizmo.

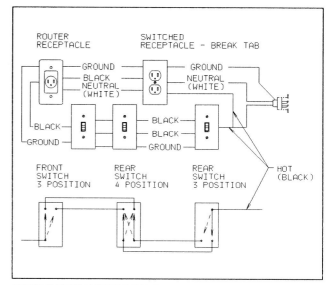

SHOP TABLE WIRING DIAGRAM

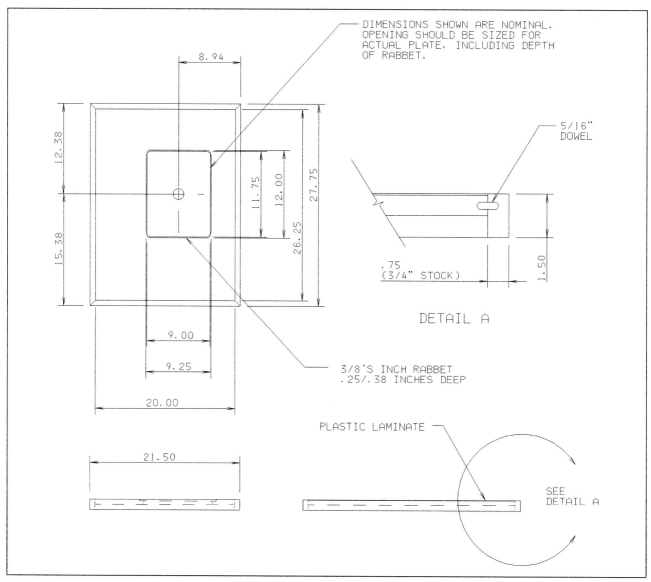

ROUTER TABLE TOP

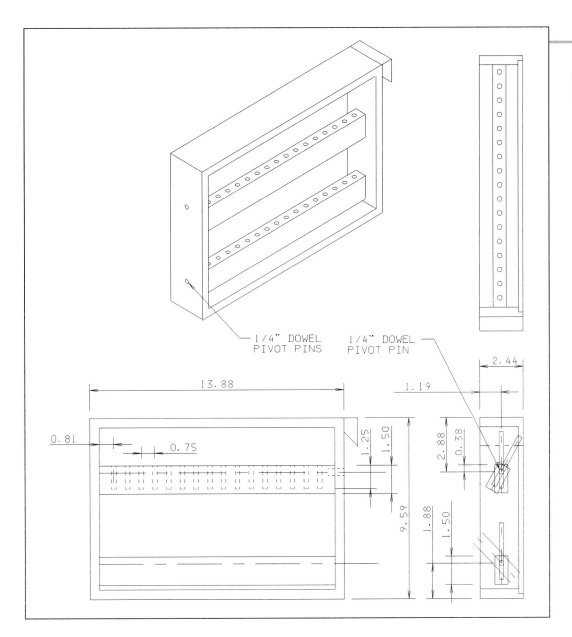

SHOP TABLE BIT
DRAWER

1/4" DOWEL
PIVOT PINS

1/4" DOWEL
PIVOT PIN

13.88

0.81

0.75

1.25

1.50

9.59

1.88

1.50

2.44

1.19

2.88

0.38

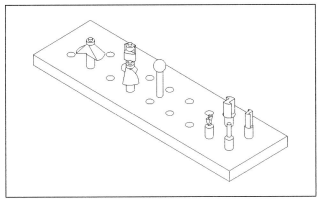

SHOP TABLE CUTTER TRAY

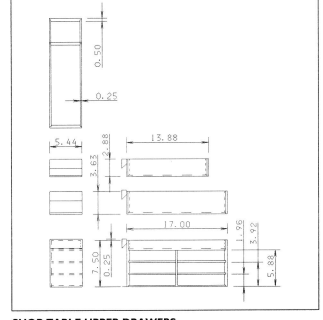

0.50

0.25

5.44

2.88

13.88

3.63

17.00

1.96

3.92

7.50

0.25

5.88

SHOP TABLE UPPER DRAWERS

Finishing

Use lacquer or polyurethane to finish the table. A smooth slick surface will stay cleaner. More for appearance than protection, I normally give the table, drawers and other pieces a coat of tung oil before applying the finish. Let the oil dry for three days, and then sand smooth before applying the finishing coats.

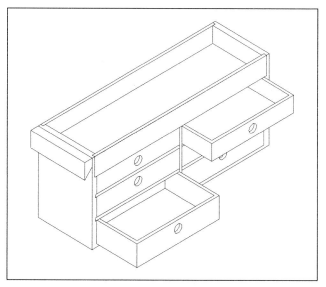

SHOP TABLE CHEST

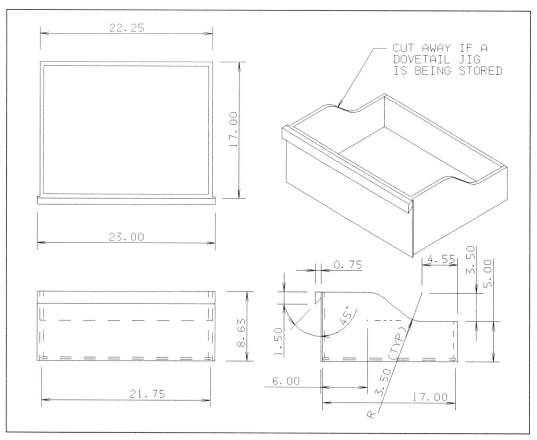

SHOP TABLE LOWER DRAWER

CHAPTER SEVEN

THE CONTRACTOR'S ROUTER TABLE

The contractor's table offers the largest working surface of the three tables. As a result all the jigs and fixtures described in chapter four must grow a little to accommodate the larger top dimensions. The table as designed will accept the Rousseau and Woodhaven router plates. Its design also allows access to the router form any side of the table.

TABLE ANATOMY

Since the table is larger, I increased the height to 36″ to accept larger wheels to make it easier to move around. Be sure this height fits with the height of the other work surfaces in your shop.

As presented, the table does not have a large storage area corresponding to the bottom drawer in the shop table or the box used with the job-site table. The space shown for router and bit storage can be converted to drawer space if desired. If you make this change, keep the base back as designed since the base back and the switch plates are the primary shear panels for any transverse load. A better option is to convert one or both of the router storage areas to individual drawers. This retains the structural integrity of the design.

The table's planned storage is for two plate-mounted routers or one plate-mounted router and two other routers, lots of router bits, the two fences and four or five drawers. The cutouts on the sides

This is the largest of the three table designs presented here and will make an attractive and functional addition to any shop.

allow the hybrid fence to be stored on the shelf, although it sticks out so you will have to watch your shins. The space below is used to store the sliding fence and whatever other jigs and fixtures will fit.

The three drawers on the left side are similar to the standard drawer used in *Build Your Own Mobile Power Tool Centers* (Betterway Books, 1995) workstations. You can also make the top drawer as shown in the drawings and then make a double-sized bottom

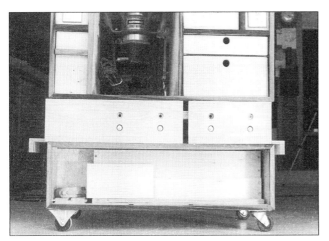

STORING THE FENCES
The contractor's table is designed to store both the hybrid fence and the sliding fence. If the hybrid fence binds in the shelf, cut away a little of the top trim strip.

TWO-DRAWER CONFIGURATION
The left-hand drawers can be either a two-drawer configuration or a three-drawer configuration. The two-drawer configuration offers the storage flexibility.

THREE-DRAWER CONFIGURATION
Here we see the three-drawer configuration. This configuration uses the standard drawer size used in *Build Your Own Mobile Power Tool Centers* (Betterway Books, 1995).

drawer instead of two standards.

If Baltic birch is used for the construction of the table, consider increasing the width of the pieces by 1½″ instead of using trim strip. The edge of the multi-layer Baltic birch is attractive and doesn't need a trim. This change will require three instead of two sheets of the Baltic birch.

The boxed dado is shown as an alternative joint to the lock miter for the construction of the table. The boxed dado will make it a little harder to assemble the carcass but it can be done.

The biggest problem I have experienced with the construction of contractor tables is the tolerance buildup when using ¹¹/₁₆″ as opposed to ¾″ stock. This drawing shows what happens.

As shown, the primary accumulation of error occurs in the center compartments. Fortunately, these errors are easy to accommodate. The router compartment grows by ⅛″ and has no consequence on the resultant table. Correct the width of the bit trays by making the tray base slightly wider. When laying out the pieces and making the cuts, let the center portions vary to compensate for the stock thickness. In other words, measure in from the outside edges and don't measure across the workpiece.

BUILDING THE CONTRACTOR TABLE

Do a dry assembly of the table, making sure the primary pieces are clamped and square before measuring for any adjustment to the secondary pieces that may be required. The primary pieces are the subtop,

bottom, sides, center and base back.

Step 1. Position the base back and center pieces to the base.

Step 2. Add the sides.

Step 3. Place the top on the sides and slide the various dividers into the frame.

Step 4. Check the dadoes you cut for the switch plates to make sure they line up.

Step 5. Remove the top and set the switch plates in the four corners.

Check for fit and square. Clamp only as tight as required to get the specified height or width. If a piece is short or a dado too deep, don't bottom the piece if it shortens the planned dimension. If necessary, shim

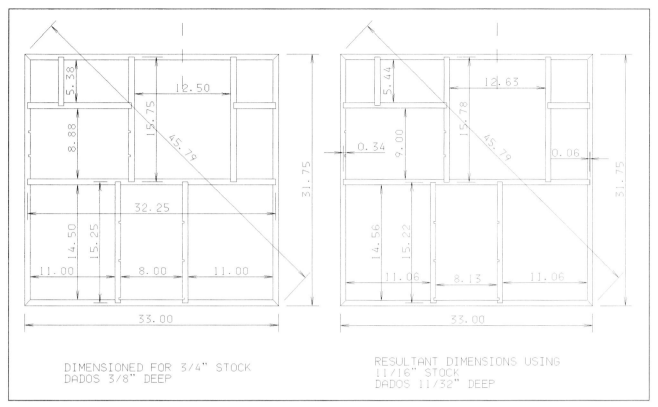

DIMENSIONED FOR 3/4" STOCK
DADOS 3/8" DEEP

RESULTANT DIMENSIONS USING
11/16" STOCK
DADOS 11/32" DEEP

TOLERANCE BUILD-UP

to hold the desired dimension. Use permanent shims so you don't forget them when you glue the case. When you like the fit, go ahead and glue the case.

Building the Top

Construct the top using any of the methods outlined in chapter two. The dimensions are shown at the end of the "Detailed Drawings" section in this chapter. As noted in chapter three, if the INCRA Jig Ultra fence is the primary fence for the table, the router plate's router cutout should be centered on the 24" axis.

Wiring the Table

Wiring the contractor's table is similar to wiring the shop table. The power panel is on the right side opposite the router receptacle. The wires to the 4-way switches on the left side of the table are brought across the subtop in the dado trench. Most of the wiring is hot " + " black wires. Like the shop table, 25' of black wire will handle it.

Step 1. Attach the receptacle and the male power connector to the power panel.

Step 2. Cut the black and ground wires to length and wire the switches.

Switch wires should have about 3" slack at each end.

LAYING OUT THE CUTTING PATTERN
Take your time when laying out the cutting patterns on the workpiece. The two sides shown here are placed like facing pages in a book. Doing the layout in this manner ensures that the right and left mirror-image cuts are on the right side of the workpiece. You don't want to end up with two lefts or two rights.

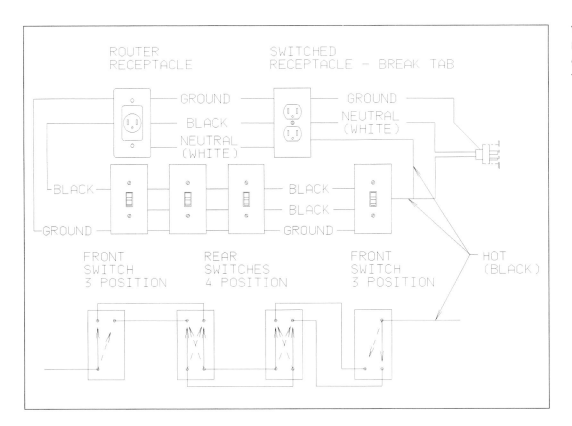

Step 3. Wire the router receptacle and feed the wires through the power panel opening.

Step 4. Wire the switched receptacle (break the black tab) and the male power receptacle. Wireless (twist) connectors can be used but are not necessary. In either case, the power panel has plenty of room behind it for the wiring.

Step 5. Do a continuity check and then a "power on" check before closing up.

Router Storage

Two forms of router storage are used. One side is a simple shelf where routers can be stored. The other side has provisions for storing a mounted router and additional router plates.

A pair of the holders of the type shown here make it possible to have slide-in slots for the plates and the mounted router.

Bit Storage

Trays are used to store bits. This design has provisions for three trays. The picture opposite, top right, shows three varieties of trays. Two are for individual bit storage while the bottom tray is for storing boxed bit sets.

The individual bit trays show two styles of handles or pulls. The bit tray drawing opposite, lower right, shows how extra long bits can be accommodated.

MEASURING THE DRY ASSEMBLY
When measuring and checking the dry assembly, first establish the square. Use both the diagonal measurement and framing squares to set the pieces.

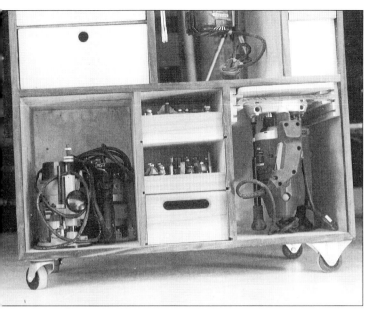

ROUTER STORAGE

Mounted routers and router plates can be stored as shown here. Other routers or tool boxes can be stored on the left side.

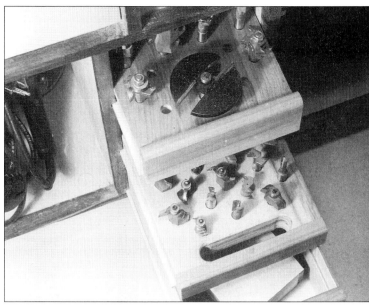

ROUTER-BIT STORAGE

Here are some variations for the storage of router bits. The top two trays are a matrix hole pattern that can accommodate almost any size bit. The bottom tray is built as a drawer for holding boxed bit sets. This picture and the router-storage picture show three variations of tray pulls. All of them work well.

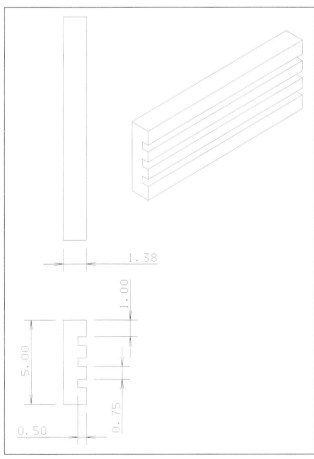

ROUTER AND PLATE HOLDERS

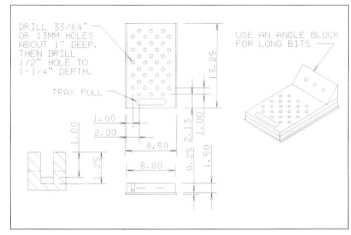

BIT TRAYS

Drawers

The pull-through drawers can be used from either side of the table. The drawings show a standard pull whereas the photographs show finger pulls. If the drawers are so full your finger won't fit through the hole, use the standard pull; otherwise, the finger pulls work fine.

Make sure the drawer edges are clean and rounded over. The Baltic birch ply, like all plys, will splinter.

The two variations of the standard drawer were shown on page 132. If you are not sure what's best, go with a two-drawer configuration.

A chest drawer is always desirable. The only problem is remembering where you put what.

The top left drawer turns out to be a good drawer size for all the other stuff. Every office, kitchen and shop needs one junk drawer. The contractor's table is the only router table with the size to afford this luxury.

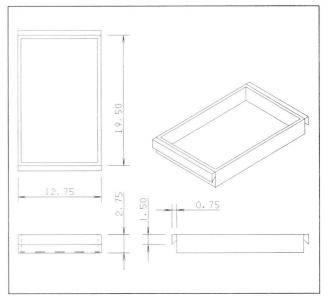

STANDARD DRAWER

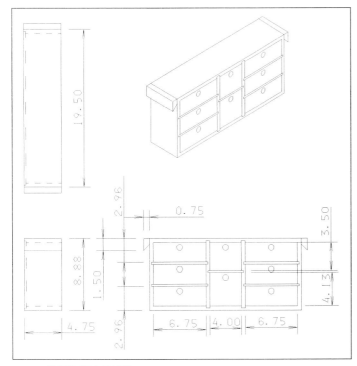

CHEST DRAWER

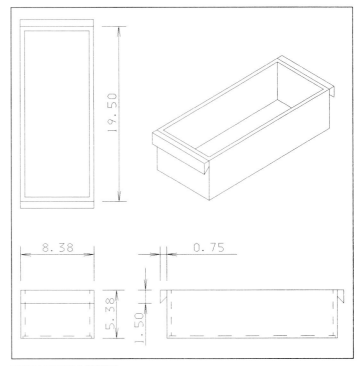

TOP LEFT DRAWER

ROUTER-TABLE DRAWER

After the drawers have been glued, round over the top edges and sand clean. That little splinter sticking out can end up under a fingernail if the edges aren't clean.

"THE OTHER STUFF" STORAGE

It looks like a junk drawer but in reality it stores some valuable aids. The Dremel MiniMite can clean cutting burns off the workpiece. The adhesive-backed weatherstrip makes super nonslip pads for push blocks and fixtures. Double-backed tape, adhesive-backed slick strips and edge banding will all find application when you make your jigs and fixtures.

OUTLINE AND MOUNTING DRAWING

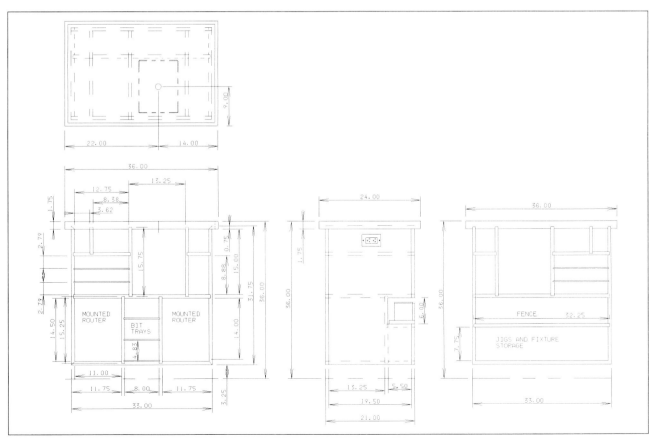

CONTRACTOR TABLE

CUTTING DIAGRAMS

These cutting diagrams are for $4' \times 8'$ or $5' \times 5'$ sheets.

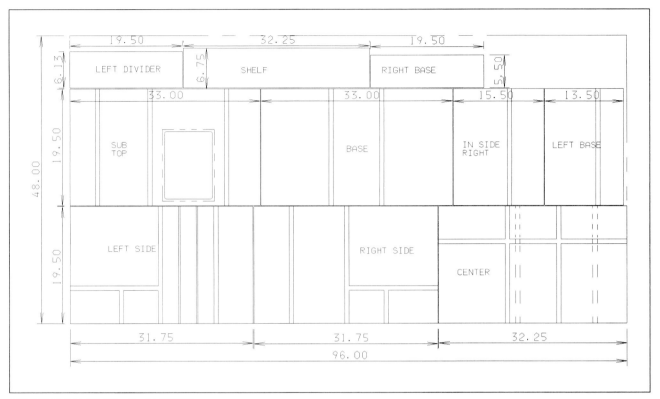

CUTTING DIAGRAM—$4' \times 8'$ SHEET

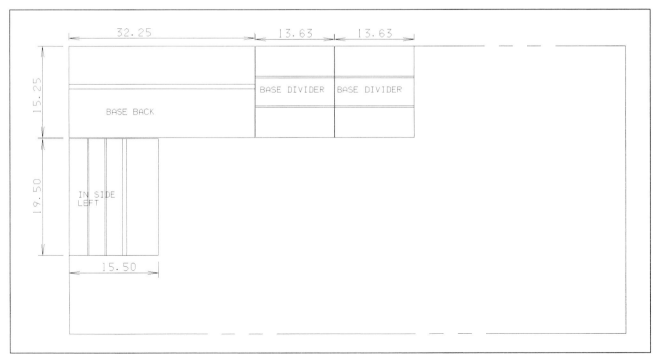

CUTTING DIAGRAM—$4' \times 8'$ SHEET

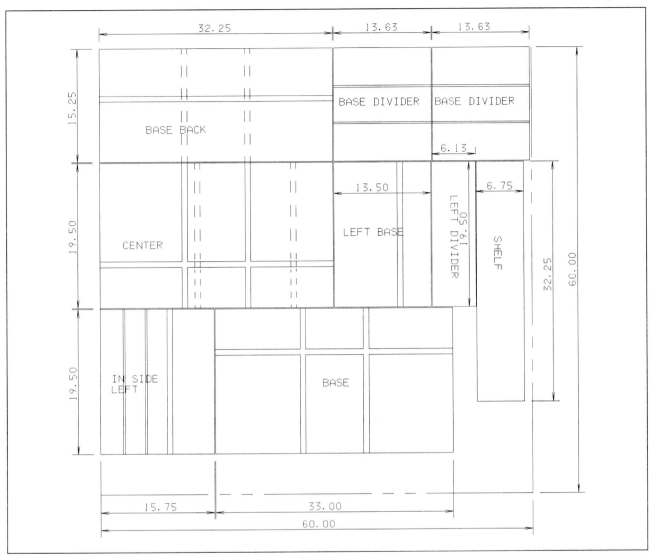

CUTTING DIAGRAM—5′ × 5′ SHEET

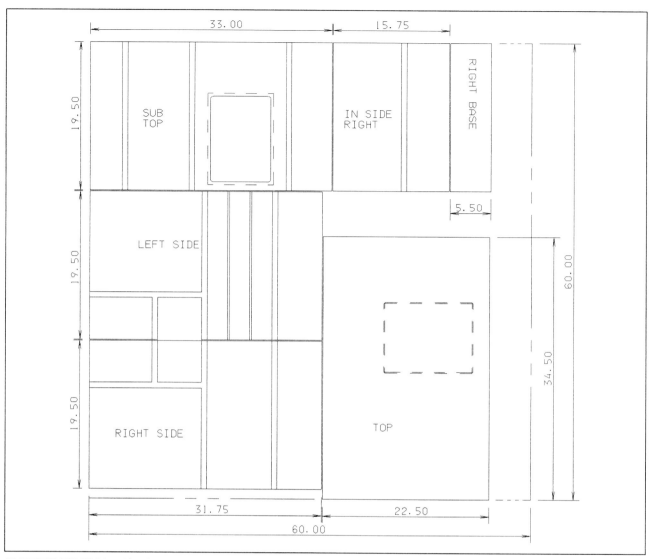

CUTTING DIAGRAM—5′ × 5′ SHEET

DETAILED DRAWINGS

Review this exploded view and study the individual pieces before you start cutting. If you are going to make changes, now is the time to do it. Decide on the changes you want to make and then mark the drawings to reflect these changes.

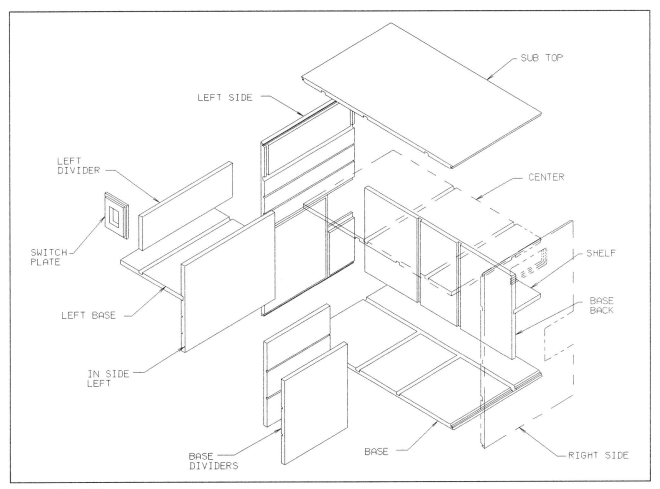

EXPLODED VIEW

SUB-TOP AND BASE DRAWING

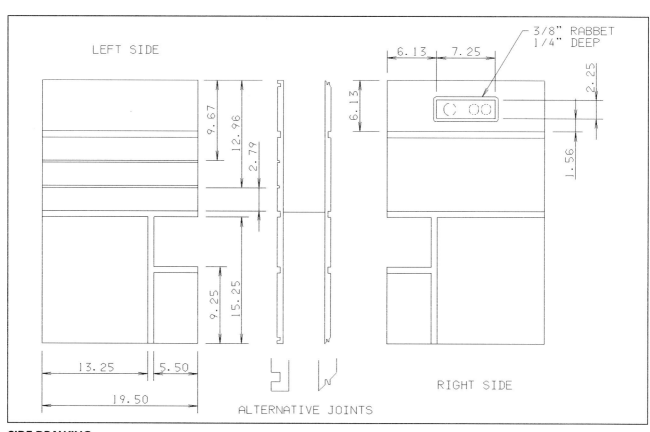

DADO TRENCH
FOR WIRING
TOP ONLY

19.50

32.25 (DADO BOX)

33.00 (LOCK MITER)

CORNER JOINTS

LOCK MITER   DADO BOX

SUB TOP

4.37   12.50   5.50

14.25

11.75   11.75

BASE

LEFT SIDE

3/8" RABBET
1/4" DEEP

6.13   7.25

6.13

2.25

9.67

12.96

2.79

1.56

9.25

15.25

13.25   5.50

19.50

ALTERNATIVE JOINTS

RIGHT SIDE

SIDE DRAWING

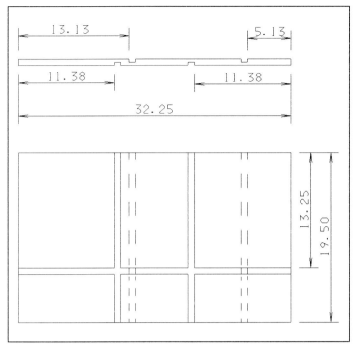

CENTER DRAWING

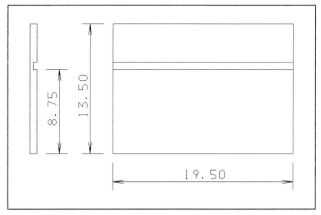

LEFT BASE DRAWING

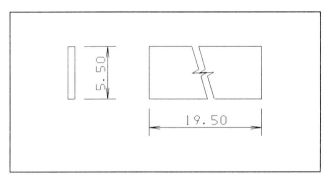

RIGHT BASE DRAWING

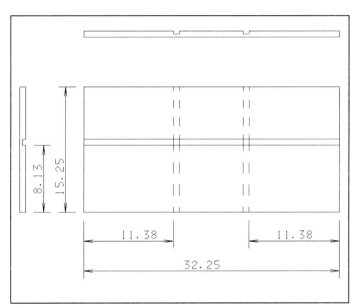

BASE BACK DRAWING

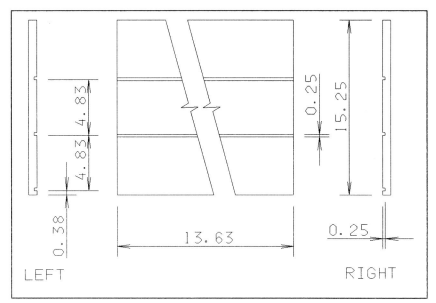

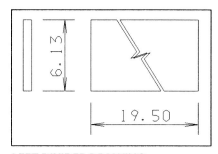

LEFT DIVIDER DRAWING

BASE DIVIDER DRAWING

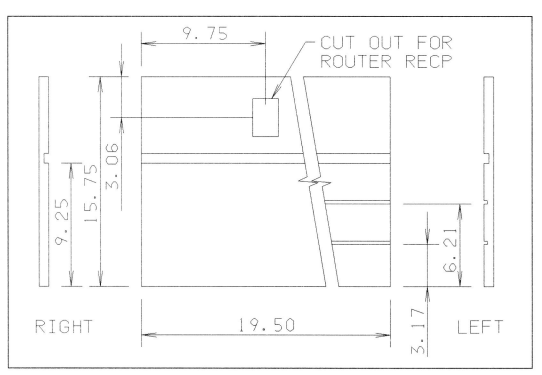

INSIDES DRAWING

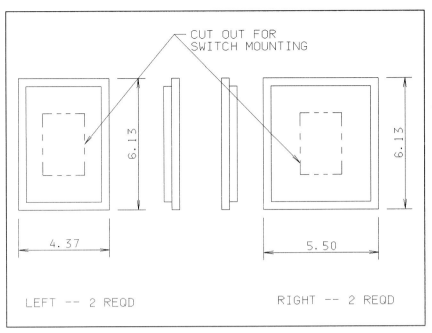

SWITCH PLATES DRAWING

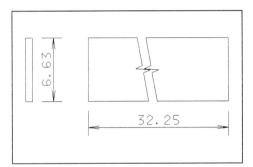

SHELF

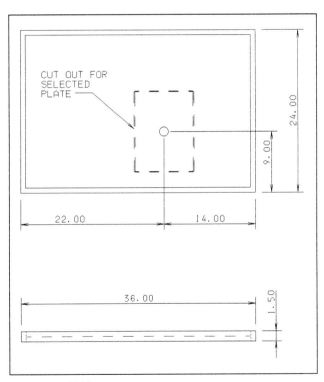

TOP DRAWING

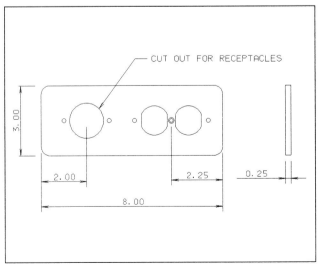

POWER PLATE DRAWING

GLOSSARY

amalgamate—To become a homogeneous blend.

backsaw—A saw with a metal rib across its back.

Baltic birch—Similar to Finnish birch. Available only in 5′ × 5′ sheets.

bar sinister—Heraldic device (diagonal bar) denoting bastardy. Actually a corruption of the blend of sinister and/or the baton that is used by modern writers.

bench dog—A metal or wooden peg fitting in holes in a bench surface. Used to retain workpiece.

bond—To cause to adhere firmly. Glue and contact cement are bonding agents.

butch plate—Used to cover or join a mistake.

carcass (also **case**)—Solid side construction as opposed to frame construction.

catch-22—In Joseph Heller's book *Catch 22* (Dell Publishing Co., Inc., New York, NY; 1961) set in World War II in Italy, there was only one catch and that was catch-22. Catch-22 "specified that a concern for one's own safety in the face of dangers that were real and immediate was the process of a rational mind. Orr [a bomber pilot] was crazy and could be grounded. All he had to was ask; and as soon as he did, he would no longer be crazy and would have to fly more missions. Orr would be crazy to fly more missions and sane if he didn't, but if he was sane he had to fly them." (p. 47).

chatter—To vibrate. Results in uneven cutting of the workpiece.

cigar boxes—Any of the small boxes or tins we use to collect the things that are too neat to throw away and, in many cases, we don't know what to do with.

circadian—Noting or pertaining to rhythmic biological cycles recurring at approximately twenty-four-hour intervals.

collet—A tapered sleeve made in two or more segments that grips the shaft of a cutter.

crosscut—To cut across the grain of the wood.

crown moulding—A moulding designed to join two normal surfaces like a room wall and ceiling.

dado—A groove cut in the workpiece.

dead-blow hammer—A hammer or mallet designed to allow a no-bounce, nonmarring striking of the workpiece surface. Used to hammer in tight joints and can be used in bonding of laminates.

fence—Any guide used to keep the cutting edge of a tool a fixed distance from the workpiece edge.

ferrule—A metal ring or collar that reinforces the connection between a tool and its handle.

Finnish birch—Multilayer plywood produced in Finland. Available in 5′ × 5′ and, for some thicknesses, 4′ × 8′ sheets. The grain in the 4′ × 8′ sheets is along the 4′ axis.

fix—To hold steady. Clamps, nails, screws, glue and double-backed tape are all materials used to fix.

fixture—A device used for fixing.

hardboard—Tempered fiberboard, such as that manufactured by Masonite. Use the "Serviced tempered" class of hardboard as defined by the American National Standards Institute (ANSI).

J-roller—Nonmarring rubber roller used to lay laminates and veneers. Typically the roller will exert about 25 psi over the roller surface.

jig—A device to position the workpiece or the tool so work can be performed accurately and safely.

laminate—(verb) To roll or compress into a thin sheet.
(noun) The plastic material resulting from this process, such as Formica.

MDF—(medium-density fiberboard) Particle board or fiberboard made with fine particles. Works well and finishes well. Fiberboard is coarser and weaker than MDF and is not a substitute for MDF.

micron—One millionth of a meter.

micron sandpaper—Sandpaper made with a grit graded in microns.

miter—A joint formed between two pieces of wood. Usually refers to the gauge or jig used to cut miters.

mussick—A goatskin water bag. With 'is mussick on 'is back / 'E would skip with our attack . . . (from "Gunga Din," by Rudyard Kipling).

noise—Irrelevant or meaningless data.

plano—Flat, i.e., no curvature. Safety-glass lens with no correction.

plant-on—A strip of edged moulding or a block pattern glued to a larger piece, used to form decorative crowns or border trims.

Procrustes—A character in Greek mythology who had an iron bed on which he compelled his victims to lie, stretching or cutting off their legs to make them fit the bed's length.

Pythagorean theorem—The square of the diagonal (hypotenuse) of a right triangle is equal to the sum of the squares of the lengths of the other two sides.

rabbet—A stepped recess along the edge of the workpiece.

rip—To cut with the grain of the wood.

Romex—Insulated copper wire, normally two conductors and one ground wire in a protective plastic coating. Used for household wiring.

runners—Strips, normally of wood, that support and guide drawers or similar structures.

shear panel—Panel structure used to counteract a force applied by a transverse load.

starting pins—Used with router tables and shapers to steady the workpiece as it is rotated into the cutter path. Without the starting pin, the cutter may grab the workpiece resulting in kickback.

template—A pattern used as a guide.

Theorem of Procrustes—Cut to fit. *See* Procrustes.

SOURCES OF SUPPLY

COMPANY	ADDRESS, TELEPHONE	PRODUCT
American Tool Companies, Inc.	108 S. Pear DeWitt, NE 68341 (402) 683-1525	Quick-Grip clamps
The Beall Tool Co.	541 Swans Road NE Newark, OH 43055 (800) 331-4718	Wood threaders, drill bits
Black & Decker, Inc.	(800) 544-6986	Workmate 300 Project Center
Bridge City Tool Works	1104 NE 28th Ave. Portland, OR 97232 (800) 253-3332	Layout and measuring tools, micro fences
Carr Lane Manufacturing Co.	P.O. Box 191970 4200 Carr Lane Ct. St. Louis, MO 63119-2196 (314) 647-6200	Components for jigs and fixtures. Excellent reference book, *Jig and Fixture Handbook*, second edition
Central Rubber Products Co., Inc.	Silver Springs Rd. South Salem, NY 10590 (914) 533-2200	Glue applicators
Delta International Machinery Corp.	(800) 438-2486	30″ Unifence
DeWalt Industrial Tools	(800) 433-9258	Industrial power tools
Dremel	4915 21st St. Racine, WI 53406 (800) 437-3635	Power tools and accessories
Eclectic Products, Inc.	(800) 767-4667	Wood fillers, bonding materials, wood stains, lacquers
Formica Corp.	155 Route 46 Wayne, NJ 07470 (800) 524-0159	Plastic laminates
Highland Hardware	1045 N. Highland Ave., NE Atlanta, GA 30306 (800) 241-6748	Woodworking tools, books and supplies, router maintenance kits
JDS Company	800 Dutch Square Blvd., Suite 200 Columbia, SC 29210 (800) 382-2638	JDS Air-Tech 2000 air filtration system, Accu-Miter precision miter gauge
Jointech, Inc.	P.O. Box 790727 San Antonio, TX 78279 (800) 619-1288	Fences, positioning systems
MicroCADAM, Inc.	355 S. Grand Ave., 23rd Floor Los Angeles, CA 90071 (213) 613-2300	Desktop computer-aided design software

COMPANY	ADDRESS, TELEPHONE	PRODUCT
Micro Fence	11100 Cumpston St., #35 North Hollywood, CA 91601 (818) 766-4367	Micro Fences for routers, circle jig attachments
MLCS Ltd.	P.O. Box 4053 Rydal, PA 19046 (800) 533-9298	Router tables, bits and accessories
Mohawk Finishing Products, Inc.	4715 State Hwy. 30 Amsterdam, NY 12010 (800) 545-0047	Finishing supplies
Pass & Seymour, Inc.	Syracuse, NY	Wiring devices and accessories, 20-amp 3-way and 4-way switches
Porter-Cable Corp.	P.O. Box 2468 Jackson, TN 38302 (800) 487-8665	Sanders, routers, router accessories, plane jointers
Onsrud Cutter, Inc.	P.O. Box 550 800 Liberty Drive Libertyville, IL 60048 (847) 382-1560	Router bits
Rousseau Co.	1712 13th St. Clarkston, WA 99403 (800) 635-3416	Router plates, fences, job-site tables
Ryobi America Corp.	5201 Pearman Dairy Rd. Anderson, SC 29625 (800) 525-2579	Power tools
Sears Shop at Home	(800) 948-8800	Craftsman tools
S-B Power Tool Company	4300 W. Peterson Ave. Chicago, IL 60646 (312) 286-7330	Sanders, routers, router bits, Skil and Bosch power tools
Taylor Design Group, Inc.	P.O. Box 810262 Dallas, TX 75381 (972) 484-5570	INCRA Fence System, INCRA Gauge, INCRA Miter Slider, INCRA Jig Ultra
3M	(800) 362-3550	Spray adhesive
Welliver & Sons, Inc.	1540 New Milford School Rd. Rockford, IL 61109 (815) 874-2400	Power tool accessories, letter sets for making signs with routers, router clamps
Woodcraft	210 Wood County Industrial Park P.O. Box 1686 Parkersburg, WV 26102-1686 (800) 225-1153	Engineer squares, router bits, router tables and accessories, shop filtration systems
Woodhaven	5323 W. Kimberly Rd. Davenport, IA 52806 (800) 344-6657	Router tables, router table accessories, router bits

ROUTER BIT USAGE, TROUBLESHOOTING AND SAFETY GUIDELINES

A. ROUTING

Routing is an effective method of machining materials such as wood and wood by-products as well as plastics, composites and nonferrous metals. The router mechanism, portable or stationary, operates at extremely high spindle speeds (10,000 to 50,000 rpms). These speeds allow for the rapid removal of material with finished edges that are remarkably smooth. With addition of template guides, a variety of sizes and shapes of router bits, and sometimes the pure imagination of the operator, the router becomes one of the most versatile machines in the industrial marketplace.

B. TOOL SELECTION

• Use high speed steel (HAS) tools for aluminum, natural woods and most plastics. High speed steel can be ground to a keener edge than can carbide and will stay sharper longer in these materials.

• Use carbide tipped (CT) tools for laminated and composition wood materials and for abrasive or resin-base products.

• Use solid carbide tools for hard woods, wood composites, plastics and other composite materials for longer tool life and faster feed rates.

• Tool materials are not equal in quality. High speed and carbide grades vary along with heat treatment and sintering processes. Onsrud Cutter tools are manufactured with quality materials which meet inspected raw material standards consistent with production routing requirements.

• Carbide grades vary. Most carbide tipped tools are C-2 or similar carbide grade. Abrasive composites require other grades of carbide. Onsrud Cutter uses only production proven micrograin carbides which meet an inspected standard.

• Diamond and ceramic tipped router bits should be considered only when the router, the environment, the material being cut and the economics of production point to their usage.

• Onsrud cutters may be coated by several proven processes. TiN and Boride are but a few. The Onsrud Cutter Engineering Department, or a field representative, will assist in the economic analysis.

• Onsrud Cutter CNC and wood rout bits are de-signed for top performance in CNC routers. Use for faster feed rates and improved tool life.

• Tool life, finish, production requirements, production environment, and price must all be considered before selection of the proper tool. Your Onsrud Cutter field representative will assist you making the proper tool selection.

C. TOOL GEOMETRY

• Use single edge router bits when speed is the primary consideration and finish is less important.

• Use double edge router bits when finish is the primary consideration.

• Use upcut spiral router bits for grooving, slotting or when fast chip removal is required.

• Use downcut spiral router bits for faster feed rates or when cutting through material.

• Use spiral, straight or shear HAS tools for natural woods depending on type of cut required.

• Use spiral, straight or shear carbide tools for composites, particle board, plywood or MDF.

• Use spiral tools when finish and/or available horsepower are problems.

• The length of the cutting edge should not be more than four times the diameter of the cutting edge. Bits with a cutting length over four times their diameter will be subject to increased breakage.

• Use the largest diameter shank practical for increased rigidity, finish and tool life.

D. TOOL LIFE

• Tools should be changed at first sign of edge deterioration causing finish degradation or increase in operator effort to maintain feed rate.

• Never allow the tools to dwell in a cut.

• Feeding work to a router bit is like feeding to a saw blade. The router bit should be fed in such a manner so that in moving through the work it has a chance to bite or cut its way freely. The operator should feel a constant and even pressure. If the material is fed too fast, strain and deflection will occur; if fed too slow, friction and burning will occur. Both decrease the life of the router bit and are common causes of breakage.

• The router mechanism must be well maintained for any cutting tool to perform properly. Routinely check the collet for wear. Inspect tools being used for collet marks indicating slipping due to wear or dust build up. Check spindle on a dial indicator for run-out. Collet and run-out problems cause premature tool failure and associated production difficulties.

• Do not use adapter bushings to reduce size of the collet on a routing or production basis. Tools will not perform properly in bushings over an extended period of time. Bushings are for prototype, experimentation, test and evaluation and not for production.

• Wherever possible, use a coolant when routing. Heat caused by action between the tool and piece part is enemy no. 1 to tool life.

• Heat is a function of surface footage per unit of time. Thus, the more dense the material, the faster the feed rate to minimize heat. A compromise must be reached, however, between finish and heat.

• Most tools can be resharpened for additional life provided the tool is removed when dull and not when the edge is destroyed.

• Tool life is affected dramatically by tool geometry. Rake and clearance angles, as well as cutting edge length, should be examined.

• Router bit breakage is most often caused by a misapplication of the router tool. Do not assume the proper tools are being used. There are many local and regional preferences which are not good routing practices. Many users switch brands when they should switch both brands and tool specs.

• The Onsrud Cutter Engineering Department and field representatives have the experience to solve tool life problems. They take pride in doing this part of their job very well. Call them for assistance when you want another educated opinion.

E. TOOL BREAKAGE

In spite of the structural and metallurgical attributes which are designed into industrial and professional router bits, breakage occurs. A detailed examination yields the following:

1. Application-Related Breakage. The review of bit selection, design and tool quality lead us to application-related failures. High speed steel tools are preferred for aluminum, nonfiber plastics and soft to medium hardness natural woods. Other materials normally require a carbide cutting edge. Cutting edge lengths should be as short as possible to accommodate length of cut required. Larger cutting edge diameters require larger shank diameters. Spiral geometry can direct chip flow and expel chips to reduce heat. When tool application is a problem, changing the type of tool is the only solution.

2. Tool Quality Shortcomings. Although most reputable manufacturers and distributors of high quality cutting tools invest measurable effort in attempting to provide trouble-free tools to the end user, tool breakage events in the field can be attributed to tool defects. Upon investigation, such failures can be caused by an internal flaw in the steel or carbide. These failures are normally random, however, if the flaw was raw material batch based, an entire batch may be a problem. Same is true for heat treating. Too high a hardness can lead to premature edge failure. This is generally confined to one batch of tools. Geometry-induced fractures usually are related to improper rake and clearance angles as manifested in the bit riding the cut. The resulting heat generated by friction shortens edge life, tends to create burn marks and may cause material being cut to accumulate behind each cutting edge, and culminates in fracture. Shank out of round conditions prohibit effective colleting, and do not permit the tool to turn in a concentric manner. When considering this condition at 20,000 rpm, the whipping action generated is catastrophic to bit life and failure by fracture is imminent.

3. Router Collet Integrity. A router bit is rendered nearly useless if the mechanics of gripping and rotating the tool are not on the same plateau of accuracy as the tool. Operators have snapped five or six tools in succession before inspecting colleting conditions. Overt signals such as breakage and dark markings on the shank of the bit warrant immediate investigation. Inspect the collet for out of round or bell mouthed conditions. Operators often overlook inspecting new collets based on the assumption a new collet is geometrically correct. Tool manufacturers are aware, and openly share, the subtle nature of this problem. Collet performance can also be affected by dirt, dust, bonding agents and sap which occupy space and accelerate wear.

4. Machine Inspection. Given that the cutting tool being utilized is geometrically within tolerances as well as elimination of detectable collet abnormalities, a thorough inspection of the router's interface components is in order. Start the inspection process by inserting a dowel pin or hardened piece of drill rod into the collet. To facilitate accurate measurement of potential run-out, position a "recently calibrated" dial indicator against the pin. The integrity of this process can be enhanced by using a pin or drill rod that is 3½″ in overall length with 2″ projecting from the collet. At this point, judiciously rotate the spindle by hand and monitor the dial indicator reading. Additionally, while turning the spindle by hand, be sensitive to any "catch" or intermittent "resistance" to turn which enunciates bearing problems. Dial indicator run-out should not exceed .1002″ or as otherwise delineated in the machine's technical manual. It would be convenient at this point to check the spindle for sideplay by pressing on the spindle sideways to detect movement. Again, close tolerance results are mandated in a maximum sideplay of .001-.002″ on floating spindle machines. Finally using a dial indicator, inspect the vertical thrust movement. Although often overlooked, it is extremely important to check when one considers the opposite wear tendencies of the bearing when vacillating between upcut and downcut routing. Moreover, excessive thrust movement will cause excessive vibration and short tool life.

Procedurally the next event requires removal of the collet assembly to facilitate inspection of the spindle inside taper for run-out. This can be accomplished by presenting the sensing point of the dial indicator to the surface of the inside taper. Run-out should not exceed .002″ or as otherwise specified by a technical bulletin for the machine. In the event of excessive run-out, repairs should only be accomplished by an original equipment manufacturer or highly qualified authorized agent.

5. Operator Breakage. If router bit and prime mover parameters are within specifications, tool breakage can still occur through violation of standard routing techniques. Specifically, feeding the workpiece to the bit must be accomplished such that the router bit is permitted to "bite" or "cut" its way freely. If the workpiece is fed too fast, excessive strain is imposed on the tool. Conversely, if the workpiece is fed too slow, excessive friction will be generated causing destructive heat build-up. In both situations, tool life is significantly shortened or, in sustained conditions, tool fracture is imminent. Any router bit can be broken should that choice be made in the operation of the router.

Direction reversals also set the stage for router bit fracture, if one fails to consider that a cutting tool as applied to the workpiece experiences "spring" or elasticity. When reversing direction of the cut, care must be exercised to preclude excessive strain on the tool, particularly beyond its elastic metallurgical limits. Reversals of a jarring nature or taking a running start as a knot in the workpiece are simplistic events but are known to cause tool breakage.

F. SUGGESTED PROCEDURE

Should all of the above examinations be inconclusive, it is important to retain both new and expended sample tools (all pieces if broken). Please contact the Onsrud Cutter Engineering Department, or your field representative and inform them of your problem and status. The following information should also be provided: router type, material being cut, spindle speed, approximate feed rate, description of problem and circumstances and sample of material cut when breakage or problem occurs. This date should provide enough clues for a solution to the tool breakage problem. Resolution of any router bit breakage or performance problem must be handled through your local distributor to assure proper credit and shipment.

G. COLLET MAINTENANCE

Collet maintenance is one of the most common causes of inadequate tool life or breakage. There are four, and sometimes five links in the chain that make up this critical tool holding system called a collet. As a chain is only as strong as the weakest link, a router bit can only be as good as the system that holds it properly. The small amount of time spent to regularly inspect and clean the collet system will be more than offset in productivity increases reducing overall costs. The five critical components are as follows:

1. The most important is the inside of the collet. A brown resin build-up often accumulates on the inside end of the collet. Resin migrates up through the slits in the collet and then deposits itself inside the collet. This resin build-up, if not removed causes the collet to grip improperly on the tool shank. It prevents the collet from applying equal pressure throughout the entire grip range of the collet. This causes pressure points at the end of the collet which allow the tool to

resonate inside, and allow the tool to slip within the collet. Slippage then causes what's better known as "collet burn," a condition when resins are deposited on the shank of the tool in the form of brown or black markings. Resin buildup can be easily removed from the collet interior with a brass tube-type brush. These brushes are nondestructive, yet adequately remove the resins that solvents or high pressure air guns cannot.

2. The inside taper of the spindle is also a critical surface which accumulates resin build up and should be cleaned periodically as well.

3. The outside taper on the collet, both large and small, require regular inspection and should be cleaned of all deposits each time the tool is changed.

4. The inside taper of the nut should be clean and free from burrs on the surface which, if present, not only skew the collet but can ruin a new collet. At times collets are replaced only to be ruined in the first use by a collet nut in poor condition.

5. Some collet nuts also have an integrated thrust bearing connected to the inside taper. This bearing serves to reduce friction wear between the collet and nut as the nut is tightened. It is very critical, for if it is rough in movement or, worse yet, frozen, it will cause run out or out of tolerance conditions. These bearings should be kept in smooth operating condition. (Thrust bearing nuts are found on most of the larger Perske spindles as well as some C R Onsrud inverted routers.)

Additional critical components of routing with pneumatic routers are:

Some air routers contain a tool support bearing inside the nose cone. These bearings are critical for tool stability and require a longer shank tool to seat properly. The router bit must also be undersize to pass through the bearing and should have shank length enough to fill at least 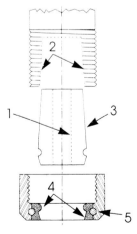 75 percent of the collet depth. Standard router bits will cause the collet to collapse and create substantial runout which will shorten both collet and tool life.

All five of these components are critical and should be regularly maintained. Another item not to be overlooked is the fact that collets should be replaced on a regular basis. This means inspection on each tool change to look for metallic damage such as bell-mouthing or burrs inside. If metallic damage is visible, the collet should be discarded and replaced. Also consider that even if there is no damage present the collet can be worn out through metal fatigue. Heat is directly transferred from the tool to the collet. These heating/cooling cycles remove the original tempering of the steel. Collets are made from spring steel allowing them to have a certain amount of elasticity to grip the tool. As the heat cycle is repeated this elasticity diminishes. This occurs with greater frequency on small air routers because of the small size of the collets and their proximity to heat from the tool. Over time, a collet requires increased tightening to maintain the tool in proper position. As over tightening increases, the collets are distorted, creating eccentricities in the tool holder. Therefore, instead of over tightening older collets and creating a number of other problems, they should be replaced. Often, the cost of a new collet can be offset by the cost of needlessly broken tools in one shift alone.

Proper positioning of the tool in the collet is critical. The tool should only be gripped on the shank portion of the tool. At no time should any portion of the flute fade out be inside the collet.

H. SAFETY GUIDELINES

These safety and operating instructions are not intended to be and are not totally comprehensive. They do not, and cannot, cover every possible safety problem which may arise in using specialized and standard tooling on varying machines and applications. These guidelines are intended to generally describe many of the basic safety and operating procedures which should be followed and to describe the types of safety considerations which should be considered in operating cutting tools.

None of the statements or information presented should be interpreted to imply any warranty or safety protection.

The drawings do not depict any particular design, type, or size of tools, equipment or machines. The drawings are illustrative only and are not to be construed to establish any exact mode, method or procedure.

All federal and state laws and regulations having jurisdiction covering the safety requirements of cutting tools at the point of usage take precedence over the statements and information presented in this publication. Users of cutting tools must, of course, adhere to all such regulations. As an aid to cutting tool users, a number of such regulations are listed below. The list does not include all regulations that may apply.

1. The Federal Register dated June 27, 1974, Dept. of Labor, Office of Safety and Health Administration (The OSHA Act)
2. American National Standards Institute, 01.1-1975 (Safety Regulations for Woodworking Machinery)
3. American National Standards Institute, 02.1-1969 (Safety Requirements for Sawmills)
4. American National Standards Institute, P1.1-1969 (Safety Requirements for Pulp, Paper and Paperboard Mills)
5. Other ANSI, State and/or Federal Codes and Regulations which may apply in your operation

1. SAFETY RULES WHICH APPLY TO THE OPERATION OF ALL CUTTING TOOLS

• Always inspect the cutting tool completely before mounting. Never attempt to operate a tool which has chipped or bent teeth or cutting edges or teeth that are not sharp. You must be familiar with normal wear conditions for the type of tooling to be used. The tool must be completely clean to allow proper visual inspection.

• Do not attempt to operate cutting tools or machinery with which you are not familiar or have not received operational training—get assistance from your supervisor, his designated representative or a trainer who is familiar with and properly trained and experienced on the machine to insure your safety. Become completely familiar with all of the machinery manufacturer's written instructions, guide and manuals before operating machine. You must use and be familiar with all controls, safety devices and emergency stop mechanisms to operate a machine safely.

• Never operate a cutting tool that is not properly aligned to the direction of feed. Do not allow sideward, twisting or other than forward pressure on the cutting tool in feeding material into a cut.

• Make sure the tool is mounted to rotate in the proper direction before cutting any material. The tool must rotate against, rather than with, the direction of feed on all hand feed machines. Do not climb on hand feed machines.

• Do not cut materials of a type, hardness or density other than that which the cutting tool was designed to cut. Never attempt to cut materials with a tool unless you have personally checked with your supervisor to make sure the cutting tool was designed for the specific type of material you wish to cut, and for the depth of cut desired. This is particularly important when attempting to cut "stacked" material, i.e., cutting more than one piece at a time.

• Never force-feed materials into a cutting tool such that it causes the tool or machine motor to slow down below operating speeds. A safe and proper cutting operation will not require much force in feeding material. If material begins to "ride up" on the cutting tool, or requires undue pressure to feed the material into the tool, or if undue vibration is experienced, do not continue the cut—turn off all power and correct the condition.

• Keep body and clothing well clear of all cutting tools and other moving parts while the machine is in operation. Use work holding fixtures and mechanical feed devices in all possible cases. When cutting material of such size, shape or type that it necessitates close approximation to the cutter and mechanical feed mechanisms can not be used, use a wood "push stick" to feed the material so that no part of your body or clothing comes close to the cutting tool.

• Never attempt to clean a cutting tool or clear pieces of material from the cutting area while machine power is "on" or when cutting tools, material or any part of the machine is moving. Allow cutter rotation to stop by itself, or by use of a brake if supplied on the machine. Never attempt to stop or slow a rotating cutting tool by applying a hand-held or any other object to the cutter, arbor, spindle or drive as a brake.

• Do not place your body in the rotational path of a cutting tool unless absolutely necessary, and then only if there is a complete and adequate barrier between you and the cutting tool. Remember that carbide tips are very hard and therefore, brittle. The tips can break away under incorrect side thrust or twisting forces, or if foreign material is allowed to contact the tips. An operator can reduce the danger of being hurt by a "kickback" of the material if he always stands beside the material he is feeding into the machine rather than in the back of it.

• Never leave machines unattended while cutting tools are still rotating or any part of the machine or material is moving.

• Never operate a machine without using all of the hoods, guards, hold downs and safety devices for the machine being operated.

• Machines must be maintained to the manufacturer's standards and current safety standards.

• Always wear safety glasses or face shield to completely protect your eyes when operating cutting tools.

2. ROUTER TOOL MOUNTING INSTRUCTIONS

• TURN OFF AND LOCK OUT ALL MACHINE POWER. Remove the collet chuck and collet (see the machine manufacturer's instructions) and clean them. Also clean the spindle and tool. Remove all nicks and burrs by very lightly honing (do not use coarse files or coarse abrasives). When removing parts and tools from a machine, handle them carefully. Never use hard metal hammers to loosen machine parts or tools, and never allow the teeth of cutting tools to touch steel even when they are dull, for this will cause the cutting edges to be damaged.

• WITH ALL MACHINE POWER OFF AND LOCKED OUT, push the machine spindle up and down and to and fro by hand pressure (without rotating the spindle). There should be no feeling of movement. Next, rotate the spindle by hand. The bearings are in proper condition.

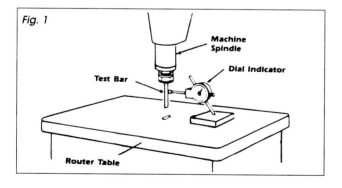

Fig. 1
Machine Spindle
Dial Indicator
Test Bar
Router Table

• WITH ALL MACHINE POWER OFF AND LOCKED OUT, check the condition of the collect chuck by mounting the collet and collet chuck in the spindle with a ground test bar positioned full depth into the chuck. A 3″ length of drill rod will serve as a test bar. Set up a dial indicator as shown above in Fig. 1, and check the runout of the test bar, turning the machine spindle by hand. Runout of the test bar in excess of machinery manufacturer's recommendation

could indicate a worn or damaged collet, or worn spindle bearings or spindle assembly. Make all corrections necessary before mounting the cutting tool.

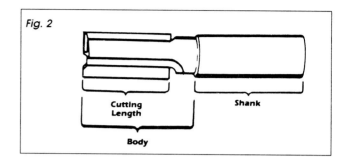

Fig. 2
Cutting Length
Shank
Body

• WITH ALL MACHINE POWER OFF AND LOCKED OUT, remove the test bar and mount the router bit or router tool in the machine after inspecting the tool. Do not mount any tool that is dull or damaged and check shank of bit to be sure it fits securely into collet. Be sure the router bit or tool is positioned completely into the collet to the full depth of the shank and clamped only on the smooth, straight surface of the shank (see Fig. 2). Never clamp only a portion of the shank to "extend" the cutting depth, or clamp on the body below the shank. If there is a radius between the tool shank and body, be sure to clamp above the radius. Check the tool with the dial indicator (as in Fig. 3). Tools that have an excess run-out (more than ±.002) or that wobble, are unsafe at the high spindle rotating speeds of router machines, and must be corrected or replaced.

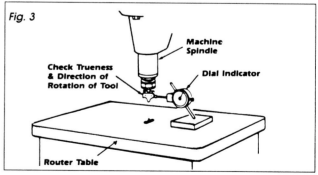

Fig. 3
Machine Spindle
Check Trueness & Direction of Rotation of Tool
Dial Indicator
Router Table

• SPECIAL NOTE: Whenever a router bit is removed from a machine, inspect the shank for collet markings (brown or black spots, or lines on the shank). If markings are present, the collet may be worn and should be checked. Worn collets cause undue vibration in the router bit, which can work harden the tool causing it to break.

3. ROUTER TOOL SPECIAL OPERATION PRECAUTIONS

• Never run router tools in machines other than router machines.

• Operate only router tools and router bits that have the shortest possible cutting edge length in order to maintain the cutting load as close as possible to the collet chuck support (never use a longer cutting edge length to "reach" the material). Material should just clear the collet chuck as it moves through the cut. Do not operate router tools with only part of the tool shank clamped in the collet to make the tool "reach" deep cuts. The entire shank must be clamped in the collet. Do not clamp the tool on any radius between the shank and body.

• Router tools are often limited in capacity of the chip pocket (area in front of the cutting edge which carries away the chip) because of the small diameter of the tool. Over-feeding (forcing material into the cut) can cause compression of chips that result in bending or breaking of the router bit of tool. Small diameter router bits are limited in the amount of clearance that can be designed and manufactured into the tool due to the need to maximize strength in the tool body. Fast feeding or router bits can result in over-loading the clearance space between the material cut and the steel behind the cutting edge. When such an operating condition occurs, dangerous, high over-loaded pressures rapidly develop that can cause bending and breakage of the tool. Don't force-feed material into these tools.

• If the cutting tool and material tend to push away from one another, or if they bounce or vibrate against each other, stop the machine immediately. Do not use force to continue the cut. Do not operate the machine until the machine or tool condition is corrected.

• Never feed material into a router tool when the material is not supported by the machine table and table guide rails, or that requires the hands or clothing to be dangerously close to the rotating parts of the machine. Keep body and clothing well clear of the cutting tool while in operating.

• Always wear safety glasses to completely protect eyes when operating routing tools.

SPECIAL NOTES ON PORTABLE ROUTERS

• Follow manufacturer's recommendations on proper inspection and operation of portable routers.

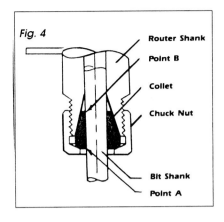

Fig. 4

Router Shank
Point B
Collet
Chuck Nut
Bit Shank
Point A

• Insure that the unit is un-plugged at all times during inspection.

• Make sure that the router motor is clamped se-curely in the base at all times.

• Insure that the router bit shank is always inserted a MINIMUM of ⅝" up into the collet.

• Total router bit runout should not exceed ± .004.

• Inspect the collet frequently. The collet should be replaced when use causes wear at point A or at point B (see Fig. 4). Continued use of such a worn collet can cause bit vibration and set up stresses that result in bit breakage.

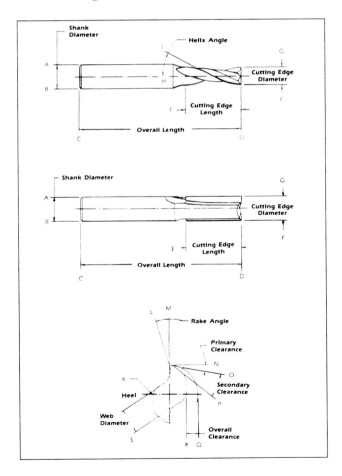

TOOL TERMINOLOGY

Shank Diameter—Diameter of that portion of a router bit shown graphically between points A and B. Shank diameter can be expressed in fractional or decimal units, such as ¼" or .250.

Overall Length (OAL)—The total length of a router bit from shank to point as shown graphically between points C and D. Overall length is usually expressed in units of inches and fractions, thereof, such as 1¼"

Cutting Edge Length (CEL)—The length of a router bit's cutting edge as shown graphically between points E and D. Cutting edge length is expressed in inches and fractions thereof.

Cutting Edge Diameter (CED)—The diameter of the cutting surface of a router bit as shown graphically between points F and G. Cutting edge diameter is expressed in decimal units or fractions.

Helix Angle—The angle of the spiral with reference to the shank as shown graphically between points H and I. Helix angle is expressed in degrees (spiral only).

Heel—The sloping base material of a router bit as shown graphically at point K.

Rake Angle—The angle formed by the cutting edge of a tool and a plane, perpendicular to the surface being worked, as shown graphically at point L and M. Rake angle is measured in degrees.

Primary Clearance—That specific clearance contained in approximately the first ¹⁄₁₆ of the cutting edge, as shown between points N and O.

Secondary Clearance—That specific clearance contained after the first ¹⁄₁₆ of the cutting edge, as shown between points O and P.

Overall Clearance—That clearance displaced from cutting edge to the center of the router bit as shown between points R and Q which comprises the heel.

Web Diameter—The diameter of the tool as shown graphically between points S and T.

THESE SAFETY GUIDELINES ARE REPRINTED BY AUTHORIZATION OF THE WOOD MACHINERY MANUFACTURERS OF AMERICA

INDEX

More Great Books for Your Woodshop!

Measure Twice, Cut Once, Revised Edition— Miscalculation will be a thing of the past when you learn these effective techniques for checking and adjusting measuring tools, laying out complex measurements, fixing mistakes, making templates and much more! *#70330/$22.99/144 pages/144 color illus.*

100 Keys to Woodshop Safety— Make your shop safer than ever with this manual designed to help you avoid potential pitfalls. Tips and illustrations demonstrate the basics of safe shopwork—from using electricity safely and avoiding trouble with hand and power tools to ridding your shop of dangerous debris and handling finishing materials. *#70333/$17.99/64 pages/125 color illus.*

Making Elegant Gifts from Wood— Develop your woodworking skills and make over 30 gift-quality projects at the same time! You'll find everything you're looking to create in your gifts—variety, timeless styles, pleasing proportions and imaginative designs that call for the best woods. Plus, technique sidebars and hardware installation tips make your job even easier. *#70331/$24.99/128 pages/30 color, 120 b&w illus.*

Good Wood Handbook, Second Edition— Now you can select and use the right wood for the job—before you buy. You'll discover valuable information on a wide selection of commercial softwoods and hardwoods—from common uses, color and grain to how the wood glues and takes finish. *#70329/$19.99/128 pages/250 color illus.*

100 Keys to Preventing & Fixing Woodworking Mistakes— Stop those mistakes before they happen—and fix those that have already occurred. Numbered tips and color illustrations show you how to work around flaws in wood; fix mistakes made with the saw, plane, router and lathe; repair badly made joints, veneering mishaps and finishing blunders; assemble projects successfully and more! *#70332/$17.99/64 pages/125 color illus.*

Build Your Own Mobile Power Tool Centers— Learn how to "expand" shop space by building mobile workstations that maximize utility, versatility and accessibility of woodshop tools and accessories. *#70283/$19.99/144 pages/250 b&w illus./paperback*

Creating Your Own Woodshop— Discover dozens of economical ways to fill unused space with the woodshop of your dreams. Self shows you how to convert space, lay out the ideal woodshop, or improve your existing shop. *#70229/$18.99/128 pages/162 b&w photos/illus./paperback*

Tables You Can Customize— Learn how to build four types of basic tables—from a Shaker coffee table to a Stickley library table— then discover how to apply a wide range of variations to customize the pieces to fit your personal needs. *#70299/$19.99/128 pages/150 b&w illus./paperback*

How To Sharpen Every Blade in Your Woodshop— You know that tools perform best when razor sharp—yet you avoid the dreaded chore. This ingenious guide brings you plans for jigs and devices that make sharpening any blade short and simple! Includes jigs for sharpening boring tools, router bits and more! *#70250/$17.99/144 pages/157 b&w illus./paperback*

The Woodworker's Sourcebook, 2nd Edition— Shop for woodworking supplies from home! Self has compiled listings for everything from books and videos to plans and associations. Each listing has an address and telephone number and is rated in terms of quality and price. *#70281/$19.99/160 pages/50 illus.*

Basic Woodturning Techniques— Detailed explanations of fundamental techniques like faceplate and spindle turning will have you turning beautiful pieces in no time. *#70211/$14.95/112 pages/119 b&w illus./paperback*

The Stanley Book of Woodworking Tools, Techniques and Projects— Become a better woodworker by mastering the fundamentals of choosing the right wood, cutting tight-fitting joints, properly using a marking gauge and much more. *#70264/$19.95/160 pages/400 color illus./paperback*

Good Wood Routers— Get the most from your router with this comprehensive guide to handheld power routers and table routing. You'll discover a world of information about types of routers, their uses, maintenance, setup, precision table routing and much, much more. *#70319/$19.99/128 pages/550 color illus.*

Tune Up Your Tools— Bring your tools back to perfect working order and experience safe, accurate cutting, drilling and sanding. With this handy reference you'll discover how to tune up popular woodworking machines, instructions for aligning your tools, troubleshooting charts and many other tips. *#70308/$22.99/144 pages/150 b&w illus./paperback*

Desks You Can Customize— Customize your furniture to fit your personal style. With Graves's instruction and detailed drawings, you'll create a unique, individualized desk as you experiment with legs, doors, drawers, organizers and much more. *#70309/$19.99/128 pages/133 b&w illus./paperback*

Make Your Woodworking Pay for Itself, Revised Edition— Find simple hints for selling your work to generate a little extra income! You'll find hints on easy ways to save on wood and tools, ideas for projects to sell, guidance for handling money and more! Plus, new information on home-business zoning and tax facts keeps you up-to-date. *#70320/$18.99/128 pages/20 b&w illus./paperback*

Marvelous Wooden Boxes You Can Make— Master woodworker Jeff Greef offers plans for 20 beautiful, functional boxes, complete with drawings, cutting lists, numbered step-by-step instructions and color photographs. *#70287/$24.99/144 pages/67 color, 225 b&w illus.*

Good Wood Joints— Learn which joints are best for specific situations and how to skillfully make them. You'll discover joints for every application, the basics of joint cutting and much more! Plus, you'll find an ingenious chart that makes choosing the right joint for the job easy. All well-illustrated with step-by-step instructions for making joinery by machine or hand. *#70313/$19.99/128 pages/550 color illus.*

Woodworker's Guide to Pricing Your Work— Turn your hobby into profit! You'll find out how other woodworkers set their prices and sell their products. You'll learn how to estimate average materials cost per project, increase your income without sacrificing quality or enjoyment, build repeat and referral business, manage a budget and much more! *#70268/$18.99/160 pages/paperback*

Display Cabinets You Can Customize— Go beyond building to designing furniture. You'll receive step-by-step instructions to the base projects—the starting points for a wide variety of pieces, such as display cabinets, tables and cases. Then you'll learn about customizing techniques. You'll see how to adapt a glass-front cabinet; put a profile on a cabinet by using molding; get a different look by using stained glass or changing the legs; and much more! *#70282/$18.99/128 pages/150 b&w illus./paperback*